THE JEWISH WOMAN:
An Annotated Selected Bibliography, 1986-1993
(With 1994-1995 Recent Titles List)

Compiled by Ann S. Masnik, M.L.S., University of Maryland

Introduction by Marcia Cohn Spiegel, M.A.

Doris B. Gold, Editor

Biblio Press   New York

TO

Eunice Clark Smith, French professor at Skidmore College, who started me on a life-long road to learning and who became my model for balancing the intellectual and the spiritual life.

And to

Melissa, Alexis and Marc who, I hope, will always be proud of their Jewish heritage.

© Copyright Biblio Press, NY, 1996
All Rights Reserved. No part of this book may be used without permission of the Publisher.

Library of Congress Cataloging-in-Publication Data

Masnik, Ann S.
The Jewish woman : an annotated selected bibliography, 1986-1993 : with recent titles list, 1994-5 / compiled by Ann S. Masnik : introduction by Marcia Cohn Spiegel : editor, Doris B. Gold.
p. cm.
Supplement to: The Jewish woman, 1900-1985 / Aviva Cantor.
Includes indexes.
ISBN 0-930395-25-5
1. Jewish women--Bibliography.   I. Gold, Doris B.   II. Cantor, Aviva. Jewish woman, 1900-85.   III. Title.
Z7963.J4C36   1987 Suppl.
[HQ1172]
016.30548'924--dc20   95-20942
CIP

Printed in the United States of America

Production/Design by Rivanne, Brooklyn, NY

Contents

Preface: Ann S. Masnik, M.L.S., University of Maryland, College Park, MD / 1

Introduction: Marcia Cohn Spiegel.M.A. / 2

I. Additions to 1900-85 Citations
   (*The Jewish Woman: 1900-85* compiled by Aviva Cantor) / 13

II. History
        A. Books / Book Chapters / 17
        B. Articles / 20

III. Holocaust and Resistance
        A. Books / Book Chapters / 24
        B. Articles / 31

IV. Religion and Biblical Studies
        A. Books / Book Chapters / 33
        B. Articles / 51

V. United States
        A. Books / Book Chapters / 74
        B. Articles / 84

VI. Israel
        A. Books / Book Chapters / 103
        B. Articles / 106

VII. Other Countries
A. Books / Book Chapters / 113
B. Articles / 116

VIII. Literature
        A. Fiction / 121
        B. Poetry / 125
        C. Short Stories / 129
        D. Collections / 130
        E. Literary Criticism—Books / 131
        F. Literary Criticism—Articles / 134

IX. Recent Titles: 1994-1995
        A. Books / Book Chapters / 143
        B. Articles / 150

X. Resources / 157

XI. Errata / 160

Indexes:
        Author / 161
        Subject / 168

ACKNOWLEDGMENTS

We wish to thank Aviva Cantor, compiler of the first bibliography in this field, *The Jewish Woman: 1900-1985* and its several earlier versions; my son Marc Masnik, my knowledgeable neighbor Joe Mayhew, my colleagues at College Park, especially in the Nonprint Media Department, at the University of Maryland, Professors Evelyn Torton Beck in Women's Studies and Hasia Diner in American Studies; Peggy Pearlstein and Sharon Horowitz at the Library of Congress; Elinor Grumet, Librarian at Stern College for Women in NYC who shared her booklist; colleagues, friends and family members who gave time and morale support; and to Doris B. Gold, editor and publisher extraordinaire of Biblio Press.

Both Biblio Press and I wish to gratefully thank the many Jewish women's organizations who sent their back issues of house organs with reminders of valued citations, and all others who responded to our call for materials.

ABOUT THE AUTHOR

Ann S. Masnik, M.L.S., University of Washington, Seattle, is currently a public service librarian, University of Maryland at College Park. She is also a graduate of Skidmore College and has studied at the University of Paris.

Ms. Masnik began as a high school library aide in New York City, and has served as an assistant librarian at the Cultural Services of the French Embassy in New York; and at community, public and Hebrew day school libraries.

She has been active in the Bibliographic Instruction Division of the American Library Association and has been a member of the Reference Awards Committee of the Association of Jewish Libraries. She recently completed a term as Chairperson of the AJL/Capital Area Chapter.

PREFACE

Purpose

My goal has been to find truths about the Jewish woman from the vast output of authors—both Jewish women writers, scholars and popular authors; both male and female, Jewish and non-Jewish, during the last ten years and to help other readers and researchers locate these riches.

Content

As its title indicates, this bibliography is selective, focusing on several perspectives—history/social issues, religion/spirituality, Jewish women's literature and literary critiques. Only works in English are included. It attempts to open doors, but is not a complete listing of these genres.

We have chosen to organize the various sections in the same format as that in Aviva Cantor's *Jewish Woman Bibliography: 1900-85;* and in Section I certain omissions have been added to those earlier citations.

The Contents page reflects the weight of the citations that were found in a variety of sources over a period of more than two years it took to create this edition. The user will find an emphasis on the annotations (except for the 1994-95 listing of recent works where there is no comment). For annotations quotes from reviews were included and frequently quotes from a work itself. Where a citation is controversial, the phrase "Judge for yourself" is intended to invite reader reaction. (Fiction, poetry and short stores are not annotated.)

There has been some coverage of arts and sciences, but for those interested in these fields as it applies to Jewish women, a reference librarian can assist the user in finding subject-specific bibliographies of indexes to these fields, as well as to *Dissertation Abstracts*. Guides to either audio or video titles on the Jewish women can be found in the final section—Resources.*

How To Use The Bibliography

1. The Contents will lead the user to broad subject sections, and to Additions as well as recent books published in 1994-1995. The alphabetical author and subject indexes will be especially important to find author or subject areas of interest. Cross-references indicate where a work could be found in more than one section—i.e., the main listing for *Daughters of the King* is in the History section, but a cross reference is also given in the Religion section.

2. The user will note that because this entire bibliography pertains to the Jewish woman, the index does not add the adjective "Jewish" or "woman" unless necessary for clarification—as in: *American Jewish women* or *Ashkenazi women;* but for artists, nurses, scientists, "Jewish woman" should be understood, as in *Feminism*. For such entries as Jews in Russia, etc. "woman" should be understood There are notes for certain terms: i.e., "conversas" for female conversos or Marranos. There are also cross-references in the subject index so that one term could be used where several were possible: i.e., *Abused women*, see "Domestic violence" or "rape."

3. In the US section are 3 "ERIC" Reports, (i.e. ED 311332). These refer to US government reports which can be found in any large library (See Reference Librarian).

4. In the Religion section are several citations to JSOT. This refers to *Journal for the Study of the Old Testament*.

Ann S. Masnik, M.L.S.
February, 1996

---

*For an exhaustive search, see the *Index to Jewish Periodicals, Rambi, MLA, American History and Life, Social Science Index, Psychological Abstracts, Uncover, Periodical Abstracts, Women's Studies Abstracts, Short Story Index, Granger's Index to Poetry,* and of course *Books in Print*. For dramatic materials, see *Plays in Collections,* or find copies of play scripts by title of produced plays which are available from Dramatists Play Service.

Introduction
Marcia Cohn Spiegel, M.A.

In 1979, Aviva Cantor's first *Bibliography on the Jewish Woman,* inspired me to read as many of the books as I could find in the local library, at our synagogue and at Hebrew Union College. It was not an unreasonable goal. Later that year, working at the National Council of Jewish Women in Los Angeles to develop a women's library, it seemed realistic to the committee that we could assemble most of the citations to become the core of our collection.

In the ensuing years, writing by and about Jewish women has increased exponentially. It seems that as many books are now being published per year as appeared in all of the previous years. My own collection of new, unread books, overflows tables and desks and cries out for time to sit down and savor their contents, their scholarship, their politics, their new slants on Jewish life. In 1995, I realize that it is an almost impossible task to keep abreast of what is now available about, by, or for Jewish women, so I welcome Ann S. Masnik's new bibliography as a guide.

In this introductory essay, I have chosen to describe the development of Jewish women's writing, the impact of geographic dislocation, changes in class and status, religious practice, as well as the recent forces of integration, assimilation, and acculturation on their writing. Books and authors referred to will be found in various sections of this bibliography.

1. Jewish Women's Writings

Jewish women's lives were changed forever when Rabbi Eliezer declared that, "If any man gives his daughter a knowledge of Torah, it is as though he taught her lewdness" (Mishna: Sotah 3:4). Later he affirmed, "It is better to burn the Torah than to teach it to your daughter." Although other sages argued that women should learn Torah, it is clear that women were excluded, not only from the study of Torah, but from other learning, including the knowledge of Hebrew, that did not directly relate to their roles as wives or mothers. The few remaining scraps of early women's writing offer only fragmentary clues to their lives, so we must become detectives in order to understand who they were, what their lives were like, and how they participated in the Jewish community.

Now that we are flooded with books, poetry, literature and scholarship by Jewish women, it is hard to reconcile ourselves to how pervasive Rabbi Eliezer's attitude was until well into the twentieth century. Not too long ago I interviewed an elderly woman, the youngest daughter of a long line of prominent rabbinic scholars, the wife of a rabbi, and the mother of rabbis. During her childhood in the *Yeshuv* (Palestine) in a Yiddish speaking family at the turn of the century, she was so eager to learn to read and write Hebrew, that her mother secretly hired a tutor for her. With her books hidden under her pinafore, she sneaked away to lessons. Unfortunately, when she was eight years old, her father caught her in the act, and confronted the teacher who assured the rabbi that he was only teaching her arithmetic, geography and history, not Torah or prayers, but the lessons stopped that day and she knew that she would never again have a chance to study. Eighty-five years later as she remembered that moment, she wept inconsolably for her loss.

While the *Tanach* (Hebrew Bible), includes prayers composed by the prophet Miriam, Deborah the judge, and Hannah; the Apocrypha includes a hymn of victory sung by Judith, and the Talmud relates the wise sayings of Breruriah and Ima Shalom, some rabbinic interpreters claim that these words were most likely written by men. Assuming that this attitude was a thing of the far distant

Introduction

past, I was shocked to hear it reiterated by a scholar of Judaica in charge of a large university collection. When I asked for his assistance in tracking down some fifteenth and sixteenth century Jewish poets, he was excited about helping me find some lost Jews, until he looked at the list of poets I handed him. "But these are all women," he said, "Their work would not have been preserved. They wrote poetry because they weren't smart enough to write prose. In prose you must use grammar and syntax. In poetry, if you don't know what to do, all you do is use a dash."

A woman needs three things in order to write: she must be literate, have the leisure time to read and write, and have access to writing materials such as pen and paper. Because we have always been a people on the move, accommodating to new communities, new environments and new languages, and because women were denied an education in Hebrew, early writing by women was often in the vernacular of the countries in which they lived, or in Yiddish or Ladino, when these became the *lingua franca*. Women who learned to read and write were often the daughters of wealthy men who did not need their daughter's labor in the family business and who hired servants to perform household chores. These girls were often taught music, art, dance, needlework and literature, not in Hebrew, but in the language of the country in which they lived. The poetry of two such sixteenth century Jewish women, Sarah Copia Sullam of Venice, and Deborah Ascarelli of Rome, reveals educated, sophisticated and literate women. (Sondra Henry and Emily Taitz, *Written out of History*). Deborah Ascarelli wrote in both Hebrew and Italian, and translated work from one language into the other. Ascarelli's poetry is the very first printed material by a Jewish woman preserved—thanks to the Italian archivists who saved even the works of women.

Rabbis and scholars who had no sons sometimes took pleasure in sharing their knowledge of Torah and Talmud with their daughters. Rashi's daughters were well educated, as was Rachel Morpurgo in nineteenth century Trieste, and Henriette Szold in Baltimore in the early twentieth century. Women who were considered unmarriageable by their parents may have been given an education so that they could earn a living. When I read about the partial blindness of Peninah Moise, author of the first collection of American Jewish hymns (Charleston, S.C. 1841), I wondered if that was how she came to be so knowledgeable (Solomon Breibart, *Peninah Moise: Southern Jewish Poetess*). In a pre-industrial world, where cottage industry prevailed, daughters working in the family trade as scribes or printers had to learn to read and write. In 1718, one such young woman wrote in Yiddish, "This pretty new prayer... I arranged with all the letters in my own hand. I, Galah, daughter of Moshe the printer... I am a virgin and almost twelve years old," (Marcia Cohn Spiegel, *Women Speak to God*). Still other women were forced to become literate when they went into the marketplace to buy and sell and earn a living for their family. The journal of Gluckel of Hameln written in 17th century Germany, gives us an insight into that world (Ellen Umansky and Dianne Ashton, *Four Centuries of Jewish Women's Spirituality*).

In the late sixteenth century, the Venetian government forced the Hebrew printers to close down; the printing presses were moved to Krakow and Prague which became the new centers for publication of Hebrew books. Because Yiddish is written with Hebrew letters, it was now possible to print Yiddish books cheaply. Books specifically written for women began to appear. The *Tsena Urena,* a collection of Biblical commentaries, stories and prayers, which could be used in the synagogue or at home, and *Techinot*, collections of women's personal prayers, were very popular. (Nina Beth Cardin, *Out of the Depths I Call To You: A Book of Prayers for the Married Jewish Woman,* Tracy Klers, *The*

Merit of our Mothers, Chava Weissler, *The Traditional Piety of Ashkenazic Women*). While it is true that some *techinas* were written by men for the growing audience of Jewish women, many, if not most, were written by women, such as Sara Bat Tovim. With the advent of the *Haskalah* (enlightenment) movement, in Eastern Europe in the mid-nineteenth century, Jews who were striving for upward mobility began to educate their daughters to take their place in a changing society. The Socialist movement and Zionism became popular with young people; some of them began to look beyond the traditional *Yeshivot* to the gymnasia and a secular education. Literacy among women and girls became more widespread, and with it an increase in memoirs, poetry and political writing.

2. Coming to America

The arrival of Jews from Eastern Europe late in the nineteenth century was not the beginning of Jewish immigration to America; Sephardic Jews, fleeing from the Inquisition, came to New York in the seventeenth century. Women writers from the Sephardic community included Peninah Moise, and Emma Lazarus whose hymn to liberty appears on the Statue of Liberty. An important Ashkenazic family, the Gratz family, arrived in Pennsylvania in the mid-eighteenth century from Poland by way of London. Rebecca Gratz, known for her energetic work in social welfare and education, was an inveterate letter writer; she is the model for Sir Walter Scott's heroine, Rebecca, in *Ivanhoe* (Jacob Rader Marcus, *The American Jewish Woman: A Documentary History*).

The next big wave of immigration came from Germany. Some of the Jewish organizations that we are familiar with today, such as B'nai Brith and the American Jewish Committee originated from this group of immigrants. Acculturated German-Jewish women involved themselves in charitable work, helping Jewish widows and orphans, and protecting Jewish women from becoming involved in the white-slave trade as prostitutes. After the 1893 Chicago World's Fair left many Jewish women stranded and out of work, the National Council of Jewish Women was founded to teach trades to the women so that they could support themselves and their children (Faith Rogow, *Gone to Another Meeting: The National Council of Jewish Women, 1893-1993*). Women were not only reading the periodicals *The Occident, The American Israelite*, and *The American Jewess*, they were writing for these periodicals as well. Strong voices spoke out for political change: in the mid-1800s, Ernestine Rose was a prominent speaker who wrote about abolitionism and feminism (Yuri Suhl, *Ernestine L. Rose: Women's Rights Pioneer*). Her zeal may have served as a role-model for Emma Goldman (Alice Wexler, *Emma Goldman: An Intimate Life)* and later Rose Schneiderman who was both a worker and organizer (Rose Schneiderman, *All for One*).

In 1881 the largest wave of immigration began as Jews fled the pogroms of Eastern Europe. Over the next forty years, Yiddish speaking Jews arrived in great numbers, settling mainly in urban areas across the country. Many women writers, poets and activists were included. By this time the earlier Sephardic and German immigrants had established themselves as Americans and created the Reform movement. The newcomers, who were largely Orthodox, found their home in the new Conservative movement. Others eschewed religion for politics, and centered their lives on the labor movement, Socialism and the Bunds. Their story is told in Susan A. Glenn's, *Daughters of the Shtetl: Life and Labor in the Immigrant Generation,* and Andrew Heinze, *Adapting to Abundance: Jewish Immigrants, Mass Consumption and the Search for American Identity.*

Introduction

For many of the immigrants *Yiddishkeit* was their secular religion. Thriving Yiddish cultural groups included the writers and poets Kadia Molodowsky, and Anna Margolin in New York, Celia Dropkin in Chicago, and Rachel Korn in Montreal. While their poems and stories reflect an honest, unromanticized examination of their lives, it was largely ignored in early anthologies of Yiddish poetry and literature; none of their short stories were translated into English or collected until the 1994 publication of *Found Treasures: Stories by Yiddish Women Writers*, edited by Frieda Forman, et al, which provides a first opportunity to examine prose by these extraordinary women. A contemporary poet, Irena Klepfiz, captures both the beauty and immediacy of Yiddish in her own bilingual works (*A Few Words in the Mother Tongue: Poems Selected and New—1971-1990*). However, most Yiddish literature and poetry is still not translated and is unavailable to the English reader.

While this bibliography is arranged by country and major themes, writing by Jewish women is difficult to neatly categorize because of the diversity of backgrounds, class, ethnicity, religious observance, political participation, geographic differences and the scope of their interests. By the turn of this century, German and Sephardic Jewish women considered themselves American-Jews and were active in social causes, education and welfare while the new immigrants were jammed into crowded ghettoes, forced to work under the most difficult circumstances to eke out a bare survival. Although they had little time left over for creating art or literature, their passion motivated some women to overcome the struggle and to write about their lives. Earlier editions of the Cantor bibliography include Mary Antin (*The Promised Land*), describing her journey to America as a child; Mamie Pinzer explaining how she became a prostitute and her subsequent struggle to survive (*The Mamie Papers*); and Anzia Yezierska expressing her anger about being an immigrant daughter in a patriarchal family (*Red Ribbon on a White Horse*). In the Masnik compilation here, Joyce Antler (*America and I*) has included short stories by Yezierska and Antin along with Edna Ferber and Fannie Hurst to describe this period of the American-Jewish experience.

3. Becoming Americans

Patterns of development and behavior of American-Jews begin to emerge in recent books, plays and stories. The assimilated American-born daughter of an American-born daughter lives a very different life from that of a newly arrived, Yiddish speaking woman. It is as difficult to identify the Jewish family in Lillian Hellman's play, *The Little Foxes*, as it is to avoid it in Anzia Yezierska's story, "The Fat of the Land," (Sylvia Barack Fishman's *Follow My Footprints: Changing Images of Women in American Jewish Fiction*). The experience of each generation is determined by the first family members to arrive in this country, where they settled, what language they spoke, how they observed or practiced Judaism. The very first immigrants usually spoke no English, had few friends or families in America, worked at menial jobs, and may have lived in urban ghettoes with other immigrants.

The children of these immigrants, raised and educated in American public schools, frequently served as go-betweens for their parents and the larger society. Sometimes they were ashamed of their parents, and this shame was transformed into blame and humiliation in the stories and novels by Jewish men, such as Philip Roth, describing their father's weaknesses and their mother's guilt producing behavior. Women of that period had their unique struggle to break free of family traditions and the expectations of a good Jewish daughter, in order to establish themselves as independent American women. Faye Moskowitz (*Her Face in the Mirror*) has selected a few of these stories in the section of her anthology entitled "In Anger and In Love". Vivian Gornick, (*Fierce Attachments: A Memoir*) and Merrill Joan Gerber (*Kingdom of Brooklyn*) give us first-hand accounts of the daughter's struggle.

The differences between the generations comes into sharp focus in these new collections of women's stories by Antler, Fishman and Moskowitz: the immigrant's story is one of struggle, survival and hope for the future; the story of the next generation is written from a place of deep ambivalence, as yearnings for assimilation vie with the importance of tradition. Many of the stories deal with disappointment and alienation from family and/or community. They reveal the confusion caused by events and relationships that have long been hidden, whether knowledge of pogroms in Europe, the Holocaust, or family secrets (Letty Cottin Pogrebin, *Debra, Golda and Me*). As we move out of the ghetto and into suburbia, immigrant grandparents become nostalgic reminders of a distant and romanticized past (Leslea Newman, *Bubbe Meisehs by Shayneh Maidelehs: An Anthology of Poetry by Jewish Granddaughters about our Grandmothers*), while parents, particularly mothers, represent conflicting values that the authors want to reject while still being accepted and loved. The recent *Jewish Women's Awareness Guide* (Janet Carnay, et al) presents a series of exercises to help women and small groups explore the origin of these feelings and how we integrate them into our lives.

The contemporary listings under "Literature" include many major American writers: Cynthia Ozick, Grace Paley, Rosellen Brown, Lynne Sharon Schwartz, Francine Prose, Anne Roiphe, in novels which explore the many facets of the lives of Jewish women in America. Marge Piercy, whose earlier novels dealt with a secular society, has turned her talents to addressing Jewish concerns. Her novel, *Gone to Soldier*, is the first epic to tell the story of World War II through the eyes of the women. Her science-fiction novel, *He, She, and It,* describes the attempts of women in the city of Tikvah (hope) to save the world by the creation of a robot, a modern *golem*. Even her poetry reflects her increasing interest in Judaism, as she translates traditional prayers into contemporary poetry.

As the twenty-first century approaches, a new generation of women who have no memory of a grandmother with a Yiddish accent are writing; women who have grown up in a world where the State of Israel always existed; women who can be rabbis or cantors, doctors or judges if they choose; women who do not see themselves as "other" because they are Jewish. Rebecca Goldstein, Pearl Abraham, Allegra Goodman and Leslea Newman are among the authors who speak for younger women. *Shaking Eve's Tree: Short Stories of Jewish Women* edited by Sharon Niederman presents some of the fiction by this group, as will Marlene Marks' forthcoming collection, *Jewish Girls: Growing Up*.

4. Changing Roles for American Women

Tradition defined the role of the Jewish woman as a dutiful daughter to her parents, a helpmate to her husband, and a doting mother to her children. There have always been women who did not accept this model, who broke free of its constraints. The immigrant woman of this century often had no choice—she may have been forced to work in order to pay the rent and put food on the table, or forbidden to work because her husband or father would lose face if it appeared he could not support his family. If she did work, she may have been so outraged by abusive working-conditions that she joined with other women to form unions, or boycotts. She may have been a warm, gentle, caring, nurturing woman; or she may have been so defeated by poverty and pressure that she became de-

Introduction

pressed, angry, and emotionally abusive to those around her. Excluded from jobs, education, or ritual involvement in the synagogue, she may have organized to help others and thereby created a world in which she could move into American society, achieve a sense of self-worth, and community status. Organizations such as Hadassah, National Council of Jewish Women, O.R.T., Pioneer Women, B'nai Brith Women and synagogue sisterhoods did more than raise funds and create social change; they were truly vehicles for assimilation and provided women a place to achieve power and a sense of personal fulfillment. Too often, however, this volunteerism was exploited by the community, and was rarely granted high status.

With the establishment of the State of Israel in 1948, the primary agenda of the Zionist organizations had been met, and their most important function now shifted to maintaining the established structures. Simultaneously, young women in large numbers had the opportunity to attend colleges and universities, and they were no longer willing to participate in the kinds of volunteer activities that had satisfied their mothers. Many of them moved outside the Jewish community for their volunteer involvement, into anti-war, anti-nuclear organizations, into abortion rights groups, into the struggle for passage of the equal rights amendment, into the National Organization for Women and the National Women's Studies Associations. The virulence of the anti-semitism expressed at the U.N. women's conferences in Copenhagen, Nairobi and Mexico City, as well as in meetings of feminist organizations, shocked Jewish women who had worked so hard, assuming that they were equals, only to find themselves isolated and alienated in the very communities that they had built. Disillusioned, some tried to repair their organizations, others turned back to the Jewish community to do the work of *tikkun olam*, repair of the world.

Unaddressed issues in the Jewish community, such as addiction and family violence, were researched in schools of Jewish communal service (Betsy Giller, "All in the Family", in Rachel Josefowitz Siegel and Ellen Cole, *Seen but not Heard: Jewish Women in Therapy* and Marcia Cohn Spiegel, "Growing up Jewish" in Ellen Umansky and Dianne Ashton, *Four Centuries of Jewish Women's Spirituality*) and Jewish women initiated efforts to change the situation. *Isha l'isha* in Israel reached out to the victims of family violence, and in the United States several Jewish family service agencies developed programs to deal with hidden problems of sexual abuse and physical violence (Ian Russ, Sally Weber, Ellen Ledley, *Shalom Bayit: A Jewish Response to Child Abuse and Domestic Violence*, Julie Ringold Spitzer, *When Love is Not Enough: Spousal Abuse in Rabbinic and Contemporary Judaism*). New organizations, founded in the last few years, the Shefa Fund, New Israel Fund, Mazon and the Jewish Fund for Justice have become social change agents using Jewish values to extend help beyond the immediate Jewish community.

Lesbian women who were once forced, by the community to remain silent, are beginning to take their place in community organizations, although their struggle for acceptance is far from over in the face of both subtle and outright homophobia. Lesbian and gay synagogues exist in many major cities, and are included on some Jewish federation boards (Christie Balka and Andy Rose, *Twice Blessed: on Being Lesbian, Gay and Jewish*; Evelyn Torton Beck, *Nice Jewish Girls: A Lesbian Anthology*). Other issues which are being confronted include antisemitism (Melanie Kaye/Kantrowitz, *The Issue is Power: Essays on Women, Jews, Violence and Resistance*), and the increasing rate of intermarriage (Rachel and Paul Cowan, *Mixed Blessings,* and Susan Weidman Schneider, *Intermarriage: The Challenge of Living with Differences between Christians and Jews*).

As women in volunteer and membership organizations age, and are not being replaced by younger women, these organizations are reexamining their agendas. Daughters no longer automatically take their mother's place in Hadassah, ORT, or Na'amat. Articles and columns in the journals of these organizations are aimed at younger women and professionals with limited time or energy to give to a cause. *Na'amat Woman* has been focusing more attention on American feminist issues, Jewish feminist scholarship, ordination of women, and recently featured articles on family violence in Jewish families. *Hadassah Magazine* is featuring new, younger writers, like Marlene Marks, and presenting the creative work of Jewish women artists. My grandmother, who was a life-member of Hadassah, would be surprised and delighted at the emerging Hadassah curriculum related to the Jewish family and women's spirituality, and their most recent publication *Voices for Change. Future Directions for American Jewish Women*. National Council of Jewish Women is addressing the needs of young families with children in daycare, and the role of working women with children. *Bridges* and *Lilith*, present issues of interest to women who represent a new set of demographics—younger, from diverse Jewish ethnic backgrounds, working class as well as middle- and upper-class, who are redefining what it means to be a Jewish woman.

5. Feminist Spirituality and Religion

The post-World-War II building- and baby-boom expanded Jewish communities out of urban areas and into suburbia; we saw the development of new synagogues, schools and Jewish institutions; youngsters in large numbers attended Jewish camps, religious schools and youth group retreats. Girls celebrated *bat mitzvah,* became equal participants in services, led prayers and read from the Torah. These young women who grew up in Jewish youth programs, exposed to a changing Judaism, anti-war activism and the feminist movement refused to accept the status quo of the religious establishment. They demanded to be included in prayer quorums and ritual, to be allowed to conduct services as cantors and to be granted admission to rabbinic seminaries. By 1985 every movement, other than the Orthodox, ordained women. By 1990 the Cantorial Association accepted women as members. But a residue of patriarchy remains: a number of male Conservative rabbis, protesting the liberalization of the Conservative movement exemplified by the ordination of women, formed the Union of Traditional Judaism. As I write this, over fifty percent of rabbinic students in non-orthodox institutions are women. ("Women Rabbis: Turning Newness into Strength," *Na'amat Woman*, May-June, 1994:4-7+). Only one woman, Laura Geller, has been appointed rabbi of a synagogue of over 1000 families; most women rabbis are still assigned as assistant rabbis or educators. Their pay is lower than the men, and 70% report being sexually harassed. The good news is that the numbers are rising; the bad news is we still have a long way to go to be accepted as equals.

The explosion of books on religion, spirituality, prayer and biblical interpretation reflects the most dramatic difference between this bibliography and the earlier editions. While the last edition in 1986 had 49 such works, this edition has 146 citations from 1986 to 1993, and even more in the listings for 1994 to 1995. The religious needs expressed by the young women growing up in the 60s and 70s, coupled with their ability to enroll in programs of higher education, probably explains the numbers of women admitted to schools of theology, rabbinic seminaries, and Jewish studies programs. Their scholarship is included in the many books listed in the section, "Religious and Biblical Studies," and is influencing academia beyond Judaism. Jewish women play an increasingly important role in the American Academy of Religion, and the Society for Biblical Studies.

Introduction

Women exploring their spiritual options are no longer satisfied addressing their prayers only to "Lord, God, King of the Universe"; they want to feel connected to a God who has other qualities of nurturing, caring, compassion. Prayer books are being rewritten to include both feminine God language and gender neutral language, and theological concepts that focus on the immanance of diety (Marcia Lee Falk, *The Book of Blessings: A Feminist Jewish Reconstruction of Prayer*, Harper/SanFrancisco forthcoming in 1996, *Kol Haneshamah, Shabbat Eve*, a Reconstructionist Prayer Book and *Or Chadash*, from Aleph: Alliance for Jewish Renewal). New rituals are being created and performed by both observant and secular Jewish women (Rabbi Debra Orenstein, *Lifecycles: Jewish Women on Life Passages and Personal Milestones*, Irene Fine, *Midlife: A Rite of Passage, and The Wise Woman: A Celebration,* Elizabeth Resnick Levine, *A Ceremonies Sampler: New Rites, Celebrations and Observances of Jewish Women*, and Lynn Gottlieb, *She Who Dwells Within: A Feminist Vision of a Renewed Judaism*). Older rituals, such as women's Rosh Hodesh celebrations, are being reintroduced (Penina Adelman, *Miriam's Well: Rituals for Jewish Women Around the Year*, Susan Berrin, *Celebrating the New Moon: A Rosh Chodesh Sourcebook*).

Women's spirituality groups are forming throughout the USA and abroad, allowing women to pray together, observe Shabbat or long weekend retreats, share in teaching, learning and creativity. Older women are being empowered by their daughters to become *Bat Mitzvah*, and full participants in synagogue services. Women are taking the new vision of Jewish renewal into their community synagogues and *havurot*. Some prefer to restrict their groups to women only, some meet outside of their synagogue or community, others, because they are Orthodox, may not be able to participate fully in their congregations. The music they are singing, by Debbie Friedman, Linda Hirschorn and Hannah Tiferet Siegel, and the prayers that they are reciting, are finding their way into more traditional settings, sometimes as alternative music or readings, later as part of the standard liturgy.

As more women study Judaism, read the texts and reinterpret the ancient words in the light of their own experience, they are creating a new body of scholarship, collections of *midrash,* and commentaries (Carol A. Newsom and Sharon H. Ringe, *The Women's Bible Commentary*; Ilana Pardes, *Countertraditions in the Bible: A Feminist Approach*; Christina Buchmann and Celina Spiegel, *Out of the Garden* and Savina Teubal, *Sarah, the Priestess* and *Hagar, the Egyptian*). A new lens is focused on traditional laws, roles and practices (Judith Romney Wegner, *Chattel or Person?: The Status of Women in Mishnah*, Susan Grossman and Rivka Haut, *Daughters of the King: Women and the Synagogue*; Judith R. Baskin, *Jewish Women in Historical Perspective*). The voices of traditional women are included as well (Tamar Frankiel's *The Voice of Sarah: Feminine Spirituality and Traditional Judaism*). Newsletters have been created to reach out to women who are involved in these studies and activities. One such new periodical, *Neshama*, presents rituals and poetry along with *midrash* and an examination of various texts. Judith Plaskow delineates a feminist approach to Jewish theology. (*Standing Again at Sinai: Judaism from a Feminist Perspective),* and Ellen M. Umansky and Dianne Ashton, *(Four Centuries of Jewish Women's Spirituality: A Sourcebook)* present a comprehensive survey of both early and contemporary sources by women. This new vision is even found in novels (Kim Chernin, *The Flame Bearers).*

Dramatic changes are being seen in Orthodoxy as women are actively creating prayer groups and Rosh Hodesh groups and girls are having *bat mitzvah* ceremonies. In the past, if an Orthodox girl had such a ceremony, it usually took place at a dinner party, when the 12 year old girl gave a commentary on the *haftorah* reading for the week. Some women wanted more for their daughters, and now in a few communities the *bat mitzvah* takes place in the sanctuary, while the men sit in the balcony or behind the *mehitza*, as the celebrant reads from the *Torah*. Women are beginning to study seriously in *yeshivot*. Although some Orthodox rabbis are opposed to these advances, they have not succeeded in stopping the spread. Norma Joseph and Blu Greenberg write about a new generation of Orthodox women. Debra Renee Kaufman explains the current return to orthodoxy by women from non-traditional families in *Rachel's Daughters: Newly Orthodox Jewish Women*.

Despite all of these positive changes, the laws regarding women's status are still rigidly interpreted, the most serious being that of the chained woman, the *agunah*. A woman whose husband refuses to give her a *get*, a religious divorce, cannot remarry and is tied to her husband, even if he batters her, commits incest or is a child abuser. Women around the world have banded together to call attention to this injustice, but to no avail. Naomi Ragen deals with these issues in her novels (*Jephte's Daughter, Sotah,* and *The Sacrifice of Tamar*). Fay Kellerman has developed a large following in a series of mysteries that tell these stories through the eyes of Rina Lazarus, an Orthodox woman (*Day of Atonement, The Ritual Bath, Sacred and Profane*). Anne Roiphe's *Lovingkindness*, explores the tensions that arise when a secular mother is confronted by her daughter's return to tradition.

6. Israeli Women

The earliest images of life in Israel presented women in a glorified light as Zionist heroines and settlers, working as full equals with men in the fields and farms to create the land and form a new nation. Contemporary books explode the myths and take a more realistic and pragmatic look at the lives of women in Israel, the truth of their struggles, the political battles they are fighting and their ongoing efforts to break free of patriarchal strictures and expectations (Deborah S. Bernstein, *Pioneers and Homemakers: Jewish Women in Pre-State Israel*, Barbara Swirski and Marilyn P. Safir, *Calling the Equality Bluff: Women in Israel*, and Tracy Moore, *Lesbiot: Israeli Lesbians Talk about Sexuality, Feminism and Judaism*). Because of their ongoing struggle to survive internal strife, the political battles over women's status, divorce, marriage, role in the army, and the feminization of poverty, Israeli women have had less time or energy to address the issues of spirituality that are so important to contemporary American women. Almost every recent issue of *Na'amat Women* has included articles about these problems ("Women, War and Peace," "The Feminization of Poverty", and "Israeli Women and their Health", all by Amy Avgar).

Recent immigration from Russia, and Ethiopia has changed the face of Israel. We can no longer stereotype Israelis as immigrants and the children of immigrants from Eastern Europe. The demographics show us a land whose people are from many places, including Yemen, Syria, Morocco, and other middle-Eastern countries. It is no longer an *Ashkenazi* culture, but now *Sephardi* and *Mizrachi* populations make up a large percentage of the population. These newcomers are faced with a myriad of problems, not only assimilating to the culture and language, but legitimizing their status as Jews. For some the issue is the acceptance of a non-Orthodox conversion, for others it may be the legal status of their children or other close relatives. They struggle to maintain some of their religious and cultural traditions in this new environment. Many of them are single mothers, trying to make it in a man's world.

Introduction

As yet there are only a handful of books and articles written about these women: Ruby Daniel (with Barbara Johnson, *Ruby of Cochin: An Indian Jewish Woman Remembers*) describes a different Jewish ethnic experience; also Lisa Gilad (*Ginger and Salt: Yemeni Jewish Women in an Israeli Town*) and Andrea King ("Is Israel Liberating for Ethiopian Women?" in *Lilith*). It is high time that we have a chance to read more about the Sephardic and Mizrachi communities and new immigrants from Iran, South Africa, South America, and other countries around the world. New scholarship and stories will expand our understanding of what it means to be a Jewish woman today.

Books in Hebrew, written by women, are still largely unavailable in translation. Carol Diament and Lily Rattok have edited *Ribcage: Israeli Women's Fiction*, a collection of translated works. Hillel Halkin has translated several novels by Shulamit Hareven, including *City of Many Days*, which describes life in Jerusalem before the state of Israel, and *The Prophet*. Mysteries are a new genre of women's writing and Batya Gur presents a rather grim picture of Israeli society in *Saturday Morning Murder: A Psychoanalytic Case*. One hopes that in the next edition of this bibliography, translations will require a section to themselves.

7. The Holocaust

In the first bibliography there were 34 citations under "Holocaust". In the second, there were 37. In this volume, there are 58 entries. Many years had to pass before women were able to move beyond the horror of the war years, to fully understand the impact it had on their lives so that they could place it into perspective in their writing. The popularity of Steven Spielberg's film, *Schindler's List*, which triggered a project to collect the oral testimony of survivors, the holocaust memorials and museums which are also preserving their experiences, and the unfortunate persistence of those who would rewrite history to erase or minimize this horror, has created an urgency to secure the facts from the remaining survivors before they age and die. In the last few years there have been an outpouring of first hand stories and collections of writing. As a young woman I could only read *Anne Frank's Diary* and identify with her experience; my granddaughter, however, can read about Anne as well as many other courageous girls and women who were caught in the *Shoah*, some who survived, some who died. Among the many new books are the lives of Janina Bauman (*Winter in the Morning: A Young Girl's Life in the Warsaw Ghetto and Beyond*), Charlotte Salomon (*To Paint Her Life: Charlotte Salomon in the Nazi Era* by Mary Felstiner), and of those brave souls who tried to save lives (*Rescuers: Portraits of Moral Courage in the Holocaust* by Gay Block and Malka Drucker and *Conscience and Courage: Rescuers of Jews During the Holocaust* by Eva Fogelman).

In a recent issue of *Ms*, (November, 1994) Andrea Dworkin wrote about her visit to the Holocaust Museum in Washington, D. C. ("The Unremembered: Searching for Women's Experiences at the U.S. Holocaust Museum"). She found little evidence of the specific cruelties inflicted on women of sexual abuse, medical experiments, torture, maiming. A graduate student currently writing a doctoral dissertation on the women who survived these experiences has been hard-put to find any written documentation. She has encountered a few daughters who believe their mothers may have been survivors of "The House of Dolls," but has been unable to confirm it. The unspeakable humiliation, degradation and terror of these women may die with them. When we think we have come to understand all of the horror, we realize that there is more that we may never know.

8. Conclusion

In this bibliography we see a burgeoning interest in the fields of religion, theology, spirituality, biblical studies, literature and the holocaust. New studies and books on stigmatized behaviors are impacting policy decisions of Jewish institutions. There are more listings of books and articles about Jewish women in politics, while the interest in the historical role of Jewish women in developing the labor movement and their contribution as community volunteers continues. What we do not find here are many scholarly studies about Jewish women in the arts, films, theater, music, medicine, science and psychotherapy, all disciplines in which Jewish women are making a major impact. New cultural, sociological and anthropological studies will surely reveal the varieties of Jewish culture with which we are unfamiliar, and preserve that which we take for granted. Translations from Hebrew and Yiddish, as well as from other languages, will help us to learn more about authors who are still unfamiliar to us. (There remain treasures of Yiddish literature, of which only a tiny remnant is available in English.)

Through citations in the bibliography we follow the changes in Jewish life in this country and abroad. Jewish women have made major inroads into seats of power in the U.S. government as Barbara Boxer and Diane Feinstein serve in the Senate, Nina Loewy in Congress, Ruth Bader Ginsburg on the bench of the Supreme Court; Ruth Messinger in Manhattan as boro president; Alice Rivlin as Secretary of Treasury. But ironically, we still struggle to gain a foothold in the seats of power in the organized Jewish community either as professionals or volunteers.

The Jewish people will never fully recover from the horrors of the holocaust. Our numbers have been diminished by six million, and even further by intermarriage, assimilation, and conversion. Educated women are marrying later, and childbirth is delayed. Both spouses today are often forced to work in order to maintain a home. Birth rates in the Jewish community are dropping below replacement, except in the Orthodox community. The percentage of Jews in America has decreased from 4% in 1945 to 2.3% in 1995. In 1902 less than 1% of Jews were intermarried; today the number approaches 50%. As intermarriage rates grow, fewer men available for those women who would like to marry a Jewish man. Some women are choosing to become single parents; lesbian women are opting to bear children; gay men are adopting children. The image of a nuclear family with an at-home mother, working father and two children bears little resemblance to most contemporary Jewish families.

We continue to struggle with archaic laws that determine women's status; family violence, sexual abuse and addiction plague the lives of too many Jewish women; family configurations are changing; the costs of being a participating member of a Jewish community are rising; women are still fighting to attain their rightful place in the executive suites and at the board table; child care and flex-time are talked about as options for Jewish professionals, but little is done to create the structures needed; homosexuals are often not welcome in our organizations and institutions.

Despite these gloomy statistics and prognostications, this bibliography gives us reason to hope. It details a growing concern about Judaism, our roles as Jewish women in contemporary society and religious life, a willingness to grapple with the complexities of scholarship and community change. We refuse to be silenced. We no longer play "Let's Pretend." We are examining the past to understand the lives of the women who lived before us, in order to create a better world for the present and future. Our writing reflects our lives.

I
Additions to 1900-1985 Citations

A. Books

Baer, Jean: **The Self Chosen: "Our Crowd" is Dead, Long Live Our Crowd**. New York: Arbor House, 1982,

> Includes Chap. 7: The Women:Tradition and Transition (history) & Chap. 8 (The Women at the Top—brief bios of successful contemporary women).

Ben-Tov, Sharona: **During Ceasefire**. New York: Harper & Row, 1985.

Breibart, Solomon: **Penina Moise: Southern Jewish Poetess in: Proctor, Samuel and Louis Schmier, eds.:** Jews of the South. Macon, Ga: Mercer University Press, 1984.

Gerber, Merrill Joan: **Honeymoon: Stories**. Urbana, IL: University of Illinois Press, 1985.

King, Stella: **Jacqueline: Pioneer Heroine of the Resistance**. New York: Sterling/Arms & Armour, 1984.

Koppelman, Susan, Ed.: **The Other Woman: Stories of Two Women and a Man**. Old Westbury, NY: Feminist Press, 1984.

> Includes "Chayah" by Martha Wolfenstein.

Kornblatt, Joyce Reiser: **White Water**. New York: E.P.Dutton, 1985.

Krause, Corinne Azen: **Grandmothers, Mothers and Daughters: An Oral History Study of Ethnicity, Mental Health, and Continuity of Three Generations of Jewish, Italian and Slavic-American Women**. New York: Institute on Pluralism and Group Identity, 1978.

Nordhaus, Jean: **A Language of Hands**. College Park, MD: SCOP Publications, 1982.

Olsen, Tillie, ed.: **Mother to Daughter, Daughter to Mother: A Daybook and Reader**. New York: Old Westbury, 1984.

> Personal selection from writers such as Paley and Steinem.

Ostriker, Alicia: **Once More Out of Darkness and Other Poems**: Berkeley, CA: Berkeley Poets' Cooperative, 1976.

Parent, Gail: **The Best Laid Plans**. New York: Putnam, 1980.

Piercy, Marge: **Braided Lives**. New York: Ballantine, 1983.

Popkin, Zelda: **Herman Had Two Daughters**. Philadelphia, PA: Lippincott, 1968.

Richardson, Brenda: **Dr Claribel and Miss Ettie: The Cone Collection of the Baltimore Museum of Art**. Baltimore, MD: Baltimore Art Museum, 1985.

Two upper-class Jewish ladies of Victorian Baltimore collected Matisse, Picasso and other important art works. One sister became a physician, the other devoted her life to her sister and to this collection.

Ruddick, Sara Daniels, Pamela, Eds: **Working it Out: 23 Women Writers, Artists, Scientists, and Scholars Talk about Their Lives and Work**. New York: Pantheon, 1977.

Includes chapters by Tillie Olsen and Anne Lasoff, Joann Green, Amelie Rorty, etc. Foreword by Adrienne Rich.

Shneiderman, S.L.: **The River Remembers**. New York: Horizon Press, 1978.

The story of Kazimierz, and other towns in Poland where Jews lived before WWII. and where the biblical history of Queen Esther was recreated in the love of Poland's King Kazimierz (14th c.) for a Jewish woman, Esterke, daughter of a tailor. Plays and stories have been written in Yiddish and Polish about her.

Sinclair, Clive: **The Brothers Singer**. New York: Schocken Books, 1983.

Includes Esther Kreitman Singer in detail.

Solomon, Barbara Miller: **In the Company of Educated Women: A History of Women and Higher Education in America**. New Haven, CN: Yale University Press, 1985.

Although this book contains no separate chapter on Jewish women in American colleges, it does give information about discrimination at these colleges, some statistics (see p.144), identity crises, participation in peace protests, etc.

Sorin, Gerald: **The Prophetic Minority: American Jewish Immigrant Radicals 1880-1920**. Bloomington, IN: Indiana University Press, 1985.

See especially chapter 6: The Women:World of Our Mothers and Others (124-141); but women are included in other parts of the book as well

Sternberg, Meir: **Viewpoints and Interpretations in: The Poetics of Biblical Narrative**. Bloomington, IN: Indiana University Press, 1985, pp 129-152; 445-75.

Sternberg writes about "The Wooing of Rebekah"—and the "Delicate Balance in the Rape of Dinah."

Wandor, Michelene: **Gardens of Eden: Poems for Eve & Lilith**. West Nyack, NY: Journeyman/Playbooks, 1984.

Whitman, Ruth: **An Anthology of Modern Yiddish Poetry: Selected and Translated by Ruth Whitman. Bi-Lingual** New York: Workmen's Circle, 1979, 2nd edition of 1966 ed.

Contains 3 women poets

B. Articles

Berrol, Selma: **Class or Ethnicity: The Americanized German Jewish Woman and her Middle Class Sisters in 1895**. New York: **Jewish Social Studies**, 47, Winter 1985, 21-32.

Bitton, Livia E.: **The Jewess as a Fictional Sex Symbol**. Bucknell Review: **21**, Lewisburg, PA, Spring, 1973, 63-86.

Discussion of stereotypes of Jewish women - as mother, as sex symbol, in fiction - from Marlowe and Shakespeare, Middle Ages plays, Flaubert, and in American literature.

Cohen, Norman: **Miriam's Song: A Modern Midrashic Reading**. Judaism: **33**, New York, Spring 1984, 179-190.

Cohen, Shaye, J.D.: **Origin of the Matrilineal**. Cambridge, MA: **Association of Jewish Studies Review**, 10, 1985, 19-53.

Damian, Natalia: **Divorce and Immigration: The Social Integration of Immigrant Divorcees in Israel**. Jerusalem: **International Migration**, 23, December, 1985, 511-522.

Friedman, Reena Sigman: **Seminary Decision To Ordain Women Signals Communal Revitalization**. New York: **Israel Horizons**, 32, Jan/Feb 1984, 19-21.

Steps taken, and analysis of vote to ordain women as rabbis, as well as implications of decision for the Conservative movement and perhaps in a wider sense.

Gelles, George: **UW's Buried Treasures**. Seattle, WA: **Seattle Weekly**, Feb 27-March 5, 1985, 40+.

> Portrait of Diane Thome, a Jewish-American woman composer who is a member of the music faculty of the University of Washington.

Horowitz, Herman L.: **Jewish Reality in the Book of Esther**. Conservative Judaism: **34**, New York, March/April 1981, 52-55.

Miller, Rabbi Judea B.: **Visiting the Women's Peace Encampment**. New York: **Jewish Currents**, February 1985, 26+.

> An anti-nuclear encampment in New York State, reported by a rabbi.

Mintz, Jacqueline A.: **The Myth of the Jewish Mother in Three Jewish American, Female Writers**. East Lansing, MI: **Centennial Review**, 22, 1978, 346-55.

Ringelheim, Joan: **Women and the Holocaust: A Reconsideration of Research**. Chicago: **Signs**, 10, Summer 1985, 741-61.
Experiences of women during the Holocaust.

Shepard, Sanford: **Prostitutes and Picaros in Inquisitional Spain**. Mouton, The Hague, Holland: **Neohelicon**, 3, 1975, 365-72.

> Historical and fictional stories of conversas who are also prostitutes in Spain at the time of the Inquisition.

II
History: 1986-1993

A. Books

Alexy, Trudi: **The Mezuzah in the Madonna's Foot.** (See Holocaust section)

Amt, Emilie: **Jewish Women in: Tallan, Cheryl: Women's Lives in Medieval Europe.** New York: Routledge, 1993, 279-296.

"Includes excerpts from chronicles, law codes, ethical wills and Responsa which reflect the lives of European Jewish women from 1096-1470."

Archer, Leonie J.: **Her Price is Beyond Rubies: The Jewish woman in Graeco-Roman Palestine.** Sheffield, England: Journal for the Study of the Old Testament Press, 1990.

Baskin, Judith: **Jewish Women in Historical Perspective.** Detroit, MI: Wayne State University Press, 1991.

Current debates on women's role in contemporary Judaism led to this collection of essays by well known contemporary scholars, on women's activities and experiences from Biblical times to the 20th century, in both their Jewish and secular lives.

Blond, Elaine: **Marks of Distinction: The Memoirs of Elaine Blond**, see Author Index.

Brown, Cheryl Anne: **No Longer Be Silent: First Century Jewish Portraits of Biblical Women.** Louisville, KY: Westminster/John Knox Press, 1992.

Portrayal of women in Philo's "Biblical Antiquities" and Josephus' "Jewish Antiquities" both of which describe "women in the Jewish tradition during the Graeco-Roman period."

Camp, Claudia V.: **The Female Sage in Ancient Israel and the Biblical Wisdom Literature: in:The Sage in Israel and the Ancient Near East. Gammie, John and Leo G. Perdue, Editors.** Winona Lake, IN: Eisenbrauns, 1990, 185-203.

Cohen, Shaye J.D. ed.: **The Jewish Family in Antiquity.** Atlanta, GA: Scholars Press, 1993.

See especially "Jewish Mothers and Daughters in the Greco-Roman World" by Ross S. Kraemer, pp. 89-112.

Cohen, Steven M. & Hyman, Paula E.: **The Jewish Family: Myths and Reality**. New York: Holmes & Meier, 1986.

Important book on Jewish family has two chapters on women: Priestess and Hausfrau: Women and Tradition in the German Jewish family by Marion A. Kaplan and The Jewish Mother: Social Constructions of a Popular Image by Gladys Rothbell.
See Author Index under Hyman.

Diner, Hasia, **A Time of Gathering: The Second Migration: 1820-1880**, see Author Index.

Dobson, Barrie: **The Role of Jewish Women in Medieval England: Presidential Address. in:Christianity and Judaism, Ed. Diana Wood.** Cambridge, MA: Blackwell Publishers, 1992, 145-168.

Flesher, Paul Virgil McCraken: **Oxen, Women, or Citizens: Slaves in the System of the Mishnah.** Brown Judaica Series. Atlanta, GA: Scholars Press, 1988.

Using the slave as subject, the Mishnah explores the Israelite woman in such topics as classes of women, rights of daughters/wives of slaveholders and women slaves.

Goitein, Shlomo Dov: **A Mediterranean Society: The Jewish Communities of the Arab World as Portrayed in the Documents of the Cairo Geniza. V.** Berkeley, CA: University of California Press, 1988.

This final (posthumous) volume of Goitein's important work covers "The Individual: Portrait of a Mediterranean Personality of the High Middle Ages as Reflected in the Cairo Geniza." Through womens' letters found in the Cairo Geniza we can learn much about people and their lives in the Jewish communities of the Middle Ages.

Gribetz, Judah Greenstein, Edward and Regina Stein: **The Timetables of History: A Chronology of the Most Important People and Events in Jewish History**. New York: Simon & Schuster, 1993.

A great source of brief information on Jewish women in world history and throughout Jewish history.

Grossman, Susan and Rivka Haut Eds. **Daughters of the King.** (See Religion Section)

Lassner, Jacob: **Demonizing the Queen of Sheba: Boundaries of Gender and Culture in Postbiblical Judaism and Medieval Islam**. Chicago: University of Chicago Press, 1993.

History

Lerner, Gerda: **The Creation of Patriarchy**. New York: Oxford University Press, 1986.

"It is the relationship of women to history which explains the nature of female subordination..." Looking at women in history in Ancient Near Eastern culture including biblical or covenant Law, we see the creation of patriarchy.

Orfali, Stephanie: **A Jewish Girl in the Weimar Republic**. Berkeley, CA: Ronin Publishing, 1987.

Autobiography of a Jewish woman relating the life of young Jews in Nuremberg at end of 19th century, departure for Palestine and U.S.(focus is on life of women).

Pantel, Pauline Schmitt, Editor: **A History of Women in the West: I. From Ancient Goddesses to Christian Saints**. Cambridge, MA: Belknap Press of Harvard University Press, 1992.

This seemingly thorough scholarly work on the history of women, Vol. I, has no particular section on Jewish women in ancient history; only a quote about them, referring to the analogy between Jewish women and the religious roles of Roman women. Josephus is mentioned several times. However, there are 3 pages on Jewish women in the Christian Era in Chapter 9: pp.416-18. Is this a book about ALL women?

Raphael, Chaim: **Minyan: 10 Jewish Lives in 20 Centuries of History**. P.O. Box 4071, Malibu, CA 90264: Pangloss Press, 1992.

Dona Gracia Nasi, Gluckel of Hameln and Emma Lazarus are included in this volume of Jewish historical figures as "benchmarks of Jewish experience."

Shepherd, Naomi: **A Price Below Rubies: Jewish Women as Rebels and Radicals**. Cambridge, MA: Harvard University Press, 1993.

Researches the history of Jewish women from biblical times to the beginning of current century. Includes useful biographical information on radical Jewish women (especially Bertha Pappenheim).

Tallan, Cheryl: **Opportunities for Medieval North European Jewish Widows in the Public and Domestic Sphere: in: Upon my Husband's Death, Ed. Louise Mirrer**. Ann Arbor, MI: University of Michigan Press, 1992, ,115-127.
"The position of medieval Jewish widows can be described as intermediate between that of married Jewish women and adult Jewish men."

Weatherford, Doris: **Foreign and Female: Immigrant Women in America, 1840 - 1930**. New York: Schocken Books, 1986.

Gives glimpses of Jewish women immigrants: their work, their marriages, childbearing and other life experiences.

B. Articles

Aschkenasy, Nehama: **Lost Love, 1000 B.C.E.** New York: **Lilith**, No.18, Winter 1987-8, 14-15.

Basinger, Suzanne & Eisen, George: **Sport, Recreation and Gender: Jewish Immigrant Women in Turn-Of-The Century America (1880-1920).** Radford, VA: **Journal of Sport History**, 18, 1991, 103-120.

Benjamin, Jessica: **Feminist Perspectives Session: Victimology.** Oakland, CA: **Tikkun**, 4, March/April 1989, 75-77.

Guilt, suffering; its use and misuse.

Benson, Evelyn R.: **Jewish Women and Nursing: An Overview of Early Nursing.** Albany NY: **Journal of the New York State Nurses Association**, 23, December 1992, 16-19.

Contribution of Jewish women to the development of nursing starting with biblical midwives Shiphrah and Puah to modern times with examples such as Rachel Varnhagen, Penina Moise and Lillian Wald.

Cruise, P.E.: **The Problem of Being Simone Weil.** New York: **Judaism**, 137, Winter 1986, 98-106.

Cruise tries to show the Jewish threads in Weil's brief, martyred life as a convert to Judaism.

Frager, Ruth A.: **Class and Ethnic Barriers to Feminist Perspectives in Toronto's Jewish Labour Movement: 1919-1939.** Ottawa, Canada: **Studies in Political Economy [Canada]**, No. 30, Autumn, 1989, 143-165.

Friedman, Theodore: **The Shifting Role of Women, From the Bible to the Talmud:** New York: **Judaism**, 36, Fall 1987, 479-487.

Description of women's participation in political, economic, social and religious life of biblical era as compared with their exclusion in Talmudic era.

Grossman, Avraham: **Medieval Rabbinic Views on Wife-beating: 800-1300.** Haifa: **Jewish History**, 5, Spring 1991, 53-62.

Historic rabbinic attitudes changed about wife-beating. Article states that "the economic role of the Jewish woman and Ashkenazi/Hasidic traditions influenced the judgments of the German rabbis."

History 21

Hertz, Deborah; Arnold, Jane & Rubin, Julie H.: **Jewish Women in Europe: 1750-1932: A Bibliographic Guide**. Haifa: **Jewish History**, 7, Spring 1993, 127-153.

"Reconciling feminism with historical Jewish practices" in order "to uncover obscure women in modern European history." Women in England, Germany are mentioned, but those in France, Italy and Spain are not. Memoirs are annotated, fiction is simply listed.

Horn, Dara: **The March of the Living**. New York: **Hadassah**, November 1992, 16+.

Thousands of Jewish teenagers who never knew a world without Israel are being introduced to the past firsthand. One 15-year-old girl tells the story of what they are seeing and feeling.

Kaplan, Bernice: **Written Out of History: Disempowering the Jewish Woman**. Johannesburg: **Jewish Affairs**, 48, Winter 1993, 43-47.

Koonz, Claudia: **Reading about the Writing on the Wall**. New York: **Lilith**, #17, Fall 1987, 12-14.

German Jewish women recognized the Nazi threat—perhaps before men would acknowledge it.

Kraemer, Ross Shepard: **Monastic Jewish women in Graeco-Roman Egypt: Philo Judaeris on the Therapeutudes**. Chicago, IL: **Signs**, 14, Winter 1989, 342-370.

"Almost no examples of communities of Jewish women in late antiquity." Appendix to Kraemer's dissertation on religion and women in Graeco-Roman world (Maenads, Martyrs, Matrons, Monastics). Philo emphasizes the presence of both genders in ancient monastic communities. Philo on marriage and childbearing for men and women. Mention of other communities which included women.

Kray, Susan: **Orientation of an "Almost White Woman": The Interlocking Effects of Race, Class, Gender and Ethnicity in American Mass Media**. Annandale, VA: **Critical Studies in Mass Communication**. 10, Dec 1993, 349-366.

This study "examines the case of the missing Jewish women" in studies of oppressed women and minorities.

Magnus, Shulamit: **Out of the Ghetto: Integrating the Study of Jewish Women into the Study of the Jews**. New York: **Judaism**, 29, Winter 1990, 28-36.

Examines the way Jewish historiography has ignored the existence of women.

Marcus, Ivan G.: **Mothers, martyrs and moneymakers: Some Jewish Women in Medieval Europe**. New York: **Conservative Judaism**, 38, Spring 1986, 34-45.

An attempt to "outline some of the activities in which Jewish women were engaged in Medieval Europe;" especially, among "ordinary" people. Includes the eulogy given by Rabbi Eleazar of Worms (d. ca 230) of his wife Dulcia.

Melamed, Renee Levine: **Women in (Post-1492) Spanish Crypto-Jewish Society**: New York: **Judaism**, 41, Spring 1992, 156-168.

Examination of different roles women played in Crypto-Jewish society as opposed to the woman in traditional Jewish society. Their role of sustaining Jewish observances took greater risks, but were even more critical in sustaining traditions though more difficult even within the confines of their homes.

Meschel, Susan V.: **The Missing Link: Jewish Women Scientists and Physicians in Antiquity and the Middle Ages**. New York: **Reconstructionist**, LVI, Summer 1991, 24-26.

Min-Hahar, Shlomo: **The Participation of Women in War**. Zomet Institute, Gush Etzion, Israel: **Crossroads**, 2, 1988, 227-234.

Schneider, Susan Weidman: **Beyond Yentl: Battling Sexism in Jewish Schools**. New York: **Israel Horizons**, 32, March/April 1984, 28-31.

"Bias against women in much of religious Jewish education" set against dearth (in 1984) of serious research about Jewish women's lives and fact that this is changing, means schools need to make this literature known to all its students and encourage women to explore their feminist heritage.

Stow, Kenneth: **The Jewish Family in the Rhineland in the High Middle Ages: Form and Function**. Washington, DC: **American Historical Review**, 92, December 1987, 1085-1110.

Tallan, Cheryl: **Medieval Jewish women in History: Law, Literature and Art: A Bibliography**. Clinton, NY: **Medieval Feminist Newsletter**, 4;5,6, 1987-8, pp. 9-10; 28; 24-25 respectively.

Tallan, Cheryl: **Medieval Jewish Widows: Their Control of Resources**. Haifa: **Jewish History**, 5, Spring 1991, 63-74.

Money from kettubot, as well as earned money, could give a widow certain freedoms that non-Jewish women of same epoch did not possess.

Umansky, Ellen M.: **Critical Studies of Women in Jewish Life: Some Recent Works.** New York: **CCAR Journal**, 39, Spring 1992, 1-15.

> Analytical article about some of the important books and essays written recently on Jewish women and history.

Waldstreicher, David: **Radicalism, Religion, Jewishness: The Case of Emma Goldman.** Waltham, MA: **American Jewish History**, 80, Autumn 1990, 74-92.

> Author suggests that Emma Goldman's lifelong struggle for social justice stems also from her Jewish and socio-political identity.

Weissler, Chava: **For Women and For Men Who Are Like Women: The Construction of Gender in Yiddish Devotional Literature.** Chico, CA: **Journal of Feminist Studies in Religion,** 5, Fall 1989, 7-24.

> Perception of gender among women and men who are not Jewishly learned shown in the *tkhines* written for them and reveal a truer picture of their actual lives.

III
Holocaust and Resistance

A. Books

Alexander, Caroline: **Now You are Sarah**. Port Angeles, WA & Bentwood Bay, BC: Ben-Simon Publications, 1993.

> Personal essay by author concerning her W.W. II escape from Germany. She is currently living in Paris and is a playright. Based on a reunion of escapees.

Alexy, Trudi: **The Mezuzah in the Madonna's Foot.** New York: Simon & Schuster, 1993.

> Variations on a theme: Conversion to Catholicism, escape through the Pyrenees from the Nazis, eventually resettlement in the United States; then a desire to retrace her history. Alexy tells the story of the expulsion of the Spanish Jews and conversas—conversion to survive in different historical timeframes.

Amishai-Maisels, Ziva: **Depiction and Interpretation**: **The Influence of the Holocaust on the Visual Arts**. Oxford, U.K.: Pergamon Press, 1993.

> This important work on the Holocaust and Art includes many representations of women and especially mothers. Includes some discussion of such women artists as Lori Grundig, mentions others. Extensive bibliography.

Bauman, Janina: **Winter in the Morning**: **A Young Girl's Life in the Warsaw Ghetto and Beyond 1939-1945**. New York: The Free Press, 1986.

> Bauman wrote diaries and short stories during the war which describe her youthful experiences, "of remaining human in inhuman conditions."

Birger, Trudi & Green, Jeffrey M.: **A Daughter's Gift of Love**: **A Holocaust Memoir by Trudi Birger**. Philadelphia, PA: Jewish Publication Society, 1992.

> The story of a woman's love for her mother and of survival in the Nazi death camps.

Block, Gay & Drucker, Malka: **Rescuers**: **Portraits of Moral Courage in the Holocaust**. New York: Holmes & Meier, 1992.

> Text by Drucker and Gay Block, photographs by Block relating stories of undiscovered rescuers, "reactions against indifference."

Bock, Gisela: **No Children at Any Cost: Perspectives on Compulsory Sterilization, Sexism and Racism in Nazi Germany**. in: **Women in Culture and Politics: A Century of Change.** Bloomington, IN: Indiana University Press, 1986, 286-298.

Bonin, Adelyn I.: **Allegiances: A Memoir**. Santa Barbara, CA: Fithian Press, 1993.

Buber-Neumann, Margarete with Manheim, Ralph, Tr.: **Milena**. New York: Seaver Books, 1988.

Friendship between Kafka's love—Milena Jesenka and Margaret Buber-Neuman which ended in Ravensbruck where Milena died.

Chicago, Judy & Donald Woodman (photography): **Holocaust Project: From Darkness Into Light.** New York: Viking, 1993.

An artistic interpretation of the Shoah, using photography and a tapestry, attempting to address the connectivity of all genocide and the gender imbalance thus far shown Holocaust writings.

Delbo, Charlotte & Lamont, Rosette, tr. **Days and Memory**. Marlboro, Vt: Marlboro Press, 1990.

Delbo as "A valiant woman and Auschwitz survivor' speaking as "the living voice of memory."

Deutschkron, Inge: **Outcast: A Jewish Girl in Wartime Berlin**. New York: Fromm, 1990.

Drucker, Olga Levy: **Kindertransport**. New York: Henry Holt, 1992.

Autobiography of a young girl who was one of the many Jewish children sent to England on the Kindertransport.

Eibeschitz, Jehoshua and Anna Eilenberg-Eibeshitz, Comp./Tr.: **Women in the Holocaust: A Collection of Testimonies**. Brooklyn, NY: Remember, 1993.

Personal narratives of Jewish women during the Holocaust.

Erpel, Simone: **Struggle and Survival: Jewish Women in the Anti-Fascist Resistance in Germany**. in: **Leo Baeck Institute Yearbook: Vol. XXXVII** London: Secker & Warburg, 1992, 397-414.

Essay based on lives of four German-Jewish women who fought against National Socialism.

Foster, Edith: **Reunion in Vienna**. Riverside, CA: Ariadne Press, 1991.

>Growing up in Vienna, Foster tells her story of the WWII Period and of reunion with other non-Jews in Austria many years later.

Frank, Anne: **The Critical Edition**. New York: Doubleday, 1989. Netherlands State Institute for War Documentation.

>Different translations of text of diary, with photographs of actual pages from diary, investigations of those who helped them hide for 2 years and who might have betrayed the Frank family; information on Anne's father, all shed light on this famous family and their tragedy.

Friedman, Peska: **Going Forward: A True Story of Courage, Hope and Perseverance**. Brooklyn, NY: Mesorah, 1994.

>Personal narrative of the Holocaust.

Friedman, Saul S.: **Holocaust Literature: Handbook of Critical, Historical and Literary Writings.** Westport, CT: Greenwood Press, 1993, 161-175, 176-193, 521-532.

>Reference book which contains 3 women's interest chapters: #9 on Arendt, Davidowicz, Levin, Yahi, Fogelman; #10 on Jewish women in the Holocaust Resistance; #25 on Frank and Senesh diaries. Other: Fiction and Poetry in the Holocaust, i.e., Sachs and Kolmar, among others.

Fromm, Bella: **Blood and Banquets**: **A Berlin Diary 1930**. New York: Touchstone/ Simon & Schuster, 1992.

Games, Sonia: **Escape into Darkness**: **The True Story of a Young Woman's Extraodinary Survival during World War II**. New York: Shapolsky, 1991.

>Autobiography of a Jewish woman who took on the identity of a Polish Christian in order to survive the Shoah.

Gies, Miep Gold, & Alison Leslie: **Anne Frank Remembered**: **The Story of the Women Who Helped Hide the Frank Family**. New York: Simon and Schuster, 1987.

>Readable book about those Righteous Gentiles, including Miep Gies, who hid the Franks and other Jews, especially in Amsterdam.

Goldenberg, Myrna: **Different Horrors, Same Hell**: **Women Remembering the Holocaust. in: Thinking the Unthinkable: Meanings of the Holocaust. ed. Roger S. Gottlieb** New York: Paulist Press, 1990, 150-166.

Hay, Peter: **Ordinary Heroes**. New York: Paragon, 1989.

Heinemann, Marlene E.: **Gender and Destiny**: **Women Writers and the Holocaust**. New York: Greenwood Press, 1986.

Heller, Fanya Gottesfeld: **Strange and Unexpected Love**: **A Teenage Girl's Holocaust Memoirs**. Hoboken, NJ: KTAV Publishing House, 1993.

> This Holocaust biography is as much a story of love and relationships as about survival.

Isaacson, Judith Magyar: **Seed of Sarah**: **Memories of a Survivor**. Urbana, IL: University of Illinois Press, 1990.

> Growing up in Hungary, then, "life" in a Nazi concentration camp.

Jurman-Appelman, Alicia: **My Story**. New York: Bantam Books, 1988.

> Memoir of a survivor of Holocaust through her early life in Poland, the war, escape and participation in rescues and in helping Polish Jews to get to Palestine.

Kahn, Annette: **Why My Father died**: **A Daughter Confronts her Family's Past at the Trial of Klaus Barbie**. New York: Summit, 1991.

Kalib, Goldie Szachter with Ken Wachsberger & Sylvan Kalib: **The Last Selection**: **A Child's Journey Through the Holocaust**. Amherst, MA: The University of Massachusetts Press, 1991.

King, Stella: **Jacqueline**: **Pioneer Heroine of the Resistance**. New York: Sterling/Arms & Armour, 1989.

Klepfisz, Irena: **Dreams of an Insomniac.** see Author index.

Koonz, Claudia: **Mothers in the Fatherland**: **Women, the Family, and Nazi Politics**. New York: St. Martin's Press, 1986.

> Although not about Jewish women, Koonz includes them in her study: esp. Chap. 1 "Jewish Women between Survival and Death," pp. 345-383, and in relation to intermarriage, assimilation, converts, resistance, etc.

Kron, Inge Deutsch & Steinberg, Jean, tr.: **Outcast**: **A Jewish Girl in Wartime Berlin**. New York: Fromm, 1989.

> From not knowing one is Jewish, then deciding to live as a non-Jew, Deutsch eventually left Berlin to go to England.

Krutein, Eva: **Eva's War**: **A True Story of Survival**. Albuquerque, NM: Amador, 1990.

Kubar, Zofia S.: **Double Identity**: **A Memoir**. New York: Hill and Wang, 1989.

Kun, Rita: **Talking About Silence**: in: **German Women Recall the Third Reich by Alison Owings**. New Brunswick, NJ: Rutgers University Press, 1993, ,451-467.

> A German-Jewish woman who lived through the Holocaust.

Lebow, Barbara: **A Shayna Maidel**: New York: Dramatists Play Service, 1988.

Lewis, Helen: **A Time to Speak**. Belfast, N. Ireland: Blackstaff Press (U.S.Distributor, Dufour Editions), 1992.

> Autobiography of Lewis as a testimony of a woman who "survived the unsurvivable."

Linden, R.Ruth: **Making Stories, Making Selves**: **Feminist Reflections on the Holocaust**. Columbus,OH: Ohio State University Press, 1993, *Holocaust.

> A feminist's critical approach to recording the stories of Holocaust survivors while, at the same time, discovering her own Jewish identity.

Lindwer, Willy with Meersschaert, Alison, tr.: **The Last Seven Months of Anne Frank**: New York: Pantheon Books, 1991.

> Six women who knew Anne Frank retell their last memories of her together with their own stories of surviving concentration camps and World War II.

Mack, John E. & Rogers, Rita S.: **The Alchemy of Survival**: **One Woman's Journey**. Redding, MA: Addison-Wesley, 1989.

> Story of Roger's deportation experiences during and after the war.

Miller, Judith: **One, by One, by One**: **Facing the Holocaust**. New York: Simon & Schuster, 1990.

Minco, Marga: **Bitter Herbs**: **The Vivid Memories of a Fugitive Jewish Girl in Nazi-Occupied Holland**. London: Penguin, 1991.

Novack, Judith: **The Lilac Bush**. New York: Shengold, 1989

> Novack's personal story of the Holocaust.

Ringelheim, Joan: **Thoughts about Women and the Holocaust, in: Thinking the Unthinkable: Meanings of the Holocaust. ed. Robert S. Gottlieb**. New York: Paulist Press, 1990, 141-149.

Rittner, Carol, and Roth, John K. eds.: **Different Voices: Women and the Holocaust**. New York: Paragon House, 1993.

> In countering the "male dominated" Holocaust literature, Rittner has compiled a volume of women's experiences before, during and after the Holocaust: autobiographical accounts, scholarship, some statistics and reflection; "voices of experience and interpretation."

Rosenberg, Blanca: **To Tell at Last: Survival Under False Identity, 1941-45**. Urbana, IL: University of Illinois Press, 1993.

> Story of Blanca Rosenberg's survival in the Polish ghettoes using a false identity and the strength of friendships.

Schloss, Eva & Kent, Evelyn Julia: **Eva's Story: A Survivor's Tale**. New York: St. Martin's Press, 1988.

> Personal narrative of Anne Frank's stepsister (born to Anne Frank's father and his second wife).

Schwarz, Renee Fodor: **Renee**. New York: Shengold, 1991.

> Autobiography of Schwarz who is a survivor and today a psychologist in the United States.

Schwertfeger, Ruth: **Women of Theresienstadt: Voices from a Concentration Camp**. New York: St. Martin's Press, 1989.

Sendyk, Helen: **End of Days: A Memoir of the Holocaust**. New York: St. Martin's Press, 1992.

Szwajger, Adina Blardy: **I Remember Nothing More: The Warsaw Children's Hospital and the Jewish Resistance**. New York: Touchstone, Simon and Schuster, 1990.

> A first person account of the work of Adina Szwajger in the Warsaw ghetto and then in the Jewish resistance.

Szeman, Sherri: **The Kommandant's Mistress.** see Author index (Holocaust Fiction)

Tedeschi, Guiliani with Parks, Tim, tr.: **There is a Place on Earth**: New York: Pantheon, 1992.

> Tedeschi, an Italian-Jewish woman tells her story of surviving Birkenau and Auschwitz.

Van der Rol, Ruud & Verhoeven, Rian: **Anne Frank: Beyond the Diary**: **A Photographic Remembrance**. New York: Viking, 1993.

Family and early pictures of Anne Frank with commentary and actual pages from diary add to our knowledge of this remarkable young woman and her family and protectors.

Verdoner, Hilde; Verdoner, Yoka & Verdoner Kan, Francesca, eds: **Signs of Life**: **The Letters of Hilde Verdoner-Sluizer from Nazi Tansit Camp Westerbrok 1942-44**. Washington DC: Acropolis Books, 1990.

Letters from Nazi camp in Holland where this Jewish mother and housewife was interned until she was transferred to Auschwitz where she died in 1944.

Wardi, Dina Goldblum with Naomi, Tr.: **Memorial Candles**: **Children of the Holocaust**. N.Y.: Tavistock/Routledge, 1992.

Report of the work of a psychotherapist in private practice in Jerusalem with the children of Holocaust survivors.

Waterford, Helen H.: **Commitment to the Dead**: **One Woman's Journey Toward Understanding**. Frederick, CO: Renaissance House, 1987.

One woman's survivor story of expulsion from Germany, hiding in Holland then deportation to Auschwitz. Now she and a former Nazi lecture as eyewitnesses.

Westheimer, Dr. Ruth & Yagoda, Ben: **An Autobiography**: **All in a Lifetime**. New York: Warner, 1990.

The autobiography of psychotherapist Dr. Ruth, who fled Nazi Germany as a ten year old.

Wyden, Peter: **Stella**. New York: Simon & Schuster, 1992.

Wyden describes the youth and personality of Stella Goldschlag which led to her collaborating with the Gestapo; the effect on others who knew her, and especially the daughter who now lives in Israel.

Zassenhaus, Hiltgunt: **Walls**: **Resisting the Third Reich - One Woman's Story**. Boston: Beacon Press, 1993 (new edition).

B. Articles

Abramowitz, Molly: **Tales of Courage and Valor: Three Uncommon Women Tie the Past with the Present in Memoirs**. New York: **Women's American ORT Reporter**, Winter 1993, 6-9.

> Three Jewish women memoirists (Trudi Berger, Helen Lewis and Adelyn Bonin); each Holocaust survivors, and their published memoirs.

Axelrod, Toby: **New Data on Women and the Holocaust**. New York: **Lilith**, 19, 1988, 5.

Bernstein, Richard: **Lucy S. Dawidowicz, 75, Scholar of Jewish Life and History, dies**: New York: **New York Times**, 140, Dec 6, 1990, B12 (N) D21 (L).

> Obituary of famed scholar/writer.

Boas, Jacob: **Amsterdam to Auschwitz: The Diaries of Romance and Suffering**. New York: **Lilith**, 14, Spring 1989, 24-26.

Cantor, Aviva: **She Fought Back: An Interview with Vilna Partisan Vitke Kempner**. New York: **Lilith**, #16, Spring 1987, 20-24.

Felman, Jyl Lynn: **Chicago's Holocaust Project**: New York: **Lilith**, 18, 1993, 15-16.

> Felman critiques Judy Chicago's art work, "Confronting the Holocaust;" of her success in making "connections between women's oppression and Jewish oppression."

Fuchs-Kreimer, Nancy: **Sister Edith Stein: A Rabbi Reacts**. New York: **Lilith**, 16, Winter 1991, 6-7,28.

> Stein, a philosopher and mystic, died at Auschwitz.

Gilman, Sander L.: **The Dead Child Speaks: Reading "The Diary of Anne Frank"**. Kent, OH: **Studies in American Jewish Literature**, 7, Spring 1988.

> Not only did the diary of Anne Frank show the world that "not all Jews were passive and silent about their fate," but the author herself "provided a ready-made definition of the Jew as author (Anne Frank) and the Jewish author as mute victim after the Holocaust." Brief discussion of the character "Amy" in Philip Roth's novel "The Ghost Writer" who is revealed as an Anne Frank who never perished.

Isser, E.R.: **Toward a Feminist Perspective in American Holocaust Drama**. Indiana, PA: **Studies in the Humanities**, 17, Dec 1990, 139-48.

Kaplan, Marion: **Jewish Women in Nazi Germany: Daily Life, Daily Struggles, 1933-1939**. College Park, MD: **Feminist Studies**, 16, Fall 1990, 579-606.

As Nazis took over Germany specific changes occurred to Jewish women. This article details some of those difficulties.

Kozodoy, Neal: **In Memoriam: Lucy S.Dawidowicz**. New York: **Commentary**, 93, May 1992, 35-40.

Essay about Dawidowicz, student of the Holocaust, who though not involved with feminist issues, is an essential name to add to list of Jewish women scholars. (In opinion of writer, as scholar, wife, Jew and human being.)

Lowy, Beverly. **The Full Extent of the Damage: The Hidden Children of the Shoah**; **On the Issues: The Progressive woman's quarterly**, Vol.XXI, Winter 1991, pp10+.

The emotional and religious identity scars of those who were hidden during the Holocaust, whether in convents or in Gentile families, seen from the perspective of a hidden man's spouse.

Lustig, Vera: **Out of the Depths**: **Vera Lustig on Holocaust Fictions**. London, UK: **Plays and Players**, No.440, July 1990, 15-17.

Lustig writes about several Holocaust plays including Lebow's Shayna Maidel and various women characters in other plays.

Manes, Edna: **Disorder and Early Sorrow**: **A Childhood without Parents**. New York: **Lilith**, 14, Fall 1989, 25-27.

Ringelheim, Joan: **The Holocaust**: **Taking Women into Account**. London: **Jewish Quarterly**, 39, 1992, 19+.

An important probing addition to the writings of this Holocaust specialist, now affiliated with the Holocaust Museum, Washington, D.C. on the omissions and problems of recording aspects of women's activism and victimization.

Schwartz, Lauren: **The Righteous Ones**. New York: **NCJW Journal**, 15, Spring 1992, 13-16.

Interview with Malka Drucker, author of "Rescuers: Portraits of Moral Courage in the Holocaust" and in-depth analysis and excerpts from the book.

Wilner, Lori: **The Paradoxical Heroism of Chana Senesh**. New York: **Lilith**, No. 20, Summer 1988, 22-23.

Wisenberg, S.L.: **Anne Franks in Texas**: **Personal Essay**. Oakland, CA: **Tikkun**, 6, September/October 1991, 47-48.

Imagining one was enduring the Holocaust - living, dying like Anne Frank.

Wohlgelernter, Maurice: **Facing Medusa Without Mirrors**: **Three Women Reflect on the Holocaust: A Review Essay**. Baltimore, MD: **The Johns Hopkins University Press**, 12, February 1992, 85-103.

IV
Religion and Biblical Studies

A. Books

Abramov, Tehilla: **The Secret of Jewish Femininity: Insights into the Practice of Taharat HaMishpachah**. Southfield, MI & Spring Valley, NY: Targum: Feldheim, 1988.

Ackerman, Susan: **Under Every Green Tree: Popular Religion in Sixth-Century Judah**. Atlanta, GA: Scholars Press, 1992.

Adelman, Penina V.: **Miriam's Well: Rituals for Jewish Women Around the Year**. New York: Biblio Press, 1990.

Revised edition of this popular book celebrating Rosh Chodesh: the new moon and other festivals. Suggests how groups, usually, but not necessarily only women, can find new spiritual meaning by joining together in ancient and new rituals.

Aiken, Lisa: **To Be a Jewish Woman**. Northvale, N.J.: Jason Aronson, 1992.

Shows how modern Jewish women find meaning in life through study of Jewish history and by being Torah observant. Though Aiken as psychologist may sincerely believe her thesis, modern American women will question traditional women's restrictions: i.e., that a woman with brothers cannot say kaddish for her parents.

Anderson, Sherry Ruth: **The Feminine Face of God**. New York: Bantam, 1991.

Austern, Esther: **Silence is Thy Praise: The Life and Ideals of Rabbanit Batya Karelitz**. Brooklyn, NY: Mesorah Publications, 1990.

Bach, Alice: **Good to the Last Drop: Viewing the Sotah (Numbers 5.11-31) as the Glass Half Empty and Wondering How to View it Half Full. in: The New Literary Criticism and the Hebrew Bible** Sheffield, England: JSOT Press, 1993, ,26-54.

"Woman's fate as determined by men": Ritual of the Sotah as part of the discussions currently taking place in feminist rereadings of the Bible.

Baker, James: **Women's Rights in Old Testament Times**. Salt Lake City, UT: Signature Books, 1992.

Biblical law in terms of "the social and historical context of Hebrew women". Consistency between the Bible and contemporaneous, external legal codes is emphasized.

Bal, Mieke: **Lethal Love: Feminist Literary Readings of Biblical Love Stories**. Bloomington, IN: Indiana University Press, 1987.

Baskin, Judith R. **Jewish Women in Historical Perspective**, see Author index/or History Sec.

Berkovits, Eliezer: **Jewish Women in Time and Torah**. Hoboken, NJ: KTAV, 1990.

> Jewish women moved from being "an impersonal adjunct of the male" to a more personal identity through the evolution of social customs, education and a sharing of community responsibilities. Berkovits discusses contemporary halakhic issues and suggests creating new *minhagim* (customs) for today's society to reinvigorate Judaism and recognize "the human dignity of the Jewish woman of today."

Berkowitz, William, editor: **Dialogues in Judaism: Jewish Dilemmas Defined, Debated, and Explored**. Northvale, NJ: Jason Aronson, 1991.

> This collection of essays by experts in Jewish topics includes a fascinating paragraph by Steinsaltz on "the woman question".

Berner, Leila, ed.: **Or Chadash: A New Light**. Philadelphia: P'nai Or Religious Fellowship, 1989.

Bershtel, Sara and Graubard, Allen: **Saving Remnants: Feeling Jewish in America**. New York: Free Press/Macmillan, 1992.

> Interviews with young American men and women both assimilated and religious.

Biale, David: **Eros and the Jews: From Biblical Israel to Contemporary America.** see Author index.

Bloom, Harold with Rosenberg, David tr.: **The Book of J**. New York: Vintage Books, 1990.

> A new translation of portions of Bible purportedly from the "J" version, together with Bloom's analysis showing that not only does this part of the Torah include many heroines, but could actually have been written by a woman.

Boyarin, Daniel: **Carnal Israel: Reading Sex in Talmudic Culture**. Berkeley, CA: University of California Press, 1993.

> Boyarin, a noted Talmudic scholar and committed feminist, finds "protofeminist values in the Talmud" and stresses the importance of both body and spirit in Judaism.

Bradshaw, Paul F. & Hoffman, Lawrence A. eds.: **The Changing Face of Jewish and Christian Worship in North America**. Notre Dame, IN: University of Notre Dame Press, 1991.

"Evidence of how the symbols of liturgy connect to the lives and realities of women's lives." Good overview of changes in liturgy and interpretation, and the way both Jewish and Christian services are led. Esp. p. 35+ about "The changing role of women in the [Conservative] Synagogue."

Breitowitz, Irving A.: **Between Civil and Religious Law: The Plight of the Agunah in American Society**. Westport, CT: Greenwood Press, 1993.

The thesis in this authoritative book is not so much the problems with Jewish law, but the "consequences of family breakdown and disintegration." Author includes all of the halacha, many footnotes to both Jewish and secular law, and options for interpreting halacha to deal with the situation of the agunah and Jewish divorces. However, he tries to justify why the laws still exist: to "protect" Jewish women and free will. Judge for yourself!

Brenner, Athalya & Van Dijk-Hemmes, Fokkelien: **On Gendering Texts: Female and Male Voices in the Hebrew Bible**. Leiden: E.J.Brill, 1993.

"Differences within"...the Hebrew Bible lead to new scholarship on questions of authorship and on gender as represented.

Broner, E.M.: **The Telling: Including the Women's Haggadah** by E. M. Broner and Naomi Nimrod. San Francisco: Harper, 1992.

A fascinating rendering of seders attended by diverse women V.I.P.'s, with prayers and traditions reshaped by their own stated needs.(The Haggadah has also been published separately, see 1994-1995 listing here).

Bronner, Leila L.: **Biblical Prophetesses Through Rabbinic Lenses**. New York: **Judaism**, 40, Winter 1991, 171-183.

Bruder, Judith: **Convergence: A Reconciliation of Judaism and Christianity in the Life of One Woman**. New York: Doubleday, 1993.

The autobiography of a woman from an observant Jewish family who is drawn to and converts to Catholicism.

Bulka, Reuven P.: **Jewish Divorce Ethics**. Ogdensburg, NY: Ivy League Press, 1992.

Burns, Rita Jean: **Has the Lord Indeed Spoken Only Through Moses?: A Study of the Biblical Portrait of Miriam. No. 84** Atlanta, GA: Society of Biblical Literature, 1987 (new edition).

Cardin, Rabbi Nina Beth, Editor and Translator: **Out of the depths I call to you: A Book of Prayers for the Married Jewish Woman**. Northvale, NJ: Jason Aronson, 1992.

Original text, translations of prayers written for Yehudit Coen, an Italian Jewish woman (late 18th century) by her husband, Dr. Giuseppe Coen. The commentaries describe the life of Jewish women of the period. Contains Hebrew prayers for candle lighting, the mikveh, pregnancy, birth and nursing. Pleasing format.

Clines, David J.A.: **Reading Esther from Left to Right: Contemporary strategies for reading a Biblical text**, in: **The Bible in Three Dimensions, edited by David Clines** Sheffield, UK: Journal for the Study of the Old Testament, 1990, 31 52.

Covenant of the Heart: Prayers, Poems and Meditations from the Women of Reform Judaism. 838 Fifth Avenue, New York: National Federation of Temple Sisterhoods, 1993.

Sisterhood's prayers for their own occasions: for communal events as well as individual personal prayers.

Cowan, Rachel & Paul: **Mixed Blessings**. New York: Penguin, 1988.

Darr, Katheryn Pfisterer: **Far More Precious Than Jewels: Perspectives on Biblical Women**. Louisville, KY: Westminster/John Knox Press, 1991.

Critical, rabbinical and feminist perspectives on issues relating to four biblical women: Ruth, Sarah, Hagar and Esther.

Davidman, Lynn: **Tradition in a Rootless World: Women Turn to Orthodox Judaism**. Berkeley, CA: University of California Press, 1991.

A study containing interviews with women in counseling or visiting a Lubavitch community (Bais Chana) or Lincoln Square (Orthodox) synagogue, Davidman gives substantial evidence of why many of these women consider joining " a community that assumed such strong control over its members' lives." To provide "the closeness, guidance....the women believed they had not received from their own families."

Day, Peggy L, ed.: **Gender and Difference in Ancient Israel**. Minneapolis, MN: Fortress Press, 1989.

Women in the Bible is the theme of this collection of essays by women scholars who recognize the need for the female point of view in Biblical Studies.

Diament, Carol, Ed. **Jewish Marital Status: A Hadassah Study**, see Author index.

Eck, Diana and Jain, Devaki, eds: **Speaking of Faith: Global Perspectives on Women, Religion and Social Change**. Philadelphia: New Society Publishers, 1987.

> Includes essay by Judith Plaskow.

Eilberg-Schwartz, Howard, ed.: **People of the Body: Jews and Judaism from an Embodied Perspective**. Albany, NY: State University of New York Press, 1992.

> Rather than "the people of the book," Eilberg-Schwartz suggests a reconsideration of our attitudes toward our bodies, our sexuality and its importance in Judaism. Introduction by Eilberg-Schwartz, essay by Chava Weissler on "Womens' mitzvot";"Zionism as an Erotic Revolution"by David Biale; and "Why Jewish-Princesses Don't Sweat..." by Riv-Ellen Prell; "Jewish Lesbians" by Rebecca Alpert. The book offers provocative discussions.

Encyclopedia Judaica Yearbook. 1986-87, article by Rachel Biale on women and Jewish law, full listing in U.S. section.

Esther's Suit to King Ahasauerus in behalf of the Jews: In a Letter to A Member of Parliament. New York: Clearwater Publishing Co., 1987.

> A microfilm facsimile of an English document purporting to be genuine, but actually a fake.

Exum, J. Cheryl: **Fragmented Women: Feminist (Sub)Versions of Biblical Narratives**. Valley Forge, PA: Trinity Press International, 1993.

> "Stories" of Biblical women: Michal, Samson's women; mothers Sarah and Hagar, Bathsheba; rape victims in the Bible.

Falk, Marcia: **Song of Songs: A New Translation and Interpretation**. San Francisco, Harper, 1990.

> This new translation of the Biblical love poem Song of Songs (Shir Hashirim) from the Megillah, combines Falk's skill as a poet with her feminist critique.

Fewell, Danna Nolan & Gunn, David M.: **Gender, Power & Promise: The Subject of the Bible's First Story**. Nashville, TN: Abingdon Press, 1993.

> Women in the Bible and power relations as depicted in the Bible; between the sexes, heterosexuals vs. homosexuals, and male dominance.

Fine, Irene: **Midlife, a Rite of Passage: The Wise Woman, a Celebration**. San Diego, CA: Woman's Institute for Continuing Jewish Education, 1988.

Finkelstein, Rabbi Baruch and Finkelstein, Michal: **B'Sha'ah Tovah: The Jewish Woman's Clinic and Halachic Guide to Pregnancy and Childbirth.** New York: Feldheim, 1993.

Fiorenza, Elizabeth Schussler: **But She Said: Feminist Practices of Biblical Interpretation.** Boston: Beacon Press, 1992.

Fishman, Sylvia Barack: **"Paradise Lost" as a Midrash on the Biblical Bride of God: in: From Ancient Israel to Modern Judaism, Vol IV, Marvin Fox, ed.** Atlanta, GA: Scholars Press, 1989, 87-103.

Flesher, Paul & Virgil McCracken: **Are Women Property in the System of the Mishnah: in: Fox, Marvin: From Ancient Israel to Modern Judaism.** Atlanta, GA: **Scholars Press**, I, 1989, 219-331.

Flesher, Paul and Virgil McCraken: **Oxen, Women or Citizens: Slaves in the System of the Mishnah**, full listing in History section.

Frymer-Kensky, Tikva: **In the Wake of the Goddess: Women, Culture and the Biblical Transformation of Pagan Myth.** New York: Free Press, 1992.

Author states "monotheism provided and advanced an egalitarian view of human nature...while the pagan world strictly separated male and female."

Fuchs, Rav Yitzchak Yaacov & Dombey, Rav Moshe: **Halichos Bas Yisrael: A Woman's Guide to Jewish Observance. I: from Hebrew edition, Chapters 1-14.** Oak Park, MI: Targum Press, 1987.

English translation of this guide to "practical observance for the (observant) Jewish woman." Includes information on mitzvot, prayer, modesty, Yichud, mourning, dress/hair, etc.

Frankiel, Tamar: **Voice of Sarah.** San Francisco, CA: Harper, 1990, NY: Biblio Press, 1994 pap.

Author combines traditional Judaism and feminist consciousness. Uses role models such as Sarah, Deborah, Hannah, and Judith to show the spiritual richness of these women's lives as a model for modern Jewish women. Excerpts can be found in Tikkun, vol.5, no.6, p.33-35,106-7.

Geffen-Monson, Rela, Ed.: **Celebration & Renewal: Rites of Passage in Judaism.** Philadelphia, PA: Jewish Publication Society, 1993.

Includes prayers and rituals for childbirth, abortion, infertility, marriage, divorce and many that are for both genders; chapter by Hauptman on Healing.

Religion and Biblical Studies

Gold, Yeshara: **I Lift My Eyes: True Stories of Spiritual Triumph**. Southfield, MI: Targum, 1990.

Gottlieb, Freema: **The Lamp of God: A Jewish Book of Light**. Northvale, NJ: Jason Aronson, 1989.

> See especially Part I: The Light of the Feminine. Gottlieb speaks of the shekhinah, the light of Miriam, the feminization of light, and other feminine aspects of God.

Greenberg, Blu: **How to Run a Traditional Jewish Household**. Northvale, NJ: Jason Aronson, 1989.

Greenberg, Blu: **Women and Judaism: in: Contemporary Jewish Religious Thought. Cohen, Arthur A. and Paul Mendes-Flohr, eds.** New York: Scribner, 1987, 1039-1053.

> Asks questions about paradoxes and contradictions in status of women in Judaism. Greenberg cites a "precedent of equality upon which to build, but it is the traditions that need adjustment."

Greenberg, Irving: **The Jewish Way: Living the Holidays**. New York: Summit, 1988.

> Greenberg includes in his Jewish calendar Rosh Chodesh and other opportunities for orthodox women's participation.

Greenberg, Simon, Ed.: **The Ordination of Women as Rabbis: Studies and Responsa**. New York: Jewish Theological Seminary of America, 1988.

> Conservative Responsa explains that there is nothing in Jewish law disallowing women's admission to the rabbinate. This is the most thorough and authoritative book on the history of Conservative women rabbis.

Greenstein, Edward L.: **A Jewish Reading of Esther in: Judaic Perspectives on Ancient Israel, Edited by Jacob Neusner, Baruch A. Levine and Ernest S. Frerichs**. Philadelphia, PA: Fortress Press, 1987, ,225-243.

Greisman, Nechama and Miller, Moshe, ed.: **The Nechama Greisman Anthology**. Jerusalem: Machon Chaya Mushka, 1992.

Grob, Leonard Riffat Hassan and Haim Gordon, Eds.: **Women's and Men's Liberation: Testimonies of Spirit**. New York: Greenwood Press, 1991.

> Inspired by Buber, editor Leonard Grob tries to "sow seeds of redemption" which will show that traditions do not need to be abandoned, but act as guides to keep "in seeking to realize equality and justice for women...from within..to dialogue, explore and teach..." Relevant essays by Frymer-Kensky (Women Jews); Grob (male-female dialogue); Swidler (on Yeshua/Jesus); and Haim Gordon (education).

Grossman, Susan & Rivka Haut, eds.: **Daughters of the King: Women and the Synagogue**, New York: Jewish Publication Society, 1992. see index.

One of the most important works in this bibliography. Describes history of women's roles in Judaism, the Temple and the ancient synagogues.

Gruber, Mayer I. : **The Motherhood of God and other Studies**. Atlanta, GA: Scholars Press, 1992.

Collection of essays that "attempt to bring to the light of day Hebrew Scripture's teaching about womanhood"; discuss distortions or interpretations of Biblical texts which have led people to accept as "god-given", laws which were really set down by men.
Interviews with 75 Jewish women who have recently turned to orthodoxy.

Gunn, David & Fewell, Donna Nolan: **Narrative in the Hebrew Bible**. Oxford, UK: Oxford University Press, 1993, See esp: 34-45; 90-100 and 194-205.

Interesting interpretations of role of women in Bible: Tamar and Judah and his relations with his wives; Abraham and Sarah; Trible on women as portrayed in the Bible.

Gurock, Jeffrey: **The Men and Women of Yeshiva: Higher Education, Orthodoxy and American Judaism**. New York: Columbia University Press, 1988.

See especially Chapter 10.

Haas, Peter J, ed.:**Recovering the Role of Women: Power and Authority in Rabbinic Jewish Society.** Atlanta,GA: Scholars Press, 1992.

Examination of traditional portrayal of Jewish women. Shows women assumed a more authoritative role than previous research reveals.

Hertzberg, Arthur: **Judaism: The Key Spiritual Writings of the Jewish Tradition**. New York: Touchstone: Simon & Schuster, 1991, 115-130.

Hertzberg makes distinctions between men and women from various Jewish points of view.

Holman, Phyllis Weisbard & David Schonberg, eds. **Jewish Law: Bibliography of Sources and Scholarship in English**. 10368 West Centennial Road,Littleton, CO: Fred B. Rothman, 1990.

"Bibliography of Jewish law research....including status of women."

Huwiler, Elizabeth: **Biblical Women: Mirrors, Models and Metaphors**. Cleveland, OH: United Church Press, 1993.

Biblical texts are likely to describe times when women's status was lowest. This book looks for the surprises in the text - giving examples of unexpected roles shown by such women as Huldah, Noadiah, Rebekah, Ruth and the Matriarchs. Although written for Christian readers, Huwiler's book gives another dimension to reinterpreting the women of our biblical history.

Hyman, Paula E.: **The Introduction of Bat Mitzvah in Conservative Judaism in Postwar America**: in: **Yivo Annual**. Evanston, IL: Northwestern University Press, vol. 19, 1990, 133-146.

Starting with Mordecai Kaplan's daughter's bat mitzvah in 1922, the tradition has grown (Reform Movement in 1931) and the Conservative movement has gradually accepted it (1/3 by 1948) until today, when even American Orthodoxy is addressing the issue.

Jacob, Walter: **Contemporary American Reform Responsa**. New York: Central Conference of American Rabbis, 1987.

New responsa directly relating to women, except on abortion, fetal issues, some conversion and marriage issues; Jewish lesbians, some relevant medical ethics issues; the mikveh; men and women lighting candles; on Jewish bridesmaids in non-Jewish weddings. [See Vol. II: American Reform Responsa] The index for both volumes is in this book.

Jeansonne, Sharon Pace: **The Women of Genesis: From Sarah to Potiphar's Wife**. Minneapolis, MN: Fortress, 1990.

Jobling, David: **Ruth Finds a Home: Canon, Politics, Method in: The New Literary Criticism and the Hebrew Bible.** Sheffield, England: JSOT Press, 1993, 5-139.

"Hannah and the Presentation of Women" is followed by the story of Ruth and its representation of women in the Bible.

Kaufman, Debra Renee: **Patriarchal Women**: A Case Study of Newly Orthodox Jewish Women **in: Sociological Slices:Introductory Readings from the Interactionist Perspective** Greenwich, CT: JAI Press, 1992, 233-248.

Kaufman, Debra Renee: **Rachel's Daughters: Newly Orthodox Jewish Women**. New Brunswick: Rutgers University Press, 1991.

Study of women who turn to Orthodoxy with their reasons for joining the patriarchal tradition.

Kaufman, Michael: **The Woman in Jewish Law and Tradition**: Northvale, NJ: Jason Aronson, 1993.

Though Kaufman states that Jewish women have shaped the Jewish experience, his book seems to be more of a rationalization of Jewish laws and customs rather than an objective work about the importance of Jewish women in family and society. Judge for yourself!

Kaye, Evelyn: **Hole in the Sheet**. Secaucus, NJ: Lyle Stuart, 1987.

A modern woman looks at Orthodox and Hasidic Judaism in a sensational tone.

Koltuv, Barbara Black: **Weaving Women: Essays in Feminine Psychology From the Notebooks of a Jungian Analyst**. York Beach, ME: Nicholas-Hays, 1990.

See especially chapter 2: Mothers and Daughters; chapter 4: Sisters and Shadows.

Koskoff, Ellen: **The Sound of a Woman's Voice: Gender and Music in a New York Hasidic Community in: Women and Music in Cross-Cultural Perspective: Koskoff, Ellen, ed.** Westport, CT: Greenwood Press, 1987, 213-223.

Kraemer, Ross Shepard: **Her Share of the Blessings: Women's Religions among Pagans, Jews and Christians in the Graeco-Roman World**. New York: Oxford University Press, 1992.

Women's religions in the world of Graeco-Roman antiquity; the links between them and the social constraints under which women lived. See esp. Chap. 8:93-105 (Rabbinic Sources) and 9, 106-127 (Jewish Women's religious lives and positions.)

Krause, Deborah: **A Blessing Cursed: The Prophet's Prayer for Barren Womb and Dry Breasts in Hosea 9 in: Fewell, Donna Nolan, ed. Reading Between Texts: Intertextuality and the Hebrew Bible.** Louisville, KY: Westminster/John Knox Press, 1992, 191-202.

Discussion of a biblical request for "dry breasts and a miscarrying womb." Is this a prayer or a judgment?

Krauss, Chaim: **A Compilation in English of Halachos Pertaining to the [shivah nekiyim] and the Nedikos of [yom ha-vest]**. Brooklyn, NY: C.Krauss, 1986.

Krois, Hayim ben Y.: **Kuntress ha-tevilah: A Compilation in English of the halachos pertaining to tevilas noshim.** Brooklyn, NY: G. Krauss, 1986.

Book outlines the halacha concerning the mikveh.

LaCocque, Andre: **The Feminine Unconventional: Four Subversive Figures in Israel's Tradition**. Minneapolis, MN: Fortress Press, 1990.

Lassner, Jacob: **Demonizing the Queen of Sheba: Boundaries of Gender and Culture in Postbiblical Judaism and Medieval Islam.** Chicago: University of Chicago Press, 1993.

Lepon, Shoshan: **No Greater Treasure: Stories of Extraordinary Women Drawn From the Talmud and Midrash**. Southfield, MI: Feldheim, 1990.

Levine, Elizabeth Resnick, ed.: **A Ceremonies Sampler: New Rites, Celebrations and Observances of Jewish Women**. San Diego, CA: Women's Institute for Continuing Jewish Education, 1991.

Linafelt, Tod: **Talking Women in Samuel: Readers/Responses, Responsibility**. in: Fewell, **Reading Between Texts: Intertextuality and the Hebrew Bible.** Louisville, KY: John Knox Press, 1992, 99-113.

Theme of "taking of women as a sign of male power" is discussed in a critical analysis of the narrative in Book of Samuel.

Long, Asphodel P.: **In a Chariot Drawn by Lions: The Search for the Female in Diety**. Freedom, CA: Crossing Press, 1993.

"Textual evidence and focuses on biblical and Hellenistic times..showing the historic importance of goddesses...and the hidden female aspect of God in the Western tradition."

Malmgreen, Gail, ed.: **Religion in the Lives of English Women, 1760-1930**. Bloomington: Indiana University Press, 1986.

The Merit of Our Mothers: A Bilingual Anthology of Jewish Women's Prayers. trs. Klirs, Selevan, Fishman and others. Cincinnati, Ohio: Hebrew Union College Press, 1992.

First bilingual edition of *tkhines:* a collective endeavor to bring together Yiddish and English prayers, many written by women especially but not exclusively for women; with notes, translations and glossary.

Meyers, Carol: **Discovering Eve: Ancient Israelite Women in Context.** see Author index.

Miller, Yisrael: **Guardian of Eden**. New York: Feldheim, 1993.

Nadell, Pamela S.: **Conservative Judaism in America: A Biographical Dictionary and Sourcebook**. Jewish Denominations in America (Series): Westport, CN, Greenwood Press, 1988.

The ordination of Conservative women rabbis is mentioned among sketches of male rabbis (eg: David Gershon Cohen) who were involved in the process of ordination Surprisingly omitted is Amy Eilberg, the first ordained Conservative woman rabbi, but mentioned. Use index for relevant pages. (See Simon Greenberg's book for a more informative treatment of the subject.) Good on Mathilde Roth Schechter (1860-1920), Founding President of the National Women's League of the United Synagogue and on the Women's League for Conservative Judaism, as well as the National Women's League of the United Synagogue of America.

Newsom, Carol A. and Sharon H. Ringe, Eds.: **The Women's Bible Commentary**. London and Louisville, KY: Westminster/John Knox Press, 1992.

Ground-breaking commentary by many outstanding women scholars.

Niditch, Susan: **Underdogs and Tricksters: A Prelude to Biblical Folklore**. San Francisco, CA: Harper, 1987.

Because of "Israel's peculiar history as underdog and trickster," Niditch has studied the Hebrew Bible for examples such as wives and sisters in Genesis and The Book of Esther.

Noam, Rahel: **View from Above**. Princeton, NJ: Bristol, Rhein & Englander (CIS Communications), 1993.

Noam becomes a Ba'alot teshuvah.

Ochs, Vanessa: **Words on Fire: One Woman's Journey Into the Sacred**. San Diego, CA: Harcourt Brace Jovanovich, 1990.

"An accessible portrait of the clash between feminism and Judaism as part of Och's own religious journey." A moving as well as informative book.

Ostriker, Alicia: **Feminist Revision and the Bible: Bucknell Lectures in Literary Theory**. Cambridge, MA: Blackwell Publications, 1993.

Literary studies have led to re-evaluation of religion in light of women's experiences and with aim of resurrecting that part of the female narrative in the Bible which had been repressed. Also includes series of poems on Lilith.

Pardes, Ilana: **Countertraditions in the Bible**: **A Feminist Approach**. Cambridge, MA: Harvard University Press, 1992.

After a review of past feminist criticism of the Bible, Pardes presents her own scholarly yet readable analysis in which she discusses some of the heterogeneity she feels has been overlooked in the Bible. Includes Miriam, Rachel, Zipporah, Leah, Rachel and Job's wife.

Patai, Raphael: **The Hebrew Goddess**. Detroit, MI: Wayne State University Press, 1990.

Patai, Raphael & Patai, Jennifer: **The Myth of the Jewish Race**. Detroit, MI: Wayne State University Press, 1989.

Important information on halacha and interpretations of intermarriage, conversion, slavery, concubinage and rape, and its effect on Jewish women and their offspring, from Sumerian times to the 19th century. See esp. Parts IV & V. Interesting photos and descriptions of Jewish males and females from many countries showing different physical features which belie the Jewish stereotype.

Phipps, William E.: **Assertive Biblical Women**: **Contributions in Women's Studies**. **No. 128.** Westport, CN: Greenwood Press, 1992.

Examples of "self-expression" by women in ancient societies: Sarah, Tamar, Shiphrah and Puah, Miriam, Naomi, Ruth, Huldah, Vashti, Esther, Jezebel and others. One special example: Miriam's role in the exodus from Israel!

Pirani, Alix: **The Absent Mother**: **Restoring the Goddess to Judaism and Christianity**. London: Mandala, 1991.

This collection offers us some of the missing aspects of Judaism in essays and poems about the shekinah, goddesses, Lilith and Miriam.

Plaskow, Judith: **Standing Again at Sinai**: **Judaism From a Feminist Perspective**. San Francisco: Harper, 1991.

An important work exploring the "implications of women's increasing involvement in shaping and transforming Judaism." Examples include feminist work in synagogues, Rosh Hodesh groups and the deepening Judaism of many different women. (See: Tikkun, vol 1, No. 2: pp. 28-34 for overview or introduction to book.

Plaskow, Judith & Christ, Carol P., eds.: **Weaving the Visions: New Patterns in Feminist Spirituality**. New York: Harper, 1992.

Essays by Plaskow and Umansky on Jewish feminism and Marcia Falk on feminist blessings.

Prell, Riv-Ellen: **Prayer & Community: The Havurah in American Judaism**. Detroit, MI: Wayne State University Press, 1989.

> Women were vital in the development of havurot; not just in the "Minyan", a California havurah. See especially, "Community, Visibility and Gender in Prayer," pp. 273-315.

Preserving the Covenant: A Challenge for Jewish Women. in The Life of Covenant: The Challenge of Contemporary Judaism. Edelhert, Joseph A., ed. Chicago, Il: Spertus College, 1986, 1-6.

Radcliffe, Sarah Chana: **Aizer k'negdo: The Jewish Woman's Guide to Happiness in Marriage**. Spring Valley, NY: Targum Press, 1988.

Rapoport-Albert, Ada and Zipperstein, Steven J. eds.: **On Women in Hasidism: S. A. Horodecky and the Maid of Ludomir Tradition** in: **Jewish History: Essays in Honor of Chimen Abramsky**. London: Peter Halban, 1988, 495-525.

> Review of Horodecky's mostly apologetic position on women in Judaism, and in particular, Hasidic women. He claims it appeals to them as an "emotional" religion and they are, in fact, more equal in Hasidism. It is true there were women tzadiks—but not, Rapoport-Albert shows, equal in many ways. However, she does mention the late Rabbi Shneerson's call for participation of women: was he actually giving women their due?

Rashkow, Ilona N.: **Daughters and Fathers in Genesis: Or, What is Wrong with this Picture?** in: **The New Literary Criticism and the Hebrew Bible.** Sheffield, UK: JSOT Press, 1993, 250-265.

> How families, and especially daughters, were portrayed in the Bible in relation to their fathers.

Rashkow, Ilona N.: **Intertextuality, Transference, and the Reader in/of Genesis 12 and 20**: in: **Fewell, Danna Nolan, ed., Reading Betwen Texts: Intertextuality and the Hebrew Bible.** Louisville, KY: Westminster/John Knox Press, 1992, 57-73.

> Deals with issue of Israeli matriarchs as seen in Genesis.

Riskin, Shlomo: **Women and Jewish Divorce: The Rebellious Wife, the Agunah, and the Right of Women to Initiate Divorce in Jewish Law, a Halakhic Solution**. Hoboken, NJ: KTAV, 1989.

Romanoff, Lena and Hostein, Lisa: **Your People, My People: Finding Acceptance and Fulfillment as a Jew by Choice**. Philadelphia, PA: The Jewish Publication Society, 1990.

Religion and Biblical Studies

Rosengarten, Sudy: **Worlds Apart: The Birth of Bais Yaakov in America, a Personal Recollection**. Spring Valley, NY: Targum Press, 1992.

Rosenthal, Rabbi Dovid Simcha: **Joyful Mother of Children: A Compilation of Prayers, Suggestions and Laws of the Jewish Expectant Family**. Spring Valley, NY: Feldheim, 1988.

Ruether, Radford, Rosemary Keller & Rosemary Skinner, eds.: **Women and Religion in America**: 3, New York: Harper, 1990.

This volume covers 1900-1968.

Sabar, Shalom: **Mazal Tov: Illuminated Jewish Marriage Contracts from the Israel Museum Collection**. Jerusalem: Israel Museum, 1993.

Exhibit catalog with marvelous illustrations.

Sahgal, Gita: **Jewish Fundamentalism and Women's Empowerment** in: **Refusing Holy Orders: Women and Fundamentalism in Britain.** London: Virago Press, 1992, 198-226.

Continuation of the traditional Jewish life requires the need for women's cooperation in maintaining orthodox ways of life, but this conflicts with women's desire for more independence.

Sara, Elizabeth: **Biblical Account of the First Woman: A Jewish Feminist Perspective. in: Elwes, Teresa, ed.: Women's Voices: Essays in Contemporary Feminist Theology** London: Marshall Pickering, 1992.

Schneider, Susan Weidman: **Intermarriage: The Challenge of Living with Differences Between Christians and Jews**. New York: Free Press, 1989.

"Comprehehensive study of interfaith couples pays special attention to sex-role socialization."

Schoenfeld, Stuart: **Integration into the Group and Sacred Uniqueness: An Analysis of Adult Bat-Mitzvah: in W.P.Zenner, ed., Persistence and Flexibility: Anthropological Studies of American Jewish Identities and Institutions**. Albany, NY: New York State University Press, 1988.

Sered, Susan Starr: **Women as Ritual Experts: The Religious Lives of Elderly Jewish Women in Jerusalem.** New York: Oxford University Press, 1992.

Although separated by gender, these Middle Eastern Jewish women have rich religious lives, full of rituals and deep meaning.

Sheres, Ita: **Dinah's Rebellion: A Biblical Parable for Our Time**. New York: Crossroad Publishing, 1990.

"An expresson of a rigidly tribal ideology that emphasized male Jewish 'chosenness' and exclusivity at the expense of foreigners and women."

Siegel, Hanna Tifferet: **Sacred Garment, Sacred Light: A Woman's Journey into the Jewish Ritual Garments of Tefillin and Tallit**. 8 Carter St., Hanover, NH 03755: Hanna Tifferet Siegel, 1989.

Slobin, Mark: **Engendering the Cantorate**. In **Yivo Annual**, Evanston, IL: Northwestern University Press, 19, 1990, 147-167.

Taking some data from author's <u>Chosen Voices: The Story of the American Cantorate</u> this shows the connection between the experiences of female cantors and those of other American women from 1950s to 1980. Interesting data: first Reform woman cantor accepted in 1976 and Conservative in 1987.

Spiegel, Marcia Cohn & Kremsdorf, Deborah Lipton: **Women Speak to God: The Prayers and Poems of Jewish Women**. San Diego, CA: Women's Institute for Continuing Jewish Education, 1987.

Spitzer, Rabbi Julie: **When Love is not Enough: Spousal Abuse in Rabbinic and Contemporary Judaism**. New York: Federation of Temple Sisterhoods, 1993 (revised edition).
Ground-breaking research on this important topic.

Stern, Chaim, ed.: **Gates of Prayer for Shabbat: A Gender Sensitive Prayerbook**. New York: Central Conference of American Rabbis, 1992.

This new prayerbook goes one step further than the Reform prayerbook, "Gates of Prayer" of 1974, in which English references to human beings were gender inclusive, and now does the same for all references to G-d.

Taking the Fruit: Modern Women's Tales of the Bible. San Diego: Women's Institute for Continuing Jewish Education, 1989.

Interpretations by women of biblical women's texts.

Teubal, Savina J.: **Hagar the Egyptian: The Lost Tradition of the Matriarchs**. New York: Harper & Row, 1990.

An essay about Hagar in a different mode. Teubal shows Hagar as a companion of the priestess Sarah — a matriarch for Hebrew and Islamic culture.

Teutsch, David A. ed.: **Kol Ha-Neshamah: Shirim U-Verakhot: Kol Haneshamah Songs, Blessings and Rituals for the Home**. Wyncote, PA: Reconstructionist Press, 1991.

Torjesen, Karen J.: **When Women were Priests**. San Francisco: Harper, 1993.

Studies women's leadership in the first centuries before they were marginalized by the church.

Umansky, Ellen & Dianne Ashton: **Four Centuries of Jewish Spirituality: A Sourcebook**. Boston: Beacon Press, 1992.

One of the most important books of the last ten years for and about Jewish women. Letters, fragments of diaries, poems, prayers and other writings show the spiritual richness of Jewish women's beliefs from 1560 to today.

Vanderkam, James C.: **No One Spoke Ill of Her: Essays on Judith. Series: Early Judaism and its literature:No.2,** Atlanta, GA: Scholars Press, 1992.

A collection of critiques of the biblical Judith showing her resourcefulness, courage and religiosity. Author sees her as a role model of an independent woman of great character. We view her from religious, feminist and historical perspectives and especially as frequently depicted in art.

Walfish, Barry Dov: **Esther in Medieval Garb: Jewish Interpretation of the Book of Esther in the Middle Ages**. Albany, NY: State University of New York Press, 1993.

Essay on Esther; the Shekhinah, the modest woman. Discusses various midrashic sources of the Middle Ages. Several pages devoted to Vashti, and mentioned throughout.

Weems, Renita J.: **The Hebrew Women are not Like the Egyptian Women: The Ideology of Race, Gender and Sexual Reproduction in Exodus**. 1, 59: Atlanta, GA: Semeia, 1992.

Wegner, Judith Romney: **Chattel or Person? The Status of Women in the Mishnah**. New York: Oxford University Press, 1988.

"The Mishnah treats all women as persons some of the time, and some women as persons all of the time." Exploration of women's status in the Mishnah; asks for restoration of women's personhood in Jewish law.

Weiss, Avraham: **Women at Prayer: A Halakhic Analysis of Women's Prayer Groups**. New York: KTAV, 1990.

> Presentation of the halacha pertaining to women's prayer groups and affirmation that there is no contradiction in women praying together in organized groups, but not together with men!

Weissler, Chava: **Making Davening Meaningful, in: Yivo Annual,** 19. Evanston, IL: Northwestern University Press, 1990, 255-282.

> This chapter describes the havurah movement and the important role of women in its development, and its importance for the new ways in which women are praying and finding their creative participation in the Jewish service.

Weissler, Chava: **The Traditional Piety of Ashkenazic Women, in: "Jewish Spirituality". ed.: Arthur Green**. 2, New York: Crossroad, 1986, 245-275.

> Weissler raises the issue of the spiritual life of Ashkenazic women who, "as a group, have been perhaps the most neglected area of the history of Jewish spirituality." She looks into the sources, such as the Yiddish *tkhines* to study them.

Weissler, Chava: **Traditional Yiddish Literature: A Source for the Study of Women's Religious Lives. Jacob Pat Memorial Lecture,** Cambridge, MA: Harvard University Library, 1988.

> Lecture on techines/Yiddish prayers for private devotion, now printed in pamphlet form. Some of these prayers were actually written by women and they enlighten us as to women's religious lives.

Wikler, Meir: **Bayis Ne'eman b'Yisrael: Practical Steps to Success in Marriage**. Jerusalem: Feldheim, 1988.

Willey, Patricia K.: **The Importunate Woman of Tekoa and How She Got Her Way,** in **Fewell, Donna Nolan, ed. Reading Between Texts: Intertextuality and the Hebrew Bible.** Louisville, KY: Westminster/John Knox Press, 1992, 115-131.

> "What motivates the Tekoan woman? Why does she speak as she does?" Willey discusses her along with King David and other "players" in this story.

Wolkstein, Diane: **Song of Songs: The First Love Stories: From Isis and Osiris to Tristan and Iseult**. New York: Harper Perennial, 1992, 93-109.

> A retelling of this famous love story which revitalizes the sensual dialogue between man and woman. Wolkstein's introduction describing storytelling sessions of Jewish content is also interesting.

Young, Serinity, ed.: **An Anthology of Sacred Texts by and about Women**. New York: Crossroad, 1993.

Zakutinsky, Rivka.: **Techines: A Voice from the Heart: A Collection of Jewish Women's Prayers. "As Only a Woman Can Pray."** Brooklyn, NY: Aura Press, 1992.

Techines from two "popular" collections, Shas Tehine Hadoshe and Shas Tehine Rav Peninim as well as some prayers that were traditionally said in Hebrew by women. The volume is in Yiddish and English and has a guide for reading the Yiddish but the reviewer (see Breger) states that a "more complete translation" would have improved the work.

Zolty, Shoshana Pantel: **And All Your Children Shall be Learned: Women and the Study of Torah in Jewish Law and History**. Northvale, NJ: Jason Aronson, 1993.

Analysis of halakhic literature, Mishnah, Talmud, etc. in which the author traces Jewish education for traditional women.

B. Articles

Adelman, Penina V: **The Golden Calf Jumps Over the New Moon: Mythmaking Among Jewish Women**. Chambersburg, PA: **Anima**, 16, Fall 1989, 31-39.

Adelman discusses "how ritual is used to rejuvenate the human spirit," via Jewish women's myths and stories, especially those connected to Rosh Chodesh.

Adler, Rachel: **Feminist Folktales of Justice: Robert Cover as a Resource for the Renewal of a Halakhah.** New York: **Conservative Judaism,** XLV, Spring 1993, 40-55.

"The project of feminist Jews is what Cover called Jurisgenesis." His objective was to transform the "normative" universe Jews inhabit. His theme: the need for halacha to engender Judaism.

Adler, Rachel: **In Your Blood, Live: Re-visions of a Theology of Purity**. Oakland, CA: **Tikkun**, 8, Jan/Feb 1993, 38-41.

Adler, Rachel: **The Virgin in the Brother and Other Anomalies: Character and Context in the Legend of Beruriah**. Oakland, CA: Tikkun, 3, Nov/Dec 1988, 28-32, 102-105.

Story/legend of Beruriah; rabbinic attitudes toward her and lessons we can learn from this story.

Allison, Marla Ruth: **Bat Mitzvah in the Divorce Crossfire**. New York: **Lilith**, 15, Spring 1990, 23-24.

> Struggle over Jewish identity/versus self-identity.

Ashton, Dianne: **Grace Aguilar and the Female Response to Evangelists**. Oberlin, OH: **Jewish Folklore and Ethnology Review**, 12, 1990, Special Issue: Jewish Women.

Axelrad, Albert S.: **Let Principle Encounter Principle: Conservative Judaism and Religious Egalitarianism**. New York: **Conservative Judaism**, 38, 1986, 77-79.

Bal, Mieke: **The Elders and Susanna**. Leiden: **Biblical Interpretation**, 1, 1993, 1-19.

Balka, Christie: **In Search of the Ideal Shul**. New York: **Lilith**, 16, Fall 1991, 10-12+.

Bell, Roselyn: **Coming Apart Jewishly**. New York: **Hadassah**, March 1991, 21.

> While most American Jews ask a rabbi to officiate at marriages, when divorcing, it does not occur to them to go to a rabbi, with consequences that are sometimes tragic.

Berkovits, Berel: **Divorce and Gittin in the 1990s**. Part I. London: **L'Eylah**, 34, April 1992, 20-22.

> Proposals for reform of current English divorce laws, compared with Jewish laws. Examines "current halakhic problems within the realm of Jewish divorce law, gittin and agunah."

Berkovits, Berel: **Divorce and Gittin in the 1990s**. Part II. London: **L'Eylah**, 34, Sept. 1992, 20-22.

> Berkovits "shows how the proposed English [divorce] law reforms are moving closer to the Jewish concept of divorce."

Berkowitz, Gila: **Lifting the Yoke: Is There Hope for Ending Jewish Legal Discrimination against Women**, see Author Index.

Berkowitz, Adena: **Thinking about Women in Abortion Controversies**. New York: **S'vara**, 2, Winter 1991, 25-28.

Berkowitz, Adena: **The Prisoners of Divorce**. New York: **Lilith Special Report**, 18, Winter 1987-8, 18-23.

> Jewish divorces in Jerusalem

Berman, Joshua: **Balancing the Bimah**: **The Diaspora Struggle of the Orthodox Feminist**. New York: **Midstream**, Aug/Sept 1990, 20-24.

"Self-inspection of American Orthodoxy concerning the presence of feminist activity within the movement."

Berman, Rabbi Donna: **The Feminist Critique of Language**. New York: **CCAR Journal**, 39, Summer 1992, 5-14.

Biale, Rachel: **Abortion**: **Abortion in Jewish Law**. Oakland, CA: **Tikkun**, 4, July/August 1989, 26-28.

Bilik, Dorothy: **Tsene-rene: A Yiddish Literary Success**. New York: **Jewish Book Annual**, 51, 1993-94, 96-111.

The Tsene-rene helped Jewish women to gain traditional Jewish learning in a way that proved immensely popular to much of the Jewish population of 17-19th century Eastern Europe and showed the importance of Yiddish for Jewish women.

Bird, Phyllis A.: **The Harlot as Heroine**: **Narrative Art and Social Presupposition in Three Old Testament Texts**. Atlanta GA: **Semeia: Society of Biblical Literature**. Scholars Press, 46, 1989, 119-139.

Examines the "interrelationship of narrative art and social presupposition in three biblical texts having a harlot or assumed harlot."

Bitton-Jackson, Livia: **Prophesying Women**. New York: **Midstream**, 38, November 1992, 21-23.

Rabbinic list of prophets includes 7 women as well as the Matriarchs. "What element in their personalities or actions singled out these particular Biblical heroines for inclusion in the category of prophets.?"

Bos, Johanna W.H.: **Out of the Shadows**: **Genesis 28; Judges 4:17-22; Ruth 3**. Atlanta,GA: **Semeia**, 42, 1988, 37-67.

"This essay attempts to delineate the role of three women (Yael, Naomi and Ruth), as they challenge patriarchy from within patriarchal structures."

Braiterman, Zachary: **Trible/Rashi**: **And Never the 'Twain Shall Meet?** Los Angeles, CA: **Response**, Nos.61-2, Fall 1993, 10-17.

Breger, Jennifer: **The Prayers of Jewish Women**: **Some Historical Perspectives**. New York: **Judaism**, 42, Fall 1993, 504-513.

Questions about techines, womens' literacy and use of prayer discussed in light of new books (see: Bilik, Cardin, Zabutinsky, Klirs, Merit of our Mothers).

Brettschneider, Marla: **Feminist Judaism: Providing Models for Continuity Through Multiculturalism**. Los Angeles, CA: **Response**, Nos. 61-2, Fall 1993, 18-21.

Brin, Deborah: **Up Against the Wall: How We Answered Our Own Prayers**. New York: **Reconstructionist**, LIV, June 1989, 13-16.

Bronner, Leila Leah: **The Changing Face of Woman from Bible to Talmud**. West Lafayette, Indiana: **Shofar**, 7, Winter 1989, 34-47.

Contrast between importance of certain biblical women as compared with the social or religious role they played in the Talmudic era.

Bronner, Leila Leah: **From Veil to Wig: Jewish Women's Hair Covering**. New York: **Judaism**, 42, Fall 1993, 465-477.

Examination of "the practice of hair covering among Jewish women from a historical and cultural perspective."

Brooten, Bernadette J.: **Were Women and Men Segregated in Ancient Synagogues?** Washington, DC: **Moment**, 14, Dec.1989, 32-39.

Broyde, Michael J.: **Tradition, Modesty and America: Married Women Covering Their Hair**. New York: **Judaism**, 40, Winter 1991, 79-94.

Refutes assertions that covering hair is within halacha, and therefore, that there are no sanctions for women not covering their hair. Is question one of custom or of law?

Broyde, Michael J.: **Further on Women as Prayer Leaders and their Role in Communal Prayer: An Exchange: Communal Prayer and Women**. New York: **Judaism**, 42, Fall 1993, 387-395.

Response to Judith Hauptman's article in Judaism, vol. 42, 94-103, stating that it is Jewish law that makes it impossible for women to lead prayers since they cannot be counted in the minyan/quorum or be a shaliach/zibbur/cantor. He distinguishes between those practices to come via social change and those that require a change in the legal rules. In same article Joel B. Wolowelsky commends Hauptman on her article and the need for noting the serious prayer obligations of women.Decide for yourself!

Bycel, Lee T.: **To Reclaim Our Voice: An Analysis of Representative Contemporary Feminist Passover Haggadot**. Mississauga, Ontario: **CCAR Journal**, XL, Spring 1993, 55-71.

Camp, Claudia V: **Wise and Strange: An Interpretation of the Female Imagery in Proverbs in Light of Trickster Mythology**. Atlanta, GA: **Semeia**, 42, 1988, 14-36.

"Interconnection of wise and deceitful language" as used by women in the Book of Proverbs and demonstrating "women wisdom" in the Bible.

Carter, Carie; Merbaum, Michael & Michael J. Strube: **Constructions of Religious Symbols and Professional Roles by Male and Female North American Rabbis**. New York: **Conservative Judaism**, XLVI, Fall 1993, 70-79.

Chalmer, Judith: **Turning 12: A Menarche Ceremony**. New York: **Lilith**, 21, Sept. 1988, 17-28.

Chertok, Haim: **Sisters in Prayer: The Women at the Wall**. New York: **Congress Monthly**, 56, Nov/Dec 1989, 13-15.

Chertok, Haim: **The Book of Ruth: Complexities within Simplicity**. New York: **Judaism**, 35, Summer 1986, 290-297.

Was Ruth merely a seducer or a heroine? Virtuous or sinful? The article compares her with the biblical episode of Tamar and Judah.

Chertok, Haim: **Rachel and Esau**. Oakland, CA: **Tikkun**, 1, [1986], 54-58.

Revisiting the stories of Rachel and Leah, Jacob and Esau.

Clines, David: **What Does Eve Do to Help**. in: **What Does Eve Do to Help and Other Readerly Questions to the Old Testament**. Sheffield, UK: **Journal for the Study of the Old Testament**. Supplement Series, 94, 1990, 25-48; 85-108.

Cohen, Diane: **The Divorced Woman: Toward a New Ritual**. New York: **Conservative Judaism**, XLIV, Summer 1992, 62-68.

Suggestions for a meaningful ceremony after a woman receives a get (Jewish divorce) in order to give a sense of closure and a feeling of sharing with friends.

Cohen, Sharon: **Reclaiming the Hammer: Toward a Feminist Midrash**. Oakland, CA: **Tikkun**, 3, March/April 1988, 55-57,93-95.

Cowan, Jennifer: **Survey Finds 70% of Women Rabbis Sexually Harassed**. Washington, DC: **Moment**, 18, Oct.1993, 34-37.

Davidman, Lyn: **The Search for Family and Roots: Why Contemporary Women Choose Orthodox Judaism**. Farmington Hills, MI: **Humanistic Judaism**, XX, Summer 1992, 21-32.

Davis, Karen: **The Lavender Pulpit: Safe Haven for Women Rabbis**. Denville, NJ: **New Directions for Women in New Jersey**. 21, Jl/Ag 1992.

"Women rabbis bring about political and structural changes," yet there is a plus for gay and lesbian congregations in securing high-quality heterosexual rabbis. (Lavender is the color for gay/lesbian liberation).

Dicker, Shira: **Mikveh**. Oakland, CA: **Tikkun**, 7, Nov 1992, 62-64.

Dresner, Samuel. **Goddess Feminism**. New York: **Conservative Judaism**, XLVI, Fall 1993, 3-23.

An important overview and critique of neopaganism, WICCA, and goddess learning and some New Age practices in the women's movement which indicate a lack of knowledge of goddess facts by its practitioners. Offers references and analysis on the lack of debate by academics on the topic. Dresner's work here was stimulated by a 1989 conference at Indiana University on "Religious Alternatives."

Dresner, Samuel H.: **Barren Rachel**. New York: **Judaism**, 40, Fall 1991, 442-451.

Eisen, Arnold: **Judith Plaskow in "Jewish Theology in North America: Notes on Two Decades."** New York: **American Jewish Year Book**, 91, 1991, 27-31.

Overview of Plaskow's work in feminist Jewish theology and the "democratization of God talk."

El-Or, Tamar: **The Length of the Slits and the Spread of Luxury: Reconstructing the Subordination of Ultra-Orthodox Jewish Women Through the Patriarchy of Men Scholars**. New York: **Sex Roles: A Journal of Research**, 29, Nov. 1993, 585-598.

Preaching that takes place in ultra-orthodox communities where dress and its relationship to modesty becomes an issue of social control.

European Judaism. London, 21, 1987, Special issue.

Dialogues between Jewish, Christian and Muslim Women. Issue summarizes articles on dialogues on religious traditions, civil rights for women; from religiously committed women as well as from radical feminists.

Falk, Marcia: **Toward a Feminist Jewish Reconstruction of Monotheism**. Oakland, CA: **Tikkun**, 4, July 1989, 53+.

Falk, Marcia: **Notes on Composing New Blessings: Toward a Feminist-Jewish Reconstruction of Prayer**. Chico, CA: **Journal of Feminist Studies in Religion**, 3, Spring 1987, 39-53.

> Feminist-religious scholarship and Falk's personal journey have led Falk, a noted poet, translator and feminist scholar, to investigate a new vocabulary for blessings that would be meaningful to "klal yisrael", the entire "community of Israel."

Feeley-Harnik, Gillian: **Naomi and Ruth: Building up the House of David**. Atlanta, GA: **Scholars Press**, in: Text and Tradition:The Hebrew Bible and Folklore, ed. Susan Niditch, 1990, 163-184.

> Article and response by Edward L. Greenstein follows (185-191).

Feinhor, Noam: **Writing on the Wall: Tisha B'AV 5752**. Los Angeles, CA: **Response**, Nos. 61-2, Fall 1993, 39-41.

Fewell, Donna Nolan & Gunn, David: **Controlling Perspectives: Women, Men and the Authority of Violence in Judges 4 & 5**. Atlanta, GA: **Journal of the American Academy of Religion**, 58, 1990, 389-411.

Fishbane, Simcha: **In Any Case There Are No Sinful Thoughts: The Role and Status of Women in Jewish Law as Expressed in the Arukh Hashulhan**. New York: **Judaism**, 42, Fall 1993, 492-503.

> Evidence of concern with the status of women in the late 19th century shown in works of Y.L. Gordon and Y.L. Peretz and, here stated, in the Arukh Hashulhan.

Fishbane, Simcha: **Most Women Engage in Sorcery: An Analysis of Sorceresses in the Babylonian Talmud**. Haifa: **Jewish History**, 7, Spring 1993, 27-42.

> Talmud mentions female sorcery, although it was common to condemn women sorcerers. Author states that this may have given women an opportunity to elevate their place in society.

Fishman, Talya: **Medieval Parody of Misogyny: Judah ibn Shabbetai's "Minhat Yehudah sone hanashim"**. Baltimore, MD: **Prooftexts**, 8, 1988, 89-111.

Focus on Women and Change. New York: **Reform Judaism**, 21, Fall 1992, 22-45.

> Five articles on women in the Reform movement; God as female, Sisterhoods and women in leadership roles in the movement.

Friedman, Theodore: **On Women**. New York: **Judaism**, 37, 1988, 248-250.

Friedman, Theodore: **The Shifting Role of Women, From the Bible to the Talmud.** New York: **Judaism**, 36, Fall 1987, 479-487.

Description of women's participation in political, economic, social and religious life of Biblical era as compared with their exclusion in Talmudic era.

Frishtik, Mordechai: **Violence Against Women in Judaism**. New York: **Journal of Psychology and Judaism**, 14, Fall 1990, 131-153.

"This paper deals with the phenomenon of violence of husbands against their wives in the Judaism of the past, and with reference made to it by Jewish sages" showing that there was much evidence of such violence so the sages enacted laws to punish offenders.

Frymer-Kensky, Tikva: **The Bible, Goddesses and Sex**. New York: **Midstream**, 34, Oct 1, 1988, 20+.

Fuchs, Esther: **For I Have the Way of Women: Deception, Gender and Ideology in Biblical Narrative**. Atlanta, GA: **Semeia**, 42, 1988, 68-83.

Gender as a factor in deception in the Bible using the example of Rachel as compared with Jacob and Laban.

Fuchs, Esther: **The Literary Characterization of Mothers and Sexual Politics in the Hebrew Bible**. Atlanta GA: **Semeia: Society of Biblical Literature, Scholars Press**, 46, 1989, 151-166.

Offers a feminist critical reading of motherhood from Biblical sources.

Fuchs, Esther: **Structure and Patriarchal Functions in the Biblical Betrothal Type-Scene: Some Preliminary Notes**. Chico, CA: **Journal of Feminist Studies in Religion**, 3, Spring 1987, 7-14.

Furman, Nelly: **His Story Versus Her Story: Male Genealogy and Female Strategy in the Jacob Cycle**. Atlanta, GA: **Semeia: Society of Biblical Literature, Scholars Press**, 46, 1989, 141-149.

The woman's point of view is shown in exploring "the meaning and function of garments" in the scene between Joseph and Potiphar's wife and in other stories from the Jacob cycle.

Geller, Laura & Elwell, Sue Levi: **On the Jewish Feminist Frontier, a Report**. Port Washington, NY: **Sh'ma**, Nov. 13, 1992, 1-2.

> Survey of stages of Jewish feminists' emergence in Conservative, Reconstructionist and Conservative Movements. Two examples: Linda Zweig on her youth in the Conservative movement, and Catherine E. Coulson on studying Jewish texts from a feminist perspective.

Glancy, Jennifer: **The Accused: Susanna and Her Readers**. Sheffield, UK: **JSOT**, 58, 1993, 103-116.

Goitein, Shlomo Dov: **Women as Creators of Biblical Genres**. Baltimore, MD: **Prooftexts**, 8, 1988, 1-33.

Gold, Michael: **God in the Bedroom**. Washington, DC: **Moment**, August 1991, 36+.

> Aspects of marital sexuality.

Goldman, Ari L.: **A Bar to Women as Cantors is Lifted: Marla Rosenfeld Baruge admitted into Cantors' Assembly**. New York: **New York Times**, Sept. 19, 1990, A15 (N); B2L).

Goldman, Karla: **The Ambivalence of Reform Judaism: Kaufman Kohler and the Ideal Jewish Woman**. Waltham, MA: **American Jewish History**, 79, 1990, 477-499.

Goldman, Nechama: **Women Prepare for Their Day in Court**. Jerusalem: **Kol Emunah**, Summer, 1992, 17, 33.

> Women pleaders and the training they undergo to prepare them for a new role in the Beit Din (Jewish court of law) and thus better represent the female point of view.

Goldstein, Rabbi Elyse M.: **Take Back the Waters: A Feminist Reappropriation of Mikveh**. New York: **Lilith**, 15, Summer 1986, 15-16.

> A Reform woman rabbi describes her own "mikveh experience" and "proposes a revival...of this ancient Jewish women's ritual."

Goldston, Ruth Berger: **Separating: A Havdalah Ritual for when a Marriage Comes Apart**. New York: **Lilith**, 18, Spring 1993, 28-29.

> Concerns a ceremony for the ending of a marriage, the beginning of a new life cycle. (Includes actual ritual)

Good, Edwin M.: **Deception and Women: A Response**. Atlanta, GA: **Semeia**, 42, 1988, 117-132.

>Author responds to articles by Bos, Camp, Fuchs and Steinberg in same issue of "Semeia" and wishes that their "thesis had been a bit more radical."

Gordis, Robert: **Personal Names in Ruth: A Note on Biblical Etymologies**. New York: **Judaism**, 35, Summer 1986, 298-299.

>Some interesting remarks on Ruth, Naomi, and others in the Book of Ruth.

Gordis, Robert: **The Role of Women in Jewish Religious Life**. New York: **Midstream**, XXXII, Aug/Sept 1987, 41-44.

>Important article on women and the Jewish religion.
>See: Vol XXXII, April 1988: pgs 59-61 for responses by Mamlak and Gordis.

Gordis, Robert: **Seating in the Synagogue—Minhag**. New York: **Judaism**, 36, Winter, 1987, 47-53.

>Separate seating and the mehitzah in the synagogue—law or tradition?

Gordon, Harvey L.: **The Curse-and-a-Blessing**. New York: **Journal of Reform Judaism**, XXXVI, Summer 1989, 69-70.

Goss, Julie: **Reworking the Rabbi's Role**. New York: **Lilith**, 15, Fall 1990, 16-25.

>The entry of women into the rabbinate has changed those synagogues where they officiate as well as their own lives.

Graetz, Naomi: **Miriam: Guilty Or Not Guilty?** New York: **Judaism**, 40, Spring 1991, 184-192.

Greenberg, Blu: **Is Now the Time for Orthodox Women Rabbis?** Washington, D.C.: **Moment**, 18, December, 1993, 50-53, 74.

>Changes in Orthodox women's religious studies should now enable them to become rabbis which would prepare them to take on non-pulpit leadership roles alongside Reform, Conservative and Reconstructionist women rabbis. It is not halacha, but custom and linkages to other factors such as the minyan that has thus far prevented them from doing so.

Greenberg, Blu: **Jewish Women Today**. Washington, DC: **Jewish Monthly**, 105, Feb 1991, 8-11.

Religion and Biblical Studies

Greenberg, Blu: **Missed Connections**. New York: **Hadassah**, 74, January 1993, 20-23.

Greenberg, Blu: **For the Love of Law**. New York: **Hadassah**, 74, May 1993, 18-21.

Grossman, Lawrence: **The Women of the Wall**. New York: **American Jewish Yearbook**, 91, 1991, 202-203.

> As part of the longer report on "Jewish Communal affairs," this brief article traces the attempts by Jewish women to pray at Jerusalem's Western Wall and to consecrate their own Torah.

Grossman, Naomi: **Women Unbound: Breaking the Chains of Jewish Divorce Law**. New York: **Lilith**, 18, 1993, 8+.

> One of many articles on this pressing issue for orthodox American women and for all Israeli women.

Haberman, Bonne Devora: **A Woman's Voice**. Oakland, CA: **Tikkun**, 6, Sept./Oct/ 1991, 49+.

> Haberman's experiences trying to pray at the Kotel, and other attitudes toward Jewish women and the halacha.

Hachen, Debra: **A Rabbi's Life**. New York: **Keeping Posted**, XXXIII, April 1988, 10-11,13.

Hammer, Viva: **Jewish Marriage Protection Agreements: An Idea Whose Time Has Come**. New York: **Emunah**, Spring/Summer 1993, 15-16.

Hammer, Viva: **No More Chains**. New York: **Na'amat Women**, VIII, Mar/April 1993, 18-19+.

> Explanation of Jewish divorce obstacles in Israel and elsewhere. Cites abuses and some solutions. Author is an Australian attorney now in USA who specializes in international cases of agunot. (Na'amat itself offers legal services to them in USA and Israel).

Hauptman, Judith: **Women and Prayer: An Attempt to Dispel Some Fallacies**. New York: **Judaism**, 42, Winter 1993, 94-103.

> Discussion of obligation to pray and its influence on women praying and leading prayers.

Hauptman, Judith: **Some Thoughts on the Nature of Halakhic Adjudication: Women and Minyan**. New York: **Judaism**, 42, Fall 1993, 396-413.

> As response to Broyde's response to her original article (vol 42 94-103) she makes "a plea to the halakhic and scholarly community to re-examine contemporary synagogue practices in the light of classical Jewish texts." Extensive notes to Talmudic passages reinforce Hauptman's scholarship.

Hauptman, Judith: **Pesach**: **A Liberating Experience for Women**. New York: **Masoret**, Winter 1993, 8-9.

> Passover is a time for Jewish women who intensively must prepare; clean, cook, etc. author asks, how else could/should women participate?

Hauptman, Judith: **Maternal Dissent**: **Women and Procreation in the Mishna**. Oakland, CA: **Tikkun**, 6, Nov/Dec.1991, 81-2;94-5.

> Hauptman argues that "the rabbis fear that an obligation might dangerously empower women and lead them to replace obligations with exemptions from traditional female duties."

Helfgott, Esther Altschul: **Beth Shalom's Encounter with the Woman Question**. New York: **Conservative Judaism**, 38, Spring 1986, 66-76.

Heller, Janet Ruth: **Retelling Bible Stories to Express the Lives and Struggles of Modern Women**. Fairfax, VA: **Women and Language**, 16, Spring 1993, 35-39.

Hellig, Jocelyn: **Images of the Bride in Judaism**. Johannesburg: **Jewish Affairs**, 48, Winter 1993, 13-19.

Hollander, Vicki: **The New Improved Jewish Divorce**: **Hers/His**. New York: **Lilith**, 15, Summer 1990, 20-21.

Hyman, Frieda Clark: **Michal**: **A Liberated Woman**. New York: **Midstream**, 39, Dec 1993, 31-3.

> A careful reading of 1 and 2 Samuel and the complexities of parental involvement with matrimony. Essay contains scholarly conjectures and questions.

Hyman, Miryam: **Renewing Ritual**: **The Brit Mikvah**. Los Angeles, CA: **Response**, Nos. 61-2, Fall 1993, 22-31.

Hyman, Paula: **Gender and Jewish History**. (Historical role of women in Jewish religion) see Author Index.

Jacobs, Rebecca: **Being Part of a Transitional Generation**. Port Washington, NY: **Sh'ma**, 22, Nov.15,1991, 1-2.

Jewish Women: Redefinitions, Reaffirmations, Celebrations. New York: Melton Journal, No.22, Fall 1987, Special issue.

> Issue deals with Halacha, Miriam, women rabbinical students, Jewish education for women, etc.

Jochnowitz, Carol: **Fathers and Daughters**. New York: **Jewish Currents**, , April, 1986, 30+.

Shylock/Jessica, Isaac/Rebecca (in Ivanhoe) and other such pairs reconsidered.

Kaplan, Betsy: **The Rituals of Death**. New York: **Lilith**, 14, Winter 1989, 16-17.

Kass, Leon R. **Miriam: A Woman for All Seasons**. New York: **Commentary**, Sept 1991, 30-5.

Kass, Leon R.: **Regarding Daughters and Sisters: The Rape of Dinah**. New York: **Commentary**, 93, April 1992, 29-38.

Kaufman, Debra: **Coming Home to Jewish Orthodoxy: Reactionary or Radical Women?**. Oakland, CA: **Tikkun**, 2, July/August 1987, 60-63.

Explores some of the reasons why Jewish women turn to orthodoxy.

Kayfetz, Ben: **Canadian Law Eases Halachic Divorce For Jewish Women**. London: **Patterns of Prejudice**, 20, 1986, 37-39.

Kenel, Mary Elizabeth: **Religious Women and the Problem of Anger**. New York: **Journal of Religion and Health**, 27, Sept. 1988, 236-244.

Klagsbrun, Francine: **Feminine Spirituality**. Washington, DC: **Moment**, 17, August 1992, 14,17.

Klagsbrun, Francine : **Jewish Divorce**. Washington, DC: **Moment**, 18, Dec. 1993, 26-7.

Knight, Chris: **The Bloodiest Revolution**. Oakland: **Tikkun**, 7, May/June 1992, 45-48,88-94.

Provocative interview by anthropologist "...posing a theory for women inventing morality and symbolic culture."

Kofsky, Alina Semo:**A Comparative Analysis of Women's Property Rights in Jewish Law and Anglo-American Law**. St. Paul, MN: **Journal of Law and Religion**, 6, 1988, 317-353.

Important article discussing women's status as citizens/property owners in Jewish law as compared to secular law. It outlines how Jewish law in fact led the way in giving women "superior property rights and recognizing them as legal entities and viable citizens of the Jewish community."

Kranzler, Gershon: **The Women of Williamsburg: A Contemporary American Hasidic Community**. See Author Index.

Kraemer, David C.: **A Development Perspective on the Laws of Niddah**. New York: **Conservative Judaism**, 38, Spring 1986, 26-33.

"The modern law of Niddah stands in blatant contradiction to the spirit of the original Torah text." This article is a review of its evolution, explaining sources of confusion and fear and pleads for a more tolerant interpretation.

Krasner-Davidson, Haviva: **Why I'm applying to Yeshiva U**. Washington, D.C.: **Moment**, 18, December, 1993, 54-55, 97.

Krasner-Davidson is applying to Yeshiva University and prays with tallit and tefillin; she considers herself orthodox. She wishes to study and receive the same recognition as a man so that she can show that halacha can move and not stagnate.

Land, Randi Jo: **Changing the Face of Judaism**. New York: **Na'amat Woman**, VII, 1991, 3-5, 28.

Efforts of Israeli orthodox and Reform women to gain religious equality. Summarizes Women At The Wall since 1988 and their work as a women's prayer group; their appeal to the Israel court. Valuable information about orthodox women's progress in ritual, synagogue life and politics in Israel.

Land, Randi Jo: **Women Rabbis in Israel**. New York: **Na'amat Woman**, Sept/Oct 1990, 12-14, 24-25.

Women rabbis in Israel are a curiosity (6 in all; 5 Reform, 1 Reconstructionist), who call themselves "rabanit" (female rabbi). All remain unrecognized by the government and cannot perform rabbinic functions while they all work to break the orthodox monopoly over religious life in Israel. Article details problems of Israelis toward acceptance of women rabbis and how the rabanit is coping.

Lefkovitz, Lori: **Leah Behind the Veil: The Divided Matriarchy in Bible, Midrash, Dickens, Freud and Woody Allen**. Jerusalem: **Hebrew University Studies in Literature and the Arts**, 18, 1990, 177-205.

Sister relationships: They are tested/diminished/competing and, in fact, "silenced in their relationships to one another." Examples given are "Hannah and her Sisters," The Biblical story of Rachel and Leah, Dickens and Freud's own family.

Leibowitz, Shira and Leibowitz, Nathaniel: **Shira Leibowitz and Nathaniel Leibowitz discuss Chaim Herschenson's View of Deborah: A Justice or a Justess**. Jerusalem: **Kol Emunah**, Summer 1992, 34-5.

Current discussions of the role of religious women in public positions, with frequent reference to Deborah and her role in ancient Israel.

Lerner, Anne Lapidus: **Judaism and Feminism: The Unfinished Agenda**. New York: **Judaism**, 36, Spring 1987, 167-173.

Levine-Melammed, Renee: **The Ultimate Challenge: Safeguarding the Crypto-Judaic Heritage,** in: American Academy for Jewish Research: Vol. LIII, Jerusalem: American Academy for Jewish Research, 1986, 91-109.

Importance of the role of Jewish women or conversas in preserving the Jewish religion has been uncovered in Inquisition dossiers.

Levy, Diane: **Women as Makers of Meaning: Tradition and the Ndebele Bride**. Johannesburg: **Jewish Affairs**, 48, Winter 1993, 147-152.

Litman, Jane: **The Power of Women's Folk Judaism**. New York: **Lilith**, 16, Fall 1991, 6-8.

Looking at our foremothers to find evidence of the ways in which Jewish women practiced their religion.

Lubitch, Rivkah: **A Feminist's Look at Esther**. New York: **Judaism**, 42, Fall 1993, 438-446.

Looking at the Book of Esther and the various midrashim written about Esther we find "two different personalities in one woman..." One is the "beautiful, obedient wife" and the other "assertive, active politically and full of self-confidence."

Mamlak, Gershon: **Women and Judaism**. New York: **Midstream**, XXXIV, 1988, 59-60.

Marder, Janet: **How Women are Changing the Rabbinate**. New York: **Reform Judaism**, Summer 1991, 4+.

Mason, Ruth: **Adult Bat Mitzvah: Changing Women, Changing Synagogues**. New York: **Lilith**, 14, Fall 1989, 21-24.

Mazabow, Gerald: **Some Biblical Women: The First Woman: A Fresh Homiletic Perspective**. Johannesburg: **Jewish Affairs**, 48, Winter 1993, 20-23.

Metzger, Deena: **What Dinah Thought**. New York: **Lilith**, 15, Spring 1990, 8-12.

Milgrom, Jo: **Jewish Women's Rituals**. Oakland, CA: **Tikkun**, 2, Jan/Mr 1987, 108.

A critical review of "Miriam's Well;" its strengths and some shortcomings are detailed.

Moore, Carey A.: **Susanna: A Case of Sexual Harassment in Ancient Babylon**. Washington, DC: **Bible Review**, 8, 1992, 20-29.

Murphy, Cullen: **Women and the Bible**. Joplin, MO: **Atlantic**, 272, Aug 1993, 39-64.

Musleah, Rahel: **New Rituals and Ceremonies for Jewish Women**. New York: **Na'Amat Woman**, March-April 1992, 5-7, 26-27.

A roundup of reasoning about women's new rituals, girls' birth ceremonies, Simchat Hochmah (60th year wisdom celebration); study sessions for brides, women's prayer groups, Rosh Hodesh. Emphasis is on "new rituals grounded in Jewish sources."

A New Look at Judaism & Gender. Los Angeles, CA: **Response**, Nos. 61-2, Fall 1993 (Special issue), 10-17.

Nirenberg, David: **A Female Rabbi in Fourteenth Century Zaragoza**. Madrid: **Sefarad**, 51, 1991, 179-182.

Article about a letter published in 1325 concerning a female rabbi in Zaragoza, Aragon. She was apparently called Ceti and was the "rabbess of the female Jews of the major synagogue" in this city. Her mere existence raises more questions than there are answers.

Ochs, Vanessa: **Not In My Backyard.** Oakland, CA: Tikkun, 8, July/Aug 1993, 52-55.

Concerning Orthodox day schools for girls.

Ochs, Vanessa: **Women Finally Decode Jewish Law**. New York: **Lilith**, 15, Summer 1990, 16-18.

Orenstein, Debra: **How Jewish Tradition Treats Wife Abuse**. New York: **Lilith**, No. 20, Summer 1988, 9.

Ostriker, Alicia: **We'll Never Read the Bible the Same Way Again: Revisionist Myth-Making**. New York: **Lilith**, 14, Fall 1989, 17-20.

Plaskow, Judith: **We Are Also Your Sisters**. New York: **Women's Studies Quarterly**, 21, Spring/Summer 1993, 9-21.

Plaskow asserts that women's studies in religion are a vibrant area for research, they expose much about womens' oppression and liberation. Not only "reactionaries" do this research which also reaches "outside the academy."

Plaskow, Judith: **The Year of the Agunah**. Oakland, CA: **Tikkun**, 8, Sept/Oct. 1993, 52-3,86-7.

Plaskow, Judith: **Facing the Ambiguity of God: Jewish Feminism**. Oakland, CA: **Tikkun**, 6, September/October 1991, 70,96.

Discussion of "feminist characterizations of the sacred" and the relationship of women to God.

Plaskow, Judith: **It Is Not in Heaven: Feminism and Religious Authority**. Oakland, CA: **Tikkun**, March/April 1990, 39-40.

The feminist movement has had to fight for the right to its actions and convictions, and has had to confront authority all along the way.

Plaskow, Judith: **Standing Again at Sinai: Judaism from a Feminist Perspective**. Baltimore, MD: **Modern Judaism**, 13, October 1993, 317-320.

Plaskow, Judith: **Roundtable: A New Sexual Ethics for Judaism?** Oakland, CA: **Tikkun**, 8, Sept/Oct. 1993, 61-68,89.

Plaskow, Judith: **What's Wrong with Hierarchy?** Oakland, CA: **Tikkun**, 7, Jan/Feb 1992, 65-67.

Reimers, Paula: **Feminism, Judaism and God the Mother**. New York: **Conservative Judaism**, XLVI, Fall 1993, 24-29.

Reis, Pamela Tamarkin: **Take my Wife, Please: On the Utility of the Wife/Sister Motif**. New York: **Judaism**, 41, Fall 1992, 306-315.

Discussion of three passages in Genesis where wives are "passed" off as sisters in order to "save" their husbands or pacify strangers, or when Sarah and Rebekah act in "cruel and devious" ways.

Reisenberger, Azila Talit : **The Creation of Adam as Hermaphrodite-and its implications for Feminist Theology**. New York: **Judaism**, 42, Fall 1993, 447-452.

When studying how women are depicted in the Bible it is important to differentiate between historical texts and divine theology and to be aware of limitations of translations. Reisenberger then proceeds to study Adam and Eve as God's creations.

Resnick, David A.: **Response to the "Final Report of the Commission for the Study of the Ordination of Women as Rabbis"**. New York: **Conservative Judaism**, XLII, Winter 1989, 49-58.

Rook, James: **The Names of the Wives from Adam to Abraham in the Book of "Jubilees"**: Sheffield, UK: **Journal for the Study of the Pseudepigrapha**, 7, 1990, 105-117.

Rosenheim, Judith: **Fate and Freedom in the Scroll of Esther**. Baltimore, MD: **Prooftexts**, 12, May 1992, 125-149.

Re-examination of religiosity/vs seductiveness of Esther and other personages in Scroll.

Ross, Tamar: **Can the Demand for Change in the Status of Women be Halakhically Legitimated?** New York: **Judaism**, 42, Fall 1993, 478-491.

Author does not believe halakha can "accomodate itself to the spirit of the times," but nevertheless discusses "ideological issues of women's status vis-a-vis men in Jewish law."

Ross, Wendy & Blood, Jenny: **Evangelism: A Jewish Woman's Response: A Conversation Between Wendy Ross and Jenny Blood**. Liechenstein: **International Review of Mission**, 81, April 1992, 299-305.

Rothstein, Gideon: **The Roth Responsum on the Ordination of Women**. New York: **Tradition**, 24, Fall 1988, 104-115.

The Jewish Theolgoical Seminary decision to train women as rabbis and cantors and its conviction that the decision was made in accord with halakha, albeit a different conception of halakha than the Orthodox perspective. Rothstein also says there is "room within halakha for extending women's role in religion to its limits."

Rozenzweig, Michael L.: **A Helper Equal to Him**. New York: **Judaism**, 35, Summer 1986, 277-280.

How should we translate "k'negdo"—in the context of the "creation" of Eve - as equal and partner to Adam, or "against", facing or opposite?

Salkin, Jeffrey K.: **Dinah, the Torah's Forgotten Woman**. New York: **Judaism**, 35, Summer 1986, 284-289.

Interpretations of Dina, her silence and the painful story of Shechem's love for her.

Saltzman, Cynthia: **Jewish Women Coming of Age: The Adult Bat Mitzvah**. Oberlin, OH: **Jewish Folklore and Ethnology Review**, 12, 1990, 31+.

Sara, Elizabeth: **Judaism and Lesbianism: A Tale of Life on the Margins of the Text**. London: **Jewish Quarterly**, 40, Autumn 1993, 20-23.

The issues of Judaism and lesbianism are discussed by this Reform Jewish lesbian rabbi in an authoritative article that refers to sections of the Talmud and Maimonides.

Schnur, Susan: **Gaiac Healer, Goddess, Ecstatic Rock'n Roll Mama?: The Cult of Miriam**. New York: **Lilith**, 17, Spring 1992, 16-17.

Examination of the biblical Miriam in history and in her example to Jewish women today.

Schnur, Susan: **Reshaping Prayer: An Interview with Marcia Falk**. New York: **Lilith**, No.21, Fall 1988, 10-15.

Schnur, Susan: **Ritual Junkies United: Yo, Miriam**! New York: Lilith, 17, Spring 1992, 16.

Brings together much of the research on the biblical Miriam. Schnur cites important research as to her importance in the history of Jewish women.

Schorsch, Ismar: **Women in Dark Times**. New York: **Women's League Outlook**, Winter 1992, 13-14,30.

Schwartz, Martha: **On Becoming the Mother of a Ba'al Tshuva**. New York: **Hadassah**, March 1992, 36+.

Scolnic, Benjamin E.: **Validity of Feminist Biblical Interpretation**. New York: **Conservative Judaism**, 38, Spring 1986, 10-19.

Scolnic bids us find a usable past to reinterpret classical texts and images from a new Jewish perspective. Most commentary until this time (1986) is from a Christian point of view. He gives examples from the story of Jephtah and his daughter, and from the Sotah ritual.

Seidman, Naomi: **Burning the Book of Lamentations**. Oakland,CA: **Tikkun**, 8, July/August 1993, 59-62,91-92.

"The Mishnah treats all women as persons some of the time, and some women as persons all of the time." Exploration of womens' status in the Mishna; asks for restoration of women's personhood in Jewish law.

Sered, Susan Starr: **Food and Holiness: Cooking as a Sacred Act Among Middle-Eastern Jewish Women**. Washington, D.C.: **Anthropological Quarterly**, 61, April 1988, 129-139.

"Religiosity of Middle Eastern Jewish women in Jerusalem" to whom preparation of meals and its connection with interpersonal relationships becomes a sacred act.

Shizgal Cohen, Elaine: **Rabbi's Roles and Occupational Goals: Men and Women in the Contemporary American Rabbinate**. New York: **Conservative Judaism**, 42, 1990, 20-30.

Shulevitz, Marion: **Straining the Seam: The Impact of Death and Mourning on Converts, Intermarried Couples and Their Children**. New York: **Conservative Judaism**, 43, Summer 1991, 56-63.

Women saying Kaddish, women converting to Judaism as a result of marriage are some of the topics discussed in this article

Shulman, Sarah: **What is Our Love?: Homosexuality, Jewishness and Judaism**. London: **Jewish Quarterly**, 40, Autumn, 1993, 24-27.

"Jewish lesbians are coming out as Jews and interrogating their inheritance." Examines Jewish history, Talmud, and need for education and understanding.

Siegel, Sheila Jubelirer: **The Effect of Culture on how Women Experience Menstruation: Jewish Women and Mikvah**. Binghamton, NY: **Women and Health**, 10, Winter 1985-6, 63-74.

Simon, Rita J. & Nadell, Pamela: **Teachers, Preachers and Feminists in America: Women Rabbis**. West Lafayette, IN: **Shofar**, 10, Fall 1991, 2-10.

There are close to 200 women rabbis (Reform, Reconstructionist and Conservative at time of this article). It describes findings of study of women in rabbinate as to motivations, performances and experiences and compares them to women in Protestant ministries, and as opposed to men in the rabbinate or ministry.

Smith, Ann: **Teaching Feminist Criticism: Some Problems and Difficulties**. Johannesburg: **Jewish Affairs**, 48, Winter 1993, 63-69.

Sofer, Barbara: **Over the Wall: Women and Prayer**. New York: **Hadassah**, , Aug/Sept 1990, 22.

Spiegel, Fredelle Zaiman: **The Impact of Women's Participation on the Non-Orthodox Synagogue**. New York: **CCAR Journal**, 39, Fall, 1992, 37-46.

Spiegel makes the case that since women are part of the non-orthodox service, "the synagogue has lost some of its ability to serve as holy space." Spiegel explains the changes in synagogue rituals and innovations in Jewish education, as in Minyan Atzmi at a conservative synagogue. These changes must be examined so that the desired goals are reached, and not others that "diminish the synagogue and which are compatible with feminist goals."

Spiegel, Marcia Cohn: **Becoming a Crone: Ceremony at 60**. New York: **Lilith**, 21, Sept. 1988, 18-19.

Stahl, Abraham: **A Virtuous Woman: The Ideal Wife according to the Rabbis of the East**. Calgary, Canada: **Journal of Comparative Family Studies**. 16, Autumn 1985, 357-364.

Steinberg, Naomi: **Israelite Tricksters, Their Analogues and Cross-Cultural Study**. Atlanta, GA: **Semeia**, 42, 1988, 1-13.

"The role of the trickster in the Hebrew Bible is discussed in light of cross-cultural evidence, with special interest in women as tricksters in ancient Israel."

Tobin, Gary A.: **Intermarriage: From Alarms to Open Arms**. New York: **Hadassah**, December 1991, 22.

Trible, Phyllis: **Bringing Miriam out of the Shadows**. Washington, DC: **Bible Review**, 5, 1989, 14-25,34.

Umansky, Ellen M.: **Finding God: Women in the Jewish Tradition**. New Rochelle, N.Y.: **Cross Currents**, 41, Winter, 1991, 521-537.

Adapted from the introduction to **Four Centuries of Jewish Women's Spirituality,** this essay speaks to the "minimizing" of Jewish womens' spiritual lives. Author seeks to rectify this through examples of women through the centuries.

Van der Toorn, Karel: **Female Prostitution in Payment of Vows in Ancient Israel**. Atlanta, GA: **Journal of Biblical Literature**, 108, Summer 1989, 193-205.

It would seem that women in both ancient Israel and in the ancient Near East practiced prostitution in order to fulfill sacred duties. Biblical references show that they not only were participants in religious ceremonies, but showed their religiosity to a greater extent in their everyday life than did men.

Visotzky, Burton L.: **Midrash Eishet Hayil**. New York: **Conservative Judaism**, 38, Spring 1986, 21-25.

Discusses various Biblical verses which refer to women: deeds, blessings or other requests which, translated, empower women.

Waldman, Nahum: **The Designation of Marital Status in the Ketuba**. New York: **Conservative Judaism**, 1986, 80-82.

Walters, Stanley D.: **Hannah and Anna: The Greek and Hebrew texts of 1 Samuel I**. Atlanta, GA: **Journal of Biblical Literature**, 107/3, September 1988, 385-412.

Different translations give different emphasis: thereby lessening importance or sympathy for Anna/Hannah or Peninah and in the end different perspectives of this episode.

Weems, Renita J.: **The Hebrew Women are not Like the Egyptian Women: The Ideology of Race, Gender and Sexual Reproduction in Exodus**. Atlanta, GA: **Semeia**, 59, 1992, 25-34.

Wegner, Judith Romney: **Tragelaphos Revisited: The Anomaly of Woman in the Mishnah**. New York: **Judaism**, 37, 1988, 160-172.

Weiss-Katz, Miriam: **Lubavitch Husband (former hippie) Walks**. New York: **Lilith**, 16, Fall 1991, 16-19.

Weissler, Chava: **For Women and for Men Who are Like Women: The Construction of Gender in Yiddish Devotional Literature**. Chico, CA: **Journal of Feminist Studies in Religion**, 5, Fall 1989, 7-24.

Perceptions of gender among women and men who are not Jewishly learned shown in the techines written for them which reveal a truer picture of their actual lives.

Weissler, Chava: **Women as High Priest: Kabbalistic Prayer in Yiddish for Lighting Sabbath Candles**. Haifa: **Jewish History**, 5, Spring 1991, 9-26.

Womens' part in mystical currents is shown through a techine: a prayer for lighting of Sabbath candles.

Weissler, Chava: **The Religion of Traditional Ashkenazic Women: Some Methodological Issues**. Cambridge, MA: **Association of Jewish Studies Review**, 12, Spring 1987, 73-94.

Weissler, Chava: **Women in Paradise**. Oakland, CA: **Tikkun**, 2, April/May 1987, 43-46; 117-120.

Because "we want to recover the history of Jewish women as part of the history of Judaism, it is vital to consider issues of women's religious life within ....all religious life." By studying Askenazic Judaism and within that group, women from the 16th - 19th centuries through Yiddish literature written by and for women of this period we begin to get the complete story. (Title of article comes from Zohar which depicts a women's Paradise where they study Torah.)

Wells, D.A.: **Susanna and Nebuchadnezzar: The Susanna Fragment of the "Central Franconian Rhyming Bible"**. Belfast: **Modern Language Review**, 84, 1989, 77-82.

Winkler, Gershon: **They Called Her Rebbe**. Washington, D.C.: **Moment**, 18, December, 1993, 56-57,98-100.

> A Polish couple gave birth to a daughter, a female child prodigy, the famed Maid of Ludomir, who was taught Torah and Talmud and became so learned that she taught and started her own shul. (This book was banned by some of the mainstream Orthodox bookstores.)

Wolf, Sara Lee: **Jewish Women and Jewish Law**. New York: **Na'amat Woman**, Mar/April 1987, 10-11,27.

> Report of the December 1986 First Jerusalem Conference on Women and Judaism: Halacha and the Jewish Woman.

> While many aspects of Jewish law were discussed, religious practices of divorce were the most controversial and urgent. Lobbying rabbis to respond to women's needs was forcefully urged, especially a change in Israeli custom and law, giving a choice for civil or religious marriage rites, where now only the latter is possible. (See also summary of this conference in Biblio Press, "Jewish Women and Jewish Law" Bibliography, Supplement of 1986.)

Wolowelsky, Joel B.: **Communal Prayer and Women: Further on Woman as Prayer Leaders and Their Role in Communal Prayer: an Exchange**. New York: **Judaism**, 42, Fall 1993, 394-395.

> Women are participating in many more religious rituals such as the "seven blessings recited after each meal in honor or a new bride and groom."

Women and Jewish Lifecycles: Process and Progress. Los Angeles: **Bulletin, the Newsletter of the Susan and David Institute of Jewish Policy Studies,** Spring 1993.

Wouk, Jordan: **Is God a Woman**. New York: **Lilith**, 19, 1988, 3.

Zivotofsky, Ari Z. & Zivotofsky, Naomi T.S.: **What's Right with Women and Zimmun**. New York: **Judaism**, 42, Fall 1993, 453-464.

> Discussion of Zimmun:"the introductory invitation preceding grace after meals" and women's participation in it.

V
United States

A. Books

Ashton, Dianne: **Souls Have No Sex: Philadelphia Jewish Women and the American Challenge. in: When Philadelphia Was the Capital of Jewish America.** Cranbury, NJ: Associated University Presses, 1993.

Axsom, Richard H.: **Beyond the Plane: The Relief Paintings of Judith Rothchild.** New York: Hudson Hills Press, 1992.

Survey of an important modern artist and her work.

Baker, Adrienne: **The Jewish Woman in Contemporary Society.** see Author Index.

Balka, Christie, & Rose, Andy, eds.: **Twice Blessed: On Being Lesbian, Gay and Jewish.** Boston: Beacon Press, 1989.

Each person in this book tells of experiences of "invisibility," of struggling to be Jewish and gay in many different ways throughout their personal lives and in their liturgy in order to affirm their varied identities.

Bayme, Steven: **Introduction** in: **Cohen, Steven M., Alternative Families in the Jewish Community: Singles, Single Parents, Childless Couples, and Mixed-Marrieds.** New York: American Jewish Committee, 1989.

Beck, Evelyn T. ed.: **Nice Jewish Girls: A Lesbian Anthology.** Boston: Beacon Press, 1989.(rept.)

Revised and updated version of original (1982) anthology of poetry and essays. Continues discussions of the intersection between antisemitism, political and feminist issues,"searching for possiblities for the survival of the Jewish people in celebrating our bonds as well as our differences."

Blum, Julie: **Domestic Violence in the North American Jewish Community: Issues and Communal Programs.** New York: Council of Jewish Federations, Dept. of Planning and Resource Development, 1992.

Bletter, Diane & Grinker, Lori: **The Invisible Thread: A Portrait of Jewish American Women.** Philadelphia: Jewish Publication Society, 1989.

Brief interviews by Bletter and photos by Grinker show a variety of Jewish-American women and links to their Jewish heritage and contemporary Jewish identity.

Booker, Janice L.: **The Jewish American Princess and other Myths: The Many Forms of Self-Hatred**. New York: Shapolsky, 1991.

Braunstein,, Susan L. & Joselit, Jenna Weissman, eds.: **Getting Comfortable in New York: The American Jewish Home, 1880-1950**. New York: The Jewish Museum, 1990.

Wonderful catalogue with good information on the Jewish home, social life and Jewish domestic culture.

Brewer, Joan S., Davidman,L., & Avery E.: **Sex and the Modern Jewish Woman: A Bibliography.** New York: Biblio Press, 1986.

Davidman & Avery write essays on two essential topics; Brewer supplies many mental health and psychology citations.

Broner, E. M.: **The Telling** (Egalitarian seders in New York) see Author Index.

Brown, Cherie, R: **Face to Face: Black-Jewish Campus Dialogues**. New York: American Jewish Committee pamphlet, 1987.

Jewish women are the ones who address the problem when Black men do not admit responsibility for their statements.

Bulkin, Elly Pratt, Minnie Bruce and Smith,Barbara: **Yours in Struggle: Three Feminist Perspectives on Anti-Semitism and Racism**. Ithaca, N.Y.: Firebrand Books, 1988.

Carnay, Janet; Paster, Laura Wine; Spiegel, Marcia Cohn et al.: **The Jewish Woman's Awareness Guide: Connections for the 2nd Wave of Jewish Feminism**. New York: Biblio Press, 1992.

"A Jewish consciousness-raising guide for group and program use."

Casey, Kathleen: **A Pragmatic Discourse of Secular Jewish Women Teachers Working for Social Change in: I Answer With My Life**. New York: Routledge, 1993 ,Chap. 4, 69-105.

Jewish women educators "in their daily lives act against racism and patriarchal systems and remind us of the possibility of difference."

Chernin, Kim: **Reinventing Eve: Modern Woman in Search of Herself.** New York: Times Books, 1987.

Author seeks to change our notions about Eve and our guilt about the apple, (thus about all food) into the idea of Eve as heroine and purveyor of knowledge.

Coss, Clare: **Lillian Wald, Progressive Activist: Lillian Wald at Home on Henry St.** New York: Feminist Press, 1989.

Daniels, Doris Groshen: **Always a Sister: The Feminism of Lillian D. Wald**. New York: Feminist Press, 1989.

> A "topical biography" showing the diversity of interests of Wald's work in several fields.

Dengelegi, Lidia & Kidder, Louise H.: **Lubavitch Women: Depression and Life Satisfaction in a Traditional Community* ED207140** Arlington, VA: Annual Meeting of Eastern Psychological Association/ERIC*, 1987.

Diament, Carol: **Jewish Marital Status: A Hadassah Study**. see Author Index.

Diner, Hasia: **A Time for Gathering: The Second Migration: 1820-1880**. Baltimore, MD: Johns Hopkins Press, 1992.

> A thoroughly researched work on Jewish immigration to the United States between 1820 and 1880. Presents a more complete picture of the women than similar histories by male authors.

Eckardt, A. Roy: **Black-Woman-Jew: Three Wars for Human Liberation**. Bloomington: Indiana University Press, 1989.

> Comparison of Black and Jewish women who both endure racism and sexism. See especially Chapter 13: "Again, double jeopardy: sexism and antisemitism."

Elwell, Sue Levi, compiler: **Jewish Women's Studies Guide**. New York and Lanham, MD: Biblio Press and University Press of America, 1987.

> Eighteen syllabi collected by Sue Levi Elwell (includes E.T. Beck and others) on Jewish women studies in actual use and the importance of this field in the university curriculum.

Encyclopedia Judaica Yearbook. Jerusalem: Encyclopedia Judaica, 1986-7, 12-52.

> Feature article on Jewish women, also, Biale on women and Jewish law; Education of Jewish women by Weissmana; Status of women in Israel by Dafna Izraeli; women in Armed Forces, in the Economy and in Politics.

The Ethnic American Woman: Problems, Protests, Lifestyle. Dubuque, IA: Kendall/Hunt, 1989.

> See especially, pp. 411, 446, 450, 453, 456, 469 and 476.

Feingold, Henry L.: **Time for Searching: Entering the Mainstream, 1920-1945**. Baltimore, MD: The Johns Hopkins University Press, 1992.

In this, the 4th volume of "The Jewish People in America" series (1920-1945) information on the Depression and World War II. Women are mentioned in relation to work and the labor movement (pp. 43-47), their organizations and activism, and some women writers; but not extensive.

Fischel, Jack & Pinsker, Sanford: **Jewish-American History and Culture**. New York: Garland, 1992.

Reference book includes biographical sketches of not only the most important Jewish-American women but several from the early feminist labor movement.

Fishman, Sylvia Barack: **A Breath of Life**: **Feminism in the American Jewish Community**. New York: Free Press, 1993.

"Challenges facing contemporary American Jewish women—balancing Jewish and feminist goals." An overview of the effects of feminism on Jewish life in the United States.

Fishman, Sylvia Barack: **The Impact of Feminism on American Jewish Life**: **in:American Jewish Yearbook 1989**. Philadelphia, PA: American Jewish Committee and JPS, 1989, 23-62.

Important essay on effects of feminism on Jewish women, Jewish feminism and changes occurring in synagogue life, social and demographic effects, and educational changes (with some statistics); changes in work habits, in communal life and organizational behavior.

Friedman, Reena Sigman: **The Jewish Feminist Movement, in: Michael N. Dobkowski, ed.: Jewish Voluntary Organizations**. Westport, CT: Greenwood Press, 1986, 595.

Frondorf, Shirley: **Death of a "Jewish American Princess"**: **The True Story of a Victim on Trial**. New York: Villard Books, 1988.

Geffen-Monson, Rela: **Jewish Women on The Way Up**: **The Challenge of Family, Career and Community**. 165 E. 56th St.New York: American Jewish Committee: Institute of Human Relations, 1987.

In-depth survey of attributes of Jewish women professionals, executives, and their family lives, careers, community life and intermarriage.

Girvan, Lois Brier: **Little Known Women: The Lives of 20 Extraordinary Achievers**. Santa Barbara, CA: Ideas Unlimited, 1987, 198-205.

Has chapter on the contemporary Jewish-American composer Diane Thome.

Glenn, Susan A.: **Daughters of the Shtetl: Life and Labor in the Immigrant Generation**. Ithaca, N.Y.: Cornell University Press, 1990.

Implications of immigration and ethnicity on Eastern European Jewish women working in the garment industry, caring for families and becoming involved in unions, later political activism. See notes for older items and unpublished theses.

Gold, Michael: **And Hannah Wept: Infertility, Adoption and the Jewish Couple**. Philadelphia, PA: JPS, 1988.

Goldman, Herbert G.: **Fanny Brice: The Original Funny Girl**. New York: Oxford University Press, 1992.

A biography of the showgirl Fanny Brice, and the woman herself, "talented in many ways; wise and romantic" who became even more of a legend when Barbara Streisand portrayed her in a film.

Gornick, Vivian: **Fierce Attachments: A Memoir**. New York: Farrar Straus & Giroux, 1987.

Gornick writes of growing up in New York, her volatile relationship with her mother and a neighbor, the price of education and its effect on mother-daughter relationships.

Grossman, Barbara W.: **Funny Woman: Life & Times of Fanny Brice**. Bloomington, IN: Indiana University Press, 1991.

Study based on research as well as other written sources which reveals varied facets of Brice's career as a comedienne.

Hardy, Jan, Editor: **Sister/Stranger: Lesbians Loving Across the Lines**. Pittsburgh, PA: Sidewalk Revolution Press, 1993.

Volume includes literary contributions from women of differing backgrounds.

Hefter, Wendy C.: **Complete Jewish Wedding Planner**. Baltimore, MD: PSP Press, 1993.

Heinze, Andrew: **Adapting to Abundance: Jewish Immigrants, Mass Consumption and the Search for American Identity**. New York: New York University Press, 1990.

See index references in book to women and the *"Baleboste"* which describe Jewish women's dress, consumer habits, leisure, etc.

Henry, Sondra & Taitz, Emily: **Betty Friedan: Fighter for Women's Rights**. Hillside, NJ: Enslow Publishers, 1990.

Henry, Sondra & Taitz, Emily: **Written out of History: Our Jewish Foremothers**. New York: Biblio Press, 1990 (2nd edition).

Revised edition of this popular book of 1978 giving biographical information of obscure and well-known women. These additions include women of the 20th century, labor leaders, early feminists, women scholars and the first women rabbis.

Jones, Hettie: **How I became Hettie Jones**. New York: J.P.Dutton, 1990.

Biography of Hettie Cohen, a New York Jewish girl who married LeRoi Jones, Black writer/activist; then divorced, went back to writing and activism on her own.(Reviewed in Lilith Magazine)

Joselit, Jenna: **The Sacred Life of American Orthodox Women**, **in: Joselit, Jenna Weissman:New York's Jewish Jews: The Orthodox Community in the Interwar Years**. Bloomington, IN: Indiana University Press, 1990, Chapter 4:97-122.

A historical overview of the American Orthodox woman, her education and participation historically in the Jewish community, including the synagogue, and today.

Joselit, Jenna: **The Special Sphere of the Middle-Class American Jewish Woman, the Synagogue Sisterhood, 1890-1940: in:Jack Wertheimer, ed., The American Synagogue, A Sanctuary Transformed**. New York: Cambridge University Press, 1987, Chapter 4:206-230.

Kaminetsky, Ellen: **Hawking God: A Young Jewish Woman's Ordeal in Jews for Jesus**. Malden, MA: Sapphire Press, 1992.

Kaye/Kantrowitz. Melanie: **The Issue is Power:Essays on Women, Jews, Violence and Resistance**. San Francisco, CA: Aunt Lute Books, 1992.

Writing of antisemitism, sexism, racism, homophobia and resistance in the context of Jewish women.

Klepfisz, Irena: **Dreams of an Insomniac: Jewish Feminist Essays, Speeches and Diatribes**. Portland, OR: Eighth Mountain Press, 1990.

Explored is Klepfisz's identity as a Jew, a woman and a lesbian. Includes incisive introduction by Evelyn Beck, a powerful essay on Irena's return visit to Poland after WWII, Yiddishkeit, as well as her views on issues cited.

Keeney, Bradford & Silverstein, Olga: **The Therapeutic Voice of Olga Silverstein**: New York: Guilford Press, 1986.

Family therapy by a famed practitioner in a Jewish (unstated) environment.

Kuzmack, Linda Gordon: **Woman's Cause**: **The Jewish Woman's Movement in England and the United States, 1881-1933**. Columbus, OH: Ohio State University Press, 1990.

Focuses on women whose feminist activities directly affected the Jewish community and the mainstream in both countries.

Levitan, Tina: **Tina Levitan Bibliography**: **Books, Articles, Short Stories and other works published**. 372 Central Park West, 9H, New York: Charuth, 1990.

Lisle, Laurie: **Louise Nevelson**: **A Passionate Life**. New York: Summit Books, 1990.

A good biography of this famous artist who came from Russia to Rockland, Maine, and experienced antisemitism and also later acceptance from synagogue and other groups who commissioned her constructions and sculpture.

Marcus, Jacob Rader: **History of Jews in America**. Detroit, MI: Wayne State University Press, 1989.

Although Marcus' intention was to place women into American-Jewish history, and their different roles; to find them one must either skim the book or the index. Some interesting photos. Judge for yourself.

Markowitz, Ruth Jacknow: **My Daughter, The Teacher: Jewish Teachers in New York City Schools.** New Brunswick, NJ: Rutgers University Press, 1993.

Myerhoff, Barbara G.: **Life Not Death in Venice**: **Its Second Life. In: Goldberg, Harvey E. ed.: Judaism Viewed from Within and From Without: Anthropological Studies.** Albany, NY: State University of New York Press, 1986, 143-70.

Nadell, Pamela: **A Land of Opportunities**: **Jewish Women Encounter America. in: What is American about American Jewish History, ed. Marc Lee Raphael**. Williamsburg, VA: College of William and Mary, 1993.

Nobel Prize Women in Science. New York: Carol Publishing Co., 1993, 333-355.

Contains biography of Rosalyn Yalow, Jewish Nobel winner in Science, 1974.

Ornish, Natalie: **Pioneer Jewish Texans: Their Impact on Texas and American History for 400 years: 1590-1990**. Dallas,TX: Heritage Press, 1989.

History of "Jewish" Texas which represents women as well as men and includes a chapter, "The Changing Role of Women."

Piotrkowski, Chaya et al: **The Experience of Childbearing Women in the Workplace: The Impact of Family Friendly Policies and Practices. ERIC Report # 364603** New York: National Council of Jewish Women/ERIC, 1989.

Plaskow, Judith: **Feminist Judaism and Repair of the World, in: Ecofeminism and the Sacred: Adams, Carol J., ed**. New York: Continuum, 1993, 70-83.

Author links spirituality and concern for the natural world. She shows that *tikkun olam,* "repair of the world" always a tenet of Judaism, has particular relevance to ecological issues.

Polacheck, Hilda Satt Epstein, & Dena J. Polacheck, eds.: **I Came a Stranger: The Story of a Hull House Girl**. Urbana, IL: University of Illinois Press, 1989.

Prell, Riv-Ellen: **The Double Frame of Life History in the Work of Barbara Myerhoff, in: Personal Narratives Group, Editors Interpreting Women's Lives:Feminist Theory and Personal Narratives.** Bloomington, IN: Indiana University Press, 1989, 241-258.

"Personal narratives redefine the history of human experience" both of the interviewer and interviewee - an example being elderly Jewish-American men and women by the anthropologist Barbara Myerhoff.

Ravitz, Abe C.: **Leane Zugsmith: Thunder on the Left**. New York: International Press, 1992.

Biography of Zugsmith, An American Jewish fiction writer, but also "a vivacious conversationalist," a socially, politically and culturally savvy woman.

Rogow, Faith: **Gone to Another Meeting: The National Council of Jewish Women, 1893-1993**. Tuscaloosa, AL: University of Alabama Press, 1993.

History of first of major organizations founded after the Jewish Women's Congress at Chicago World Fair in 1893.

Rosen, Norma.: **Accidents of Influence**: **Writing as a Woman and a Jew in America**. Albany, NY: State University of New York Press, 1992.

> Personal reflections on writing as a Jewish woman in the U.S., a society in which she feels doubly alienated. She also speaks to the role of a Holocaust writer.(see article in Modern Judaism by Joan Moelis; vol. 14, p. 203)

Rubin, Stephen J.,ed. **Writing Our Lives**: **Autobiographies of American Jews, 1890-1990**. Philadelphia, PA: JPS, 1991.

> Through the writings of certain important Jewish-American women among other American Jews we learn much about their lives and those of their contemporaries.

Ruddick, Sarah: **Maternal Thinking**, see Author index on Israel section.

Sachar, Howard M.: **History of the Jews in America**. New York: Knopf, 1992.

> This work surveys some Jewish women, i.e.Friedan, etc. pp.834-838, but only the most well known who can be found in most biographical dictionaries. Does not adequately list Jewish women who contributed to American Jewish life. See Diner for fuller coverage; also, Fishman, Pogrebin etc.

Scarf, Mimi: **Battered Jewish Wives**: **Case Studies in the Response to Rape. Women's Studies: vol.2** Lewiston, N.Y.: Edwin Mellen Press, 1988.

> A book about battered Jewish women, it is also about marriage, Jewish guilt and of "its dark secrets", courage and endurance.

Schwalb, Susan J. & Sedlacek, William C.: **Student Attitudes Toward "JAPS"**: **The New Anti Semitism. ERIC Research Report: ED311332** College Park, MD: University of Maryland Research Report/ERIC, 1987.

Shapiro, Edward S.: **Time for Healing: American Jewry since World War II**. Baltimore, MD: Johns Hopkins University Press, 1992.

> Some discussion of role of Jewish women in U.S.

Shapiro, Sarah, ed.: **More of Our Lives**: **An Anthology of Jewish Women's Writings**. New York: Feldheim, 1993.

> A collection of short pieces, most autobiographical; a few of fiction; by contemporary observant Jewish women.

Showalter, Elaine: **The Rise of Gender,** in: **Speaking of Gender**. New York: Routledge, Chapman & Hall, 1989, 1-13.

Shuster, Claudia Kramer, ed. et al: **The Hard Questions in Family Day Care: National Issues and Exemplary Programs. ED336168** : New York, National Council of Jewish Women/ERIC, 1989.

Sidransky, Ruth: **In Silence: Growing Up Hearing In a Deaf World**. New York: St.Martins Press, 1990.

> Growing up in a deaf family, Sidransky found that Jewish people were as prejudiced and ignorant as others so that her family was, in fact "excluded from conventional Judaism."

Siegel, Rachel Josefowitz & Cole, Ellen, eds.: **Jewish Women in Therapy: Seen But Not Heard**. New York: Harrington Park Press, 1991.

> Collection of essays by scholars and therapists (including Evelyn Torton Beck and Susannah Heschel)on the "significance of their Jewishness" in Jewish women's counseling/psychotherapy; especially on issues of abuse, survivors of the Holocaust, "Jewish American princess", sexuality, midlife crises, etc. Also in Vol. 10, Number 4, 1990 issue of "Women and Therapy."

Simon, Kate: **A Wider World: Portraits in an Adolescence**. New York: Harper & Row, Publishers, 1986.

Simons, Howard: **Jewish Times: Voices of the American Jewish Experience**. Boston: Houghton Mifflin, 1988.

> Simons collects stories of American-Jewish families starting with early immigrants, often of mothers and grandmothers. These vivid personal stories convey a more complete picture than most histories which are often men's histories.

Single and Jewish: Communal and Personal Perspectives, Papers and Comments. New York: American Jewish Committee, Institute of Human Relations, 1989.

Suhl, Yuri: **Ernestine L. Rose: Women's Rights Pioneer.** New York: Biblio Press, 1990 (rept.)

> Updated edition of the 1959 biography of this important Jewish woman social reformer/suffragist of the 19th century.

Taylor, Jacqueline: **Grace Paley: Illuminating the Dark Lives**. Austin, TX: University of Texas Press, 1990.

> Kindershule and Jewish identity; growing up in a secular, labor-class home, feeling totally identified as a Jew and as a feminist. This is a biography of Paley, a writer of obvious skill.

Toll, William: **Women, Men and Ethnicity: Essays on the Structure and Thought of American Jewry.** Lanham MD: University Press of America, 1991.

    Collection of essays treating issues concerning Jewish women moving from domestic roles to participation in the public sphere.

Weinberg, Sidney Stahl: **The World of Our Mothers: The Lives of Jewish Immigrant Women.** Chapel Hill, NC: University of North Carolina Press, 1988.

    An oral history of the day-to-day lives of 45 Jewish immigrant women who came to the U.S. from 1896 to 1925. Education was the door-opener for many. We gain glimpses of their personal lives and challenges and can compare them to Jewish men of the same epoch about whom much more has been written.

Weisberg, Ruth: **A Circle of Life: Exhibit Catalog.** San Diego, CA: Fisher Gallery, University of Southern California, 1986.

    Catalog of the exhibit of this painter and printmaker. Her work combines autobiography and features Holocaust and other Jewish motifs; she is in fact considered a "Post-Holocaust artist."

Winegarten, Ruthe & Schechter, Cathy et al: **Deep in the Heart: The Lives and Legends of Texas Jews, A Photographic History.** Austin, TX: Eakin Press, 1990.

    Includes Jewish women.

Yezierska, Anzia: **Red Ribbon on a White Horse:** New York: Persea Books, 1987.

    Not only a vivid autobiographical account, but reveals the period in which Yezierska lived and struggled to be herself.

Zipser, Arthur & Zipser, Pearl: **Fire and Grace: The Life of Rose Pastor Stokes.** Athens, GA: University of Georgia Press, 1990.

    Rose Pastor Stokes was active between 1905 and 1925 as a feminist Socialist, speaker, political propagandist and labor/social activist. She was "a controversial woman in thought, lifestyle and politics."

B. Articles

Abzug, Bella, Letty Cottin Pogrebin and E.M. Broner: **The Playpen of the Patriarchs: Why We Needed a Conference on the Empowerment of Jewish Women.** New York: **Lilith**, 14, Spring 1989, 33-35.

United States

Adahan, Miriam: **The Pain of the Single or Childless Woman**. New York: **Jewish Observer**, XXV, Jan 1993, 17-27.

Agron, Laurence: **A Landmark Gathering**. (on Jewish Feminism) see Author Index or Other Countries section.

Albrecht, Nancy R.: **Women in Science: Differing Attitudes of Israeli and American Women**. New York: **Women's League Outlook**, 63, Summer 1993, 20-21.

Alperin, Mimi: **JAP Jokes: Hateful Humor**. West Lafayette, IN: **Humor: International Journal of Humor Research**, 2, 1989, 412-416.

Apparently also an AJC pamphlet of 1988.

Ankori, Gannit: **Yocheved Weinfeld's Portraits of the Self**: . Knoxville, TN: **Woman's Art Journal**, 10, Spring/Summer 1989, 22-27.

Aptheker, Bettina: **Teaching About Anti-Semitism and the Legacy of Jewish Women** Old Westbury, NY: **Women's Studies Quarterly**, 21, Fall 1993, 63-68+.

Arditti, Rita & Spiegelman, Donna: **Cancer Risks for Jewish Women**. Eugene, OR: **Bridges**, 2, Fall 1991, 85-88.

Arond, Miriam: **At The Center of the Storm: Jewish Women in Politics talk about the Issues**. New York: **Lilith**, 14, Fall 1989, 8-13.

Ascher, Carol; Bridenthal, Renate; Kaplan, Marion, & Grossmann, Atina: **Fragments of a German-Jewish Heritage in Four "Americans"**. Cincinnati, OH: **American Jewish Archives**, 40, 1988, 365-385.

Axelrod, Ira: **When the Problem Is Our Own**. Brooklyn, NY: **Jewish Homemaker**, 25, Dec.1993, 6-7.

Balka, Christie: **Thoughts on Lesbian Parenting and the Challenge to Jewish Communities**. Eugene, OR: **Bridges**, 3, Spring, 1993, 57-65.

Barsky, June: **Anne Pollard and Ethel Rosenberg: The Wives take the Heat**. New York: **Lilith**, 15, Winter 1990, 28-29.

Beck, Evelyn Torton: **The Politics of Jewish Invisibility**. Norwood, NJ: **NWSA Journal**, 1, Autumn 1988, 93-102.

Promoting the integration of Jewish women's history and culture into the broader feminist picture, Beck hopes they will help assure the inclusion of this area in Women's Studies classes and research with broader, more multicultural perspectives. She discusses why many Jewish women writers do not write about Jewish issues and the presence of anti-semitism in some feminist circles.

Beck, Evelyn: **From "KIKE" to "JAP"**. Cambridge, MA: **Sojourner**, 13, 1988, 18-23.

> The issue of the "Jewish-American Princess" is often marginalized; but it is truly either anti-semitism or self-hatred and needs to be considered seriously so that the stereotypes and the behavior this "label" implies can be confronted.

Bell, Roselyn: **Wide-Awake Dreamers**. New York: **Hadassah**, 70, Feb.1989, 24-27.

Bendet, Billa Tessler: **How to Prevent It**. Brooklyn, NY: **Jewish Homemaker**, 25, Dec. 1993, 8-11.

Benjamin, Jessica: **Feminist Perspectives Session: Victimology**. Oakland, CA: **Tikkun**, 4, Mar/Apr 1989, 75-77.

> Guilt, and suffering; its use and misuse.

Benson, Evelyn R.: **Jewish Women and Nursing: An Overview of Early Nursing**. Albany, NY: **Journal of the New York State Nurses Association**, Dec. 1992, 16-19.

> Contribution of Jewish women to the development of nursing starting with the midwives Shiphrah and Puah to "modern times." Examples were Rachel Varnhagen Penina Moise and Lillian Wald.

Benson, Evelyn R.: **Josephine Goldmark (1877-1950): A Biographical Sketch**. Boston, MA: **Public Health Nursing**, 4, 1987, 48-51.

> Goldmark, an early 20th century woman, was both devoted to "humanitarian causes and social reform" while pursuing a successful career in nursing.

Benson, Evelyn R. **Mathilda Scheuer (1890-1974): A Biographical Sketch**. Boston, Ma: **Journal of Nursing History**, 2, Nov. 1986, 36-42.

> Scheuer, a leader in public health nursing, dedicated her life to leadership roles in professional nursing organizations.

Benson, Evelyn R.: **Public Health Nursing and the Jewish Contribution**. Boston: **Public Health Nursing**, 10, March 1, 1993, 55-57.

Berkowitz, Gila: **And the Sages Say**. New York: **Lilith**, 15, Spring 1990, 24-25.

> Traditional views about childbearing.

Biale, Rachel: **Abortion: Abortion in Jewish Law**.see Author index or Religion section.

Biren, Joan E.: **Chosen Images: A Decade of Jewish Feminism**. Eugene, Or: **Bridges**, 1, Spring, 1990, 57-67.

Bograd, Michele: **Counter Transference: The Ways a Psychotherapist Discovers She's a Jew**. New York: **Lilith**, 14, Winter 1989, 24-25.

"A female psychotherapist faces her own Jewish identity as she treats Jewish patients."

Brown, Betty Ann & Raven, Arlene: **Turning Life into Art: Nancy Grossman, Kathy Jacobi and Ruth Weisberg**. New York: **Lilith**, 16, Spring 1991, 18-20.

Brown, Cheryl Anne & Rinn, Miriam: **The Secret Behind Closed Doors: Domestic Violence in Jewish Homes**. New York: **The Reporter: Women's American ORT**, Winter 1993, 20-23.

Well written article on wife abuse by Jewish husbands in USA, with focus on N.Y.,N.J.,Conn., metro. area services available; shelters cited, organizations and reports available on Jewish domestic violence.

Brown, Michael: **The American Element in the Rise of Golda Meir.** see Author index.

Brumberg, Stephen F.: **Jewish Higher Education and Efforts to Perpetuate Jewish Community in America**. New York: **History of Education Quarterly**, 29, 1989, 293-300.

Buelens, Gert: **State of the Art: The Jewish Immigrant Experience**. Cambridge, UK: **Journal of American Studies**, 25, 1991, 473-79.

Burch, C. Beth: **Mary Antin's "The Promised Land" and the Unspoken Failure of Assimilation**. see Author index.

Cantarow, Ellen: **Zionism, Anti-Semitism and Jewish Identity in the Women's Movement**. New York: **Middle East Report**, 18, Sept/Oct.1988, 38-43.

At various women's conferences the issue of anti-semitism has been manifested along with the issue of Zionism and racism. This has been extremely difficult for Jewish feminists to confront.

Cantor, Aviva: **Therapy and Jewish Women**. New York: **Na'amat Woman**, VIII, Jan/Feb 1993, 10-12,28.

Report on Seattle conference, Fall, 1992, of Assn. for Women in Psychology on "Judaism, Feminism and Psychology." Jewish women who seek therapy frequently get no understanding of their Jewish identity in their treatment. Reasons for omissions and misperceptions of Jewishness as important are cited, with indications for further sessions on this topic marked for AWP attention.

Cantor, Carla: **Coming Out in the Jewish Family**. New York: **Lilith**, 14, Summer 1989, 23-25.

Cantor, Debra: **One Question is Many Questions**. Port Washington, NY: **Sh'ma**, 21, Dec. 28, 1990, 26-27.

Capra, Joan: **The Italian Jewish Connection: The History of America**. Lincoln, Neb: **Sinister Wisdom**, 41, Summer/Fall 1990, 101-104.

A woman of both Jewish and Italian communities in New York City explains both those identities to the American lesbian community.

Chayat, Sherry: **JAP-Baiting on the College Scene**. New York: **Lilith**, No. 17, Fall 1987, 6-7.

Overview of issue of the "Jewish-American princess" ("JAP").

Chernin, Kim: **Feminist Consciousness Today: In the House of the Flame Bearers**. Oakland, CA: **Tikkun**, 2, July/August 1987, 55-59.

Chernin writes about her mother and grandmother, adapting or not, to American life and keeping one's Jewish traditions.

Chicago, Judy: **Women and Tikkun: The Tikkun Conference (II)**. Oakland, CA: **Tikkun**, 4, May/June 1989, 80-83.

Chiswick, Barry R.: **Labor Supply and Investment in Child Quality: A Study of Jewish and Non-Jewish Women**. New Brunswick, NJ: **Contemporary Jewry**, 9, 1988, 35-61.

Study of labor patterns of Jewish women with children of various ages that emphasizes use of their time for parenting.

Chiswick, Barry: **Labor Supply and Investment in Child Quality: A Study of Jewish and Non-Jewish Women: A Reply**. Cambridge, MA: **Review of Economics and Statistics**, LXXIV, Nov. 1992, 726-727.

Reply to article in this journal (Nov.1986:700-703) and, in Contemporary Jewry,

Chiswick, Barry: **Working and Family Life: The Experiences of Jewish Women in America**. Chicago, IL: **University of Illinois at Chicago, Department of Economics**, 1993, 1-20.

Study of Jewish-American women as part of the work force, as members of families; implications for raising children; includes statistics.

Ciolkowski, Laura E.: **A Question of Identity: Jewish Feminist Politics in the 1990s**. Los Angeles, CA: **Response**, 61-2, Fall 1993, 42-45.

Clar, Reva & Kramer, William M.: **The Girl Rabbi of the Golden West, Part I**. Santa Monica, CA: **Western States Jewish History**, 18, 1986, 99-111.

Cohn, Josephine: **Communal Life of San Francisco Jewish Women in 1908**. Santa Monica, CA: **Western States Jewish History**, 20, 1987, 15-36.

Conrad, Gertrude Hurwitz & Janet Cohen: **Child Abuse**. New York: **Hadassah**, 69, 1988, 26.

Cooper, Aaron: **No Longer Invisible: Gay and Lesbian Jews Build a Movement**. New York: **Journal of Homosexuality**, 18, 1989/90, 83-94.

The organized movement of gay and lesbian Jews has grown and is dealing with issues such as outreach, prejudice, rabbis, and kaddish prayers.

Davidoff, Donna J.: **American Jewish Women: Two Biobibliographies**. New York: **Judaica Librarianship**, 6, Spring 1991/Winter 1992, 137-139.

Biographical information in chronological form as well as books about Rebecca Gratz and Henrietta Szold.

Davies, Christie: **An Explanation of Jewish Jokes About Jewish Women**. Berlin, Germany: **Humor**, 3, 1990, 363-378.

Davis, Karen: **The Ascent of Sisterhood: The First Eight Decades**. New York: **Reform Judaism**, 21, Fall 1992, 37-39,43.

deBeer, Elizabeth R.: **Wife Abuse, Drugs and Silence**. New York: **Lilith**, No.20, Summer 1988, 6-7.

Drucker, Sally Ann: **It Doesn't Say So in Mother's Prayerbook: Autobiographies in English by Immigrant Jewish Women**. Waltham, MA: **American Jewish History**, 79, Autumn 1989, 55-71.

Four writers, Mary Antin, Anzia Yezierska, Elizabeth Stern and Rose Cohen's autobiographies reveal much about Eastern European immigrant life and the process of Americanization. A key article.

Dubofsky, Melvyn: **Some of our Mothers and Grandmothers: The Making of the 'New' Jewish Woman**. Baltimore, MD: **Reviews in American History**, 19, 1991, 385-390.

In-depth review of Glenn's "Daughters of the Shtetl".

Dubowsky, Hadar: **White Jewish Female: What Happens When I Fit Into More Than One Category?** New York: **Lilith**, 18, Summer 1993, 18-19.

How Judaism fits/or is ignored with regard to multicultural issues.

Dubrovsky, Gertrude: **Down on the Farm: The Coming of Age of a Chicken Farmer**: New York: **Lilith**, 14, Spring, 1989, 27-29.

>Realities of family life for a Jewish girl whose mother decided to farm since the 1920's.

Elkin, Michael: **Shticking Together: Jewish Comediennes Blend Humor with Heritage**. New York: **Women's American ORT Reporter**, Summer 1993, 8-11.

>Profiles of the Jewish "side" of comediennes Roseanne, Joan Rivers, Rita Rudner, Dinah Manoff, Estelle Getty, Totie Fields (dec.). Focus is on how their Jewish identity and experiences influence their humor style and content.

Elliman, Wendy: **Cushioning the Blows**. New York: **Hadassah**, 75, Oct. 1993, 30-1.

Felman, Jyl Lynn: **For Love and For Life, We're Not Going Back**. Oakland, CA: **Tikkun**, 3, Jan/Feb 1988, 64-5.

>Brief report on 1987 National March on Washington for Lesbian and Gay Rights; how all sectors of Jewish community celebrated Shabbat together and then mourned together.

Felman, Jyl Lynn: **Gay Jewish and Whole**. New York: **Jewish Currents**, Jan 1993, 5+.

Fishman, Sylvia Barack & Rattok, Lily: **Remaking Jewish Worlds: Israeli and American Jewish Women**, see Author index.

Foster, Barbara & Foster, Michael: **Adah Isaacs Menken: An American Original**. London: **Jewish Quarterly**, 40, Winter 1993-4, 54-59.

>Poet, superstar and love goddess, Menken is compared to, among others, Marilyn Monroe.

Frank, Shirley: **The New Infertility: Wanting Babies**. New York: **Lilith,** 19, 1988, 17-18.

Frankel, Estelle: **The Promises and Pitfalls of Jewish Relationships**. Oakland, CA: **Tikkun**, 5, September/October 1990, 19-22;95-8.

>Problems of "the relationship thing" in the contemporary American Jewish community.

Friedan, Betty: **Jewish Roots: An Interview with Betty Friedan**. Oakland, CA: **Tikkun**, 3, Jan/Feb 1988, 25-29.

>"Tikkun" interviews Betty Friedan to "learn about the role of Judaism in her life."

Friedman, Reena Sigman: **The Jewish Women's Movement**. New York: **Jewish Education News**, 12, Summer 1991, 26-7,29.

Friedman, Reena Sigman: **American Jewish Women: 1967-1991**. New York: **The Reporter: Women's American ORT**, Winter 1991, 10-14.

> Brief overview of important Jewish women; some issues of past 25 years: Bella Abzug, Madeline Kunin, Judith Resnick (dec.) new ordained women rabbis like Amy Eilberg, Nina Cardin, Debbie Friedman (cantor). Touches on Jewish women on boards of Jewish organizations; synagogues, new women-inspired rituals; US-Israeli women participation, etc. Writer sees period as "2nd stage for Jewish women's movement."

Gangelhoff, Bonnie: **No Laughing Matter: The Jewish American Princess**. Houston, TX: **Magazine of the Houston Post**, Nov. 15, 1987, 12-19.

> Jokes about the "Jewish American Princess" are thinly disguised anti-semitic jokes. Several women including the Texas attorney, Sherry Merfish, have lectured on this phenomenon and the alienation it causes among Jews.

Gilson, Estelle: **The Hapless JAP**. New York: **Congress Monthly**, 55, 1988, 10-11.

Gilson, Estelle: **Will Today's Woman Join Hadassah**? Washington, DC: **Moment**, 15, February 1990, 29-30,55.

Ginsburg, Faye: **When the Subject is Women: Encounters With Syrian Jewish Women**. Arlington, VA: **Journal of American Folklore**, 100, 1987, 540-547.

Goldenberg, Naomi Ruth: **Current Debate/Intermarriage: A Response to Anne Roiphe on the Jewish Family and the Problem of Intermarriage**. Oakland, CA: **Tikkun**, 2, 118-120.

> Article and response by Anne Roiphe.

Goldscheider, Calvin: **A Century of Jewish in Rhode Island**. Providence, RI: **Rhode Island Jewish Historical Notes**, 10, 1989, 335-349.

Goldstein, Alice: **New Roles, New Commitments? Jewish Women's Involvement in the Community's Organizational Structure**. New Brunswick, NJ: **Contemporary Jewry**, 11, 1990, 49-76.

Gornick, Vivian: **Twice an Outsider: On Being Jewish and a Woman**. Oakland, CA: **Tikkun**, 4, March/April 1989, 29-31,123-125.

> Gornick writes about Jewish women's exclusion by gender and by using personal examples from her own life in New York and elsewhere.

Grossman, Lawrence: **Abortion Rights**: In section on **Jewish Communal Affairs**. **American Jewish Yearbook**, 91, 1991, 191-2.

Jewish women's organization views and other institutional groups' stance on abortion is discussed.

Guberman, Jayne Kravetz: **Jewish Women Artists in Transition**. Oberlin, OH: **Jewish Folklore and Ethnology Review**, 10, 1988, 13-14.

Gutman, Janice: **Poor in Money But Not Much Else: Interview with Aura, Elana and Barbara Myerson**. Eugene, OR: **Bridges**, 3, Spring/Summer 1992, 86-90.

Hagy, James W.: **Her Scandalous Behavior: A Jewish Divorce in Charleston, South Carolina, 1788**, see index.

Hahn, Deborah Fuller: **Sharing Awareness: Women's Spirituality in Florida**. Johannesburg: **Jewish Affairs**, 48, Winter 1993, 49-54.

Hahn, Deborah Fuller: **Soviet Jewish Refugee Women: Searching for Security**. New York: **Women & Therapy**, 13, 1992, 79-87.

Hanft, Sheldon: **Mordecai's Female Academy**. Waltham, MA: **American Jewish History**, 79, Autumn 1989, 72-93.

Article about school for women in the South (early 19th c) which was a model for that of others including Penina Moise in Charleston, S.C.

Hauptman, Fred: **American Music, American Voices: Music by Diane Thome**. Seattle, WA: **Seattle Weekly**, June 14, 1989, 43.

Heschel, Susannah: **Women's Studies**. Baltimore, MD: **Modern Judaism**, 10, 1990, 243-258.

Hirshan, Marjorie Schonhaut: **The Jewish Women's Resource Center: Bringing Women Closer to Judaism and Judaism Closer to Women**. Oberlin, OH: **Jewish Folklore and Ethnology Review**, 12, 1990, 28+.

Hoffman, Michael: **High on the Hill: Jewish Women in the House and Senate**. New York: **The Reporter: Women's American ORT**, Fall 1993, 7-9.

Six Jewish women candidates running for House of Representatives or Senate.(Boxer, Margolies-Mezvinsky, Schenk, Feinstein, Lowey and Harman). These women represent diverse populations and many consider their Jewish identity a plus in building coalitions. (Author is a political writer for New Israel Fund).

Iannone, Carol: **Sex & the Feminists**. New York: **Commentary**, 96, Sept. 1993, 51-54.

Jacobs, Lynn Dimarsky and Sherry Berliner: **Jewish Domestic Abuse: Realities and Responses**. New York: **Journal of Jewish Communal Service**, 68, Winter 1991-2, 94-113.

Jewish Women in Therapy: Seen But Not Heard. New York: **Women & Therapy, Special Issue**, 10, 1990.

Various authors including Evelyn Torton Beck and Susannah Heschel write about Jewish topics: Holocaust, Anti-Semitism and the "Jewish American Princess," intermarriage, feminism and Jewish lesbians.

Jewish Women Look to the Year 2000: Shaping the Future. New York: **Na'amat Woman**, Jan/Feb 1988, 4-29.

Nine prominent women describe their agendas for action for Jewish women from their personal perspectives. Some statements are especially insightful, i.e., Blu Greenberg, Francine Klagsbrun and Letty Cottin Pogrebin.

Jewish Women Talk about Surviving Incest. Eugene, OR: **Bridges**, 2, Spring 1991, 26-34.

Jochnowitz, Carol: **Idle Tears**. New York: **Jewish Currents**, March, 1986, 33+.

It's good to cry when you have to, and Jewish women seem to know this!

Josefowitz, Rachel: **Antisemitisim and Sexism in Stereotypes of Jewish Women**. New York: **Women and Therapy**, 5, Summer/Fall 1986, 249-257.

Kahn, Yoel H.: **Hannah, Must You Have a Child?**. San Francisco, CA: **Out/Look**, NO.12, Spring 1991, 39-43.

Kaminetsky, Ellen: **Confessions of a Jews for Jesus Defector**. New York: **Reform Judaism**, 22, Winter 1993, 28-29.

Revealing and important excerpt from Kaminetsky's book. see Author index.

Karsh, Audrey R.: **Mothers and Daughters of Old San Diego**. Santa Monica, CA: **Western States Jewish History**, 19, 1987, 264-270.

Kaye Kantrowitz, Melanie: **Observations: The Next Step**. Norwood, NJ: **NWSA Journal**, 2, Spring 1990, 236-244.

Kaye/Kantrowitz, Melanie: **Body and Soul: Are You a Therapist with a Jewish Client? Read on....** New York: **Lilith**, 16, Summer 1991, 6+.

Kent, D.: **Offense Intended**: **Jap-Bashing on College Campuses**. New York: **Seventeen**, April 1990, 90+.

Kliger, Hannah and Schreier, Barbara: **Towards a Study of Jewish Immigrant Women in Boston 1880-1920**: **Clothing, Culture and Communication**. Oberlin, OH: **Jewish Folklore and Ethnology Review**, 12, 1990, 28.

Kosmin, Barry A.: **The Political Economy of Gender in Jewish Federations**. New Brunswick, NJ: **Contemporary Jewry**, 10, Spring 1989, 17-31.

Both males and females engage in charitable behavior. However, Kosmin examines the particular role of women in establishing women's divisions of Jewish Federations and their participation.

Kramer, William M. Stern, Norton B.: **Birdie Stodel**: **Los Angeles Patriot**. Santa Monica, CA: **Western States Jewish History**, 20, 1988, 109-116.

Kranzler, Gershon: **The Women of Williamsburg**: **A Contemporary American Hasidic Community**. New York: **Tradition**, 28, Fall 1993, 82-93.

A sociological study of Hasidic women who work hard, at home as well as in outside jobs, have many children (on average 8) and find their lives fulfilled and worthwhile.

Kravath, Tania: **Matriarchs**: **A Memoir**. Eugene Or: **Bridges**, 3, Spring/Summer 1992, 98-99.

Kray, Susan: **Orientation of an "Almost White" Woman**: **The Interlocking Effects of Race, Class, Gender, and Ethnicity in American Mass Media**. Annandale, VA: **Critical Studies in Mass Communication**, 10, Dec 1993, 349-366.

This study examines "the case of the missing Jewish women" in works of oppressed women and minorities.

Lamb, Lynette: **JAP Jokes are Nothing to Laugh at**: **Why Should Jewish Women Take the Rap for our Materialistic Culture?** Minneapolis, MN: **Utne Reader**, May/June 1989, 30+.

Lamoree, Karen M.: **Why Not a Jewish Girl? The Jewish Experience at Pembroke College in Brown University**. Providence, RI: **Rhode Island Jewish Historical Notes**, 10, 1988, 122-140.

Langford, J.K.: **We Will Not Endure This Progrom in Silence**. Washington, DC: **Off Our Backs**, 22, Mar 1992, 18,26.

Activism by women in Germany to fight violence against minority women and Lesbians—some Jewish, who were targeted.

Lantos, John D.; Offner, Stacy K. & Chambers, Tod S.: **The Case: What Should Leah be Told?**. Park Ridge, Il: **Second Opinion**, 18, Apr 1993, 80-97.

> Compares biblical Leah with contemporary Leahs.

Latting, Jean Elizabeth & Wolf, Laura Belkin: **Feminism, Self-Esteem and Depression among Jewish Women: An Empirical Study**. New York: **Journal of Jewish Communal Service**, 63, Spring 1987, 219-226.

Lehrer, Ruth: **No Job. With Benefits**. New York: **Hadassah**, November 1992, 32+.

Lerner, Harriet Goldhor: **Sisters and Other Family Legacies**. New York: **Lilith**, 14, Spring 1989, 11-14.

Lewis, Frieda: **Judith Epstein: In Tribute**. New York: **Hadassah**, 70, Jan 1989, 35.

Lipstadt, Helena & Mitchell, Pam: **Loving Across Differences of Class**. Eugene, OR: **Bridges**, 2, Spring 1991, 42-50; Fall 1991, 48-54.

> A two-part personal essay on barriers to relationships between women based on economic class. While somewhat naive, it provokes thought. Judge for yourself!

MacLean, Nancy: **The Leo Frank Case Reconsidered: Gender and Sexual Politics in the Making of Reactionary Populism**. New Haven, CT: **Journal of American History**, 78, 1991, 917-948.

Marks, Lara: **Dear Old Mother Levy's: The Jewish Maternity Home and Sick Room Helps Society, 1895-1939**. Oxford, UK: **Social History of Medicine**, 3, 1990, 61-88.

Martin, Douglas: **Long Search for Identity Ends in Joy: Woman Discovers Jewish Roots, Family**. New York: **New York Times**, 138, June 14, 1989, A20 (N); B1 (L).

Maynard, Fredelle Bruser: **A Mother and Two Daughters** (excerpts from **The Tree of Life**:Viking, Canada, 1988) New York: **Lilith**, #20, Summer 1988, 29-31.

Medjuck, Sheva: **From Self-Sacrificing Jewish Mother to Self-Centered Jewish Princess: Is This How Far We've Come?**. Halifax, Nova Scotia: **Atlantis: A Women's Studies Journal**, 14, 1988, 90-97.

Mitchell, Pam: **A Daughter of Communists**. Eugene, OR: **Bridges**, 3, Spring/Summer 1992, 91-97.

Morris, Bonnie: **Anti-Semitism in the Women's Movement**: **A Jewish Lesbian Speaks**. Washington, DC: **Off Our Backs**, 20, December 1990, 12-13.

> Concerned about anti-semitism in the feminist movement, Morris discusses the issues, especially in light of the Palestinian crisis.

Morrison, Abby: **The Women of B'nai B'rith**. Washington, DC: **Jewish Monthly**, 105, Feb 1991, 40-42.

Moses, Jennifer: **Women's Lib**. New York: **Commentary**, 86, 1988, 8,10.

Mosher, William and D. Williams, Linda B and David P. Johnson: **Religion and Fertility in the United States**: **New Patterns**. Chicago: **Demography**, 29, May 1992, 199-214.

Murphy, Marjorie: **Work, Protest, and Culture**: **New Work on Working Women's History**. College Park, MD: **Feminist Studies**, 13, 1987, 657-667.

Musleah, Rahel: **Jewish Feminist Scholarship**. New York: **Na'Amat,** Nov/Dec 1993, 4-7.

> An overview of a dozen-plus Jewish women academics with their essays and books and their Jewish women studies focus. The lack of writings about Jewish women in history is stated as a condition of "male scholars not writing about women's lives."

Musleah, Rahel: **When the Goddess Calls**: **Jewish Women Answer**. New York: **Lilith**, 18, Fall 1993, 8-13.

Nadell, Pamela: **Rereading Charles S. Liebman**: **Questions from the Perspective of Women's History**. Waltham,MA: **American Jewish History**, LXCXX, Summer 1991, 502-516.

Navaretta, Cynthia: **Conference: Jewish Women in the Arts (Hebrew Union College, New York)**. New York: **Women Artists News**, 13, Spring 1988, 11-12.

Nelson, Sara: **Notes from the Underground**: **An Aids Volunteer**. New York: **Lilith**, 15, Winter 1990, 13-14.

New, Elisa: **Killing the Princess**: **The Offense of a Bad Defense**. Oakland, CA: **Tikkun**, 4, March/April 1989, 17-19,114-117.

> New discusses Shirley Frondorf's "The Death of a 'Jewish American Princess' The True Story of a Victim on Trial" about a husband who killed his wife, supposedly a Jewish-American princess, and goes free, because "Jewish men are projecting their own self-hatred onto women," says New, or, this is a new kind of anti-semitism,or as in all "princesses" this is sexism at its most vicious.

Ochs, Vanessa: **Jewish Feminist Scholarship Comes of Age**. New York: **Lilith**, 15, Winter 1990, 8-12.

Pefferman, Naomi: **Star-Crossed Romance, 1987, N.B.C**. New York: **Lilith**, 18, Winter 1987-8, 16-17.

Popular perceptions of current Jewish women and romance compared with the story of Michal and David.

Pfeffer, Leo & Pfeffer, Alan: **The Agunah in American Secular Law**. Waco, TX: **Journal of Church and State**, 31, 1989, 487-525.

Pheterson, Gail: **Alliances between Women: Overcoming Internalized Oppression and Internalized Domination**. Chicago, IL: **Signs**, 12, Autumn 1986, 146-160.

Pogrebin, Letty Cottin: **From our Heads and our Hearts: Connecting with Black Women**. New York: **Lilith**, 16, Winter 1991, 13-15,28.

Pogrebin, Letty Cottin: **One Man, Two Fathers: Personal Essay**. Oakland,CA: **Tikkun**, 6, July/August 1991, 27-29,92-3.

Memories of her father, loss of her mother, and coming to terms with her place as a female in Judaism, and in her father's eyes.

Pogrebin, Letty Cottin: **Why Feminism is Good for the Jews**. New York: **Na'Amat Woman**, Sept.-Oct. 1991, 3-5, 24.

An excerpt from the author's "Deborah, Golda and Me: Being Female and Jewish in America." A good brief analysis of the importance of feminist awareness in modern Jewish life.

Prager, Karen: **Herefords, Hebrew & Me at the Feminist Ranch**. New York: **Lilith**, 18, Summer 1993, 14-17.

Personal essay of a Jewish woman at an all-women's ranch where she met women who had little if any knowledge or exposure to Jewish women.

Prell, Riv-Ellen: **The Begetting of America's Jews: Seeds of American Jewish Identity in the Representations of American Jewish Women**. New York: **Journal of Jewish Communal Service**, 69, Winter/Spring 1993, 4-23.

Rapoport, Nessa: **Jewish Feminism and the Future**. New York: **Hadassah**, January 1993, 16+.

The first step in envisioning and creating Jewish communities that reflect feminist values is to identify the problem.

Reines-Josephy, Marcia: **The Work of Their Hands: Jewish Women Artists**. Jerusalem: **World Congress of Jewish Studies**, 10, 1990, 109-116.

Rinn, Miriam: **Orthodox Feminism Arrives**. New York: **The Reporter: Women's American ORT**, Fall 1990, 6-8.

Changes in the way Orthodox women are asserting themselves; women's prayer groups, bat mitzvot, Shalom Bat (for newborn girls), childcare during synagogue services, advanced education for themselves. Mentions obstacles and controversies in Orthodox synagogues and new demands by educated women for more participation in prayer and ritual.

Roberts, Marlene: **Homecoming Queen**. New York: **Lilith**, 17, Winter 1992, 13-15.

A young, 1950's Jewish American girl grows to understand her immigrant grandmother through her own growth experience.

Rogow, Faith: **Why is this Decade Different from All Other Decades: A Look at the Rise of Jewish Lesbian Feminism**. Eugene, OR: **Bridges**, 1, Spring, 1990, 67-79.

Roiphe, Anne: **The Jewish Family: A Feminist Perspective**. Oakland, CA: **Tikkun**, 1, [1986], 70-75.

Are Jewish feminists working against Jewish survival? What responsibility do the rabbis, the synagogues, the men have in the issues of intermarriage, assimilation and the Jewish American Princess?

Rotenberg, Mattie: **Jewish Women: A Document From the Past**. Port Washington, NY: **Sh'ma**, 23, November 27, 1992, 13-15.

Follow-up article of the Nov.3, 1992 issue of Sh'ma.

Roundtable: Jewish Women Discuss Their Music. Eugene, OR: **Bridges**, 3, Spring 1993, 102-112.

Rubinstein, Judith & Allen Rubinstein: **The Graffiti Wars**. New York: **Lilith**, No. 17, Fall 1987, 8-9.

Stereotypes of Jewish women and mothers.

Sacks, Maurie: **Computing Community at Purim**. Arlington, VA: **Journal of American Folklore**, 102, 1989, 275-291.

Sanua, Marianne: **From the Pages of the Victory Bulletin: The Syrian Jews of Brooklyn during World War II**. New York: **Yivo Annual**. 19, 1990, 283-330.

Saper, Bernard: **The JAP Joke Controversy: An Excruciating Psychosocial Analysis**. West Lafayette, IN: **Humor:International Journal of Humor Research**, 4, 1991, 223+.

Sarna, Jonathan D.; Shargel, Baila R. & Mel Scult: **Henrietta Szold**. New York: **Hadassah Preludes**, 71, June, 1990, 18-24.

Seminar at JTS on Henrietta Szold's many roles, with sessions by Sarna on Szold: Szold, the editor, Shargel: Szold, the correspondent, and Scult on her rabbinic studies showing the many facets of her early adult life.

Schneider, Susan Weidman: **Feminist Philanthropy: Women Changing the World with Their Dollars**. New York: **Lilith**, 18, Spring 1993, 14-17.

Schneider, Susan Weidman: **Jewish Women's Philanthropy**. New York: **Lilith**, 18, Winter 1993, 6-12,29,38-39.

Schneider, Susan Weidman & Bart, Pauline: **Why Jewish Women Get Raped**. New York: **Lilith**, No. 15, Summer 1986, 8-12.

Schneyer, Mark: **Mothers and Children, Poverty and Mortality: A Social Worker's Priorities, 1915**. Philadelphia, PA: **Pennsylvania Magazine of History and Biography**, 112, 1988, 209-226.

Schnur, Susan: **Blazes of Truth: When is a JAP not a Yuppie?**. New York: **Lilith**, #17, Fall 1987, 10-11.

Stereotype of the "JAP" and connection with antisemitism.

Schwartz, Sharon: **Women and Depression: A Durkheimian Perspective**. New York: **Social Science and Medicine**, 32, 1991, 127-140.

Gender differences in mental disorders are studied among 200 Orthodox Jewish women in New York City. Depression levels are compared between those who are "traditional Orthodox" women and "modern Orthodox."

Scult, Mel: **The Baale Boste Reconsidered: The Life of Mathilde Roth Schechter (M.R.S.)**. Baltimore, MD: **Modern Judaism**, 7, 1987, 1-27.

Schechter was founder of the Women of Conservative Judaism.

Seller, Maxine S.: **World of our Mothers: The Women's Page of the "Jewish Daily Forward"**. Bellingham, WA: **Journal of Ethnic Studies**, 16, Summer 1988, 95-118.

The "Forward" newspaper spoke to women who were still rooted in working class, radical Yiddish culture. It also helped, them Americanize, politicize, and became very important in these immigrant womens' lives.

Seller, Maxine S.: **Defining Socialist Womanhood: The Women's Page of The Jewish Daily Forward in 1919**. Waltham, MA: **American Jewish History**, 76, 1987, 416-438.

Shluker, Zelda: **Drugs and Us**. New York: **Hadassah**, February 1991, 36+.

> Admitting our children are at risk is the first and most important step in combatting addiction - but for Jews it is a difficult one.

Siegel, Hannah Tifforot: **Jewish Feminists Ain't Just Singing the Blues**. Brookline, MA: **Neshama**, 5, Summer 1993, 1, 6-7.

Silber, Ellen, Keane, Ellen Marie & Catherine Vincie: **From Experience to Insight to Commitment**. New York: **Women's Studies International Forum**, 9, 1986, 171-181.

Silverstein, Olga & Schnur, Susan: **Olga Chats: About Life, Love and Jewish Idiosyncrasies**. New York: **Lilith**, 14, Spring 1989, 7-10.

> On Jewish mothers, on mother bashing and the "real" role of the Jewish woman, in conversation with noted family therapist Silverstein of the Ackerman Institute, NYC.

Sinkoff, Nancy B.: **Educating for "Proper" Jewish Womanhood: A Case Study in Domesticity and Vocational Training, 1897-1926**. Waltham, MA: **American Jewish History**, 77, June 1988, 572-599.

> Work of German-Jewish women in helping to educate newer Jewish immigrants, mainly from Russia, for domestic life or service.

Spencer, Gary: **An Analysis of JAP-Baiting Humor on the College Campus**. West Lafayette, in: **Humor: International Journal of Humor Research**, 2, 1989, 329-348.

Spiegel, Marcia Cohn: **Beyond Inclusion: Redefining the Jewish Family**. Boston: **Genesis 2**, Autumn 1987, 14-16.

Spiegel, Marcia Cohn: **The Last Taboo: Dare we speak about Incest**. New York: **Lilith**, No.20, Summer 1988, 10-12.

Spiegel, Marcia Cohn: **Stigmatized Behavior: The Community Responds**. Boston: **Genesis 2**, Summer 1988, 10-12.

Stanger, Sheila: **Instructions for the Birthing Team**. New York: **Lilith**, 15, Winter 1990, 21-3.

Stieglitz, Maria: **Five Women Who Shake the World**. New York: **Lilith**, 16, Summer 1991, 8-13, 30.

Stieglitz, Maria: **New Mexico's Secret Jews: Anna Rael Delay and Family**. New York: **Lilith**, 16, Summer 1991, 8-10,12.

Stone, Amy: **Jewish Career Women: Six Profiles**. New York: **Lilith**, 19, Spring 1988, 8-12.

Stone, Amy: **Struggling? Juggling?: Trying to Integrate our Multiple Roles**. New York: **Lilith**, 19, Spring 1988, 6-7.

Suchow, Betty & Suchow, Phil: **The Ways We Were: Was Mama a Virgin?** New York: **Lilith**, 16, Fall 1991, 36.

Swirsky, Joan: **Women's Lib**. New York: **Commentary**, 86, 1988, 10,12.

Tavris, Carol: **My Mother, the Feminist**. New York: **Lilith**, 14, Summer 1989, 10-11.

Tenenbaum, Shelly: **The Ways We Were: Buying Chickens, Paying Bills: Jewish Women's Loan Societies**. New York: **Lilith**, 16, Summer 1991, 32+.

Toll, William: **A Quiet Revolution: Jewish Women's Clubs and the Widening Female Sphere, 1870-1920**. Cincinnati,OH: **American Jewish Archives**, 41, Spring/Summer 1989, 7-26.

"American Jewish women's image of themselves changed during this period," giving them more freedom, and often more leadership roles. They began to define their own roles in both the home and community.

Umansky, Ellen M.: **Females, Feminists and Feminism: A Review of Recent Literature on Jewish Feminism and the Creation of Feminist Judaism**. College Park, MD: **Feminist Studies**, 14, Summer 1988, 349-365.

Essay discusses 7 important works of the 1980's by Adelman, Blu Greenberg, Beck, Koltun, Heschel, Weidman-Schneider, and Kaye/Kantrowitz.

We Play Music/We are Musicians/ or Neither: Jewish Women Discuss Their Music. Eugene, OR: **Bridges**, 3, Spring 1993, 102-119.

Weinberg, Sydney Stahl: **Jewish Mothers and Immigrant Daughters: Positive and Negative Role Models**. New Brunswick, NJ: **Journal of American Ethnic History**, 6, Spring 1987, 39-55.

Contrast between women's traditional role as caregiver/nurturer and "manager of the home" and often of family finances, and the daughters who came to America, and those who were born in USA.

Weinberg, Sydney Stahl: **Longing to Learn: The Education of Jewish Immigrant Women in New York City, 1900-1934**. New Brunswick, NJ: **Journal of Ethnic History**, 8, Spring 1989, 108-126.

For immigrant women secular education was the way up socially and economically. Since Jewish women were denied a Jewish education and many had to work, they went to school at night and took advantage of free opportunities to better themselves.

Weisman, Celia: **Comedy and Consciousness: Can WE Laugh at Joan Rivers?** New York: **Lilith**, No.16, Spring 1987, 18-19.

Joan Rivers and other Jewish female performers.

Wenger, Beth S.: **Jewish Women and Voluntarism: Beyond the Myth of Enablers**. Waltham, MA: **American Jewish History**, 79, Autumn 1989, 16-36.

Focus on German Jewish, and then later, East European women's service in the home; later as club women, organizing and sustaining such groups as Hadassah and NCJW, and developing important organizational and leadership skills at the same time.

Wenger, Beth S.: **Jewish Women of the Club: The Changing Public Role of Atlanta's Jewish Women (1870-1930)**. Waltham, MA: **American Jewish History**, 76, 1987, 311-333.

Winternight, Nancy: **What the Ark is to the Jewish Male, My Dish Cupboard is to Me: Artist Nancy Winternight**. New York: **Lilith**, 16, Fall,1991, 14-15.

Wisse, Ruth R.: **Women's Lib**. New York: **Commentary**, 86, 1988, 40-45.

Zandy, Janet: **Our True Legacy: Radical Jewish Women in America**. New York: **Lilith**, 14, Winter 1989, 8-13.

Radical women who can serve as role models for "spirituality and courageous disobedience" in the cause of justice.

Zerubavel, Yael and Esses, Dianne: **Reconstructions of the Past: Syrian Jewish Women and the Maintenance of Tradition**. Arlington, VA: **Journal of American Folklore**, 100, 1987, 528-539.

VI
Israel

A. Books

Baizerman, Suzanne: **The Jewish Kippa Sruga and the Social Construction of Gender in Israel**: in: **Dress and Gender: Making and Meaning, Ruth Barnes and Joanne B. Eicher, eds**. New York: Berg, 1992, ,92-105.

"The making and wearing of the kippa sruga (embroidered handmade skullcap, usually made by female family members) reinforces gender categories and ideologies in a subculture where gender distinctions are highly important."

Beck, Evelyn T. ed.: **Nice Jewish Girls: A Lesbian Anthology**. see U.S. section.

Bernstein, Deborah S. ed.: **Pioneers and Homemakers: Jewish Women in Pre-State Israel**. Albany, NY: State University of New York, 1992.

"Experience and action of Jewish women in the new Jewish settlement in Palestine (the Yishuv) from the last two decades of the 19th century until 1948."

Dubinki, D. with L.M. Weissman, tr.: **A Narrow Bridge**. New York: Feldheim, 1992.

Encyclopedia Judaica Yearbook. See feature article on women including status of women in Israel, see U.S. section (here).

Falbel, Rita, Klepfisz, Irena & Nevel, Donna: **Jewish Women's Call for Peace: A Handbook for Jewish Women on the Israeli/Palestinian Conflict**. Ithaca, NY: Firebrand Books, 1990.

Letters, essays and other writings express the wish that Jewish women support those who want peace and a home for both Israeli Jews and Palestinians.

Ferguson, Kathy E.: **Kibbutz Journal: Reflections on Gender, Race and Militarisim in Israel.** see Author Index.

Freedman, Marcia: **Exile in the Promised Land: A Memoir**. Ithaca, NY: Firebrand Books, 1990.

Freedman's achievements include making aliyah to Israel, activism in Israeli politics, membership in the Knesset and helping to found the feminist movement in Israel.

Ganz, Yaffa.: **All Things Considered: From a Woman's Point of View**. Brooklyn, NY: Mesorah, 1990.

Gilad, Lisa.: **Ginger and Salt: Yemeni Jewish Women in an Israeli Town. Women in Cross-Cultural Perspective Series.** Boulder, CO: Westview Press, 1989.

Adaptation of Yemeni Jewish women to life in Israel. Discusses their education, family bonds and status, both social and economic.

Gruber, Ruth: **Raquela: A Woman of Israel** (Documentary fiction) see Author Index.

Images of Women in Peace & War: in MacDonald, Sharon; Holden, Pat; Ardener, Shirley: eds.: Cross-Cultural and Historical Perspectives. Basingstoke, UK: Macmillan Education, 1987.

Two brief pages at beginning about dichotomy of Israeli women.

Kaufman, Shirley: **Rivers of Salt** (Poems about Israel) see also Literature-Poetry section.

Kaye/Kantrowitz, Melanie: **The Issue is Power: Essays on Women, Jews, Violence and Resistance**. see Author index.

Lemish, D. Tidhar,C.E.: **Women in Israel's Broadcasting Media and on Israeli Television: in: Y. Kawakami, eds., Women and Communication in an Age of Science and Technology.** Tokyo: Atom Press, 1988, 112-128.

Lev Ari, Ronit Kaplan, Lou, tr.: **After the Battering: The Struggle of Battered Women with Violence in the Family**. Tel Aviv: Na'amat, 1991.

Lipman, Beata.: **Israel—The Embattled Land: Jewish and Palestinian Women Talk About Their Lives**. Cambridge, MA: Urwin Hyman, 1988.

Interviews with Israeli Jewish women and Palestinian women which reveal their political views and their personal and religious identities.

Metzger, Deena: **What Dinah Thought**. New York: Viking/Penguin, 1986.

Biblical namesake Dinah and a modern Israeli woman: Metzger's own view of Israelis and Jews. Judge for yourself!

Rosenwasser, Penny: **Voices from a "Promised Land": Palestinian and Israeli peace activists speak their hearts: conversations with Penny Rosenwasser**. Willimantic, CT: Curbstone Press, 1992.

Israeli Jewish and Palestinian men and women, together with peace activists, in dialogue with Rosenwasser share alternative points of view.

Israel

Ruddick, Sarah: **Maternal Thinking**. Boston, MA: Beacon Press, 1989.

> Author's theme is that women's role as nurturers and preservers of life explains their role in peace movements.

Sered, Susan Starr: **Women as Ritual Experts: The Religious Lives of Elderly Jewish Women in Jerusalem**. New York: Oxford University Press, 1992.

> Although separated by gender, these Middle Eastern Jewish women have rich religious lives, full of rituals and deep meaning.

Shain, Ruchoma: **Dearest Children.** New York: Feldheim, 1992.

Strum, Philippa: **The Women Are Marching: The Second Sex and the Palestinian Revolution**. Brooklyn, NY: Lawrence Hill Books, 1992.

> A Jewish-American's subjective view of the Intifada and lives of Palestinian women from a women's perspective. Palestinian women: mothers, lawyers, prisoners.

Swirski, Barbara & Safir, Marilyn P.: **Calling the Equality Bluff: Women in Israel**. New York: Pergamon; also Teachers' College Press, 1991.

> Very important compilation of feminist essays by leading activists and academic women of Israel.

Tidhar, Chava E. & Lemish, Dafna: **Women in the Intifada: A Television News Perspective. in:"Framing the Intifada: People and Media" eds. Akiba A. Cohen & Gadi Wolfsfeld.** Norwood, NJ: Ablex Publishing Corp., 1993, Chapter 8:142-149.

> Differences in depiction or representation of women involved in the Intifada as compared with men, and also between Palestinian women and Israeli women. Neither group of women's activism has been adequately reported.

Violence against Women: Women: Israel Yearbook and Almanac (Events of 1992). 47 Jerusalem: Israel Yearbook and Almanac, 1993.

> Statistics on such subjects as gross wages of women compared with men, and article on p.269 on violence against women; also, women elect women, p.271.

Wallach, John and Janet: **Still Small Voices**. New York: Citadel Press, 1990, 12-40.

> A collection of interviews with Israelis and Palestinians, one with an Israeli woman Miriam Levinger, "The Jewish Fundamentalist: Footsteps in the Bible."

Weinbaum, Batya. **Voices of Women in Dialogue on Politics, Religion and Culture in Israel**. (151 Main St, Northampton,MA): (YPS), 1990.

> Interviews with Israeli women from both traditional and non-traditional sectors which demonstrate successes as well as struggles for Israeli feminism in both politics and religion.

Women in Israel: A Presentation of Data on Women in Israel Describing Their Social Situation. Jerusalem: Central Library of Social Work, December 1987.

> Data on Jewish and non-Jewish women in Israel including demographics, marriage, births, life expectancy and labor characteristics, from 1976-1986.

Young, Elise G.: **Keepers of the History: Women and the Israeli-Palestinian Conflict**. New York: Teachers College Press, 1992.

Zuckerman, Francine, Ed.: **Half the Kingdom: Seven Jewish Feminists**. Montreal, Quebec, Canada: Vehicule Press, 1992.

> This work, based on film of same name, shows contradictions in Israeli women's status. Interviews with film principals include E.M. Broner, Alice Shalvi, Michele Landsberg, Shulamit Aloni, Elyse Goldstein, Naomi Goldenberg, Norma Baumel Joseph.

B. Articles

Avgar, Amy: **Women, War and Peace**. New York: **Na'amat Woman**, Mar/April 1990, 11-12, 28-30.

> War reduces importance of women's issues; conflict of Israelis vs. Arabs affects both groups of women. Article compares Israeli women's and men's attitudes to conflict; its political and social effects, with women dovish and men hawkish. Hebrew Univ. study of gender attitudes toward war and peace cited; Israeli women activist groups; and right wing women responses. Brussels 1989 Women's Peace Conference and networking with Israeli and Palestinian women also discussed.

Avgar, Amy: **The Feminization of Poverty in Israel**. New York: **Na'amat Woman**, VII, Sept./Oct 1992, 5-8,19,27.

> Rise in poverty between 1980-1990 in Israel showed women to be the "principal victims." Statistical and policy analysis is presented — citing rules of the Natl Insurance Inst. of Israel which administers assistance to them.

Avgar, Amy: **Israeli Women and their Health**. New York: **Na'amat Woman**, May/June 1991, 18-19,24.

Israeli women have begun to demand more and better medical care in a universal health system that appears better than that of US—though patient rights and consumer awareness is lacking. An Israel Health Ministry study in 1988 showed women services were neglected. Na'amat proposed a Dept. of Women's Health. Information given on existing gaps, with opinion of writer that in Israel "a women's health movement" is still far off.

Benson, Evelyn R.: **Hadassah and the Nursing Connection: The Early Days**. Washington, DC: **American Association for the History of Nursing Bulletin**, No. 26, Spring 1990, 4-6.

Bergman, Miranda; Greene, Susan; Redman, Dina & Tobias, Marlene: **Painting for Peace: Break the Silence Mural Project**. Eugene, OR: **Bridges**, 1, Fall 1990, 39-57.

A group narrative about a cooperative mural project with Palestinians in Ramallah, Israel, 1989.

Berkowitz, Gila: **Lifting the Yoke: Is There Hope for Ending Jewish Legal Discrimination Against Women**? New York: **Lilith**, 16, Spring 1987, 25-6.

Problem of ending Jewish legal discrimination against women in Israel as posed at the 1986 conference in Israel on Israeli women and halacha.

Berkowitz, Linda: **Jewish Feminism in Action**. Jerusalem: **Israel Scene**, 10, Jan. 1989, 18.

Concise one page article on meeting of First International Jewish Feminist Conference in Jerusalem attended by women from 23 countries.

Brown, Michael: **The American Element in the Rise of Golda Meir**. see Author index.

Burgansky, Michael: **A Comparison Between Battered Women Living at Home and Residing in a Shelter**. Ramat Gan, Israel: **Journal of Social Work and Policy in Israel**, 2, 1989, 7-29.

Dinai, Amilia: **The Potentiality of the Israeli Youth Club and a Modernizing Agent: From Segregated Leisure to Joint Leisure**. Berkeley Hills, CA: **Urban Education**, 23, Oct 1988, 241-60.

Changes in behavior of Yemenite female adolescents socializing at traditional male social events.

Distelheim, Rochelle: **Jewish and Feminist in Jerusalem**. New York: **Congress Monthly**, 56, February, 1989, 12-14.

Dotan, Amira and Mar'i, Mariam: **A Women's Mideast Peace Dialogue**. New York: **Lilith**, 20, June 1988, 14-18.

Elliman, Wendy: **Nursing Keeps Pace**. New York: **Hadassah**, 70, Feb 1989, 28-30.

Fishman, Sylvia Barack & Rattok, Lily: **Remaking Jewish Worlds: Israeli and American Jewish Women**. New York: **Textures** (Hadassah National Jewish Studies Bulletin) 11, Oct 1992, np.

Comparison through interviews with Fishman (USA) and Rattok (Israel) about Jewish feminists: within the religious community in the U.S., i.e., legal actions and issues of daily life in Israel.

Friedman, Reena Sigman: **Challenging the Religious Establishment: Israel: Feminist Nature (Leah Shakdiel)**. New York: **Lilith**, No.20, Summer 1988, 20-21.

Golan, Galia: **Movement toward Equality for Women in Israel**. Oakland, CA: **Tikkun**, 2, 1987, 19-21.

Goldman, Nechama: **Women Prepare for Their Day in Court**. Jerusalem: **Kol Emunah**, Summer 1992, 17,33.

Women pleaders and the training they undergo to prepare them for a new role in the Beit Din to better represent the female point of view.

Greenbaum, Joanne: **IDF Women Come of Age**. New York: **The Reporter: Women's American ORT**, Summer 1991, 13-14.

Compares Israel Defense Forces women with US Army in terms of equality with males, duties, terms of service. Women serve 2 years in Israel; men, 3. Short-term training is common; question of women in combat. As Israeli women are not exposed to front lines, rank is different. Emphasis on technical training, civilian skills for later job entry. Some references to 1987-8.

Grossman, Naomi: **Women Unbound: Breaking the Chains of Jewish Divorce Law**. New York: **Lilith**, 18, 1993, 8+.

One of many articles on this pressing issue for Orthodox American women and for all Israeli women.

Hareven, Gail: **His Army/Her Army: Women in the Israeli Military**. New York: **Lilith**, 17, Winter 1992, 9-12.

Description of the Israeli military where "sexual harassment, depression in women, and doomed, ingenue/hero marriages" are a result.

Hottelet, Richard : **Interview with Yael Dayan, M.K. and Moustapha Barouli, MD**: New York: **Israel Horizons**, 41, Summer/Fall 1993, 17-20.

Israel, A Woman's Mideast Peace Dialogue: Brief comments and interviews with various women (Alice Shalvi, Amira Dotan, Ruth Gruber, Leah Shakdiel). New York: **Lilith**, No.20, Summer 1988, 13-21.

Izraela, Dafna N.: **They Have Eyes and See Not: Gender Politics in the Diaspora Museum**. New York: **Psychology of Women Quarterly**, 17, Dec 1993, 515-523.

Jochnowitz, Carol: **Israel's Planned Parenthood**. New York: **Jewish Currents**, Jan. 1986, 3+.

Report on Shiloh, an Israeli birth-control counseling center.

King, Andrea: **Is Israel liberating for Ethiopian women?** New York: **Lilith**, No.18, Winter 1987/8, 8-12.

Land, Randi J.: **Israeli Women in Politics**. New York: **Na'amat Woman**, Sept/Oct 1988, 4-5,18.

The 12th Knesset had 8 or 9 women of 120 members expected to be elected Article discusses the many reasons for the low ratio of women politicians in Israel and steps toward progress in electing women to Knesset.

Leibowitz, Shira & Leibowitz, Nathaniel: **Shira Leibowitz and Nathaniel Leibowitz discuss Rabbi Chaim Herschenson's view of Deborah: A Justice or a Justess**. Jerusalem: **Kol Emunah**, Summer 1992, 34-5.

Current discussions of the role of religious women in public positions, with frequent reference to biblical Deborah and her role in ancient Israel.

Leibowitz, Shira & Levy, Naomi: **Two Shelters, One Threat**. New York: **Lilith**, 20, Summer 1988, 8.

Leon, Masha: **Israeli Film Star Gila Almagor: Wrestles with her Mother's Demonic Past**. New York: **Lilith**, 16, Spring 1991, 21-25.

Lobel, Thelma C. et al: **Personality Correlates of Career Choice in the Kibbutz: A Comparison between Career and Non-career Women**. New York: **Sex Roles**, 29, Sept 1993, 359-370.

Maranz, Felice: **Sexual Harassment in the Army: Close Quarters**. Jerusalem: **Jerusalem Report**, IV, July 29, 1993, 18-19.

Mason, Ruth: **New Women in the Knesset**. New York: **Na'amat Woman**, VII, Nov/Dec 1992, 4-6,30.

> 1992 Israeli elections had 37 women running for the Knesset with 11 gaining seats. Those women formed a coalition to advance Israeli women's status. Several elected women and their right-wing and liberal policies are detailed in interviews.

Montel, Jessie: **Israeli Identities: The Military, the Family and Feminism**. Eugene, OR: **Bridges**, 2, Fall 1991, 99-108.

> Good summary of contradictions concerning Israel, especially feminism and nationalism

Neuman, Shoshana: **Does a Woman's Education Affect Her Husband's Earnings?: Results for Israel in a Dual Labor Market**. Washington D.C.: **World Bank**, 1990.

Orr, Emda Ben & Eliahu, Edna: **Gender Differences in Idiosyncratic Sex-Typed Self-Images and Self-Esteem**. New York: **Sex Roles**, 29, Aug 1993, 271+.

Prince-Gibson, Etta: **Politics '92: Israel: This Time More Women in the Knesset**. New York: **Lilith**, 17, Fall 1992, 16-17.

Rapoport, Nessa : **Love in Hebrew: A Writer's Story**. New York: **Textures (Hadassah National Jewish Studies Bulletin)** 11, October 1992, n.p.

> Rapoport describes everyday life in Israel in 1992 as a mother.

Schneider, Susan Weidman & Dayan, Yael: **Yael Dayan: An Interview with Susan Weidman Schneider**. New York: **Lilith**, 15, Fall 1990, 10-15.

Seginer, Rachel; Karayanni, Mousa & Mari, Mariam M.: **Adolescents' Attitudes Toward Women's Roles: A Comparison between Israeli Jews and Arabs**. New York: **Psychology of Women Quarterly**, 14, Mar 1990, 119-133.

Seligman, Ruth: **The Year of the Aguna.** New York: **Women's American ORT Reporter**, Fall 1993, 14-17.

> Details efforts of ICAR (Int'l Coaltion for Agunot Rights) that marked 1993 as "Year of the Agunah" to find resolution of Jewish religious divorce issues for 16,000 Israeli women (Figure uncertain). Explains Jewish law (halacha) and provides anecdotal information about consequences to women who are unable to remarry, etc. USA organizations, G.E.T. in Brooklyn, and its services are listed.

Sella, Shelley: **Women Protest Israeli Occupation**. New York: **Lilith**, 21, Sept.1988, 32-33.

Semyonov, Moshe & Lerenthal, Tamar: **Country of Origin, Gender, and the Attainment of Socioeconomic Status: A Study of Stratification in the Jewish Population in Israel**. Greenwich CT: **Research in Social Stratification and Mobility**, 10, 1991, 325-343.

"To what extent social and ecological factors affect the socio-economic attainment of Israeli men and women. (And how these result in differences between men's and women's status). Cites earlier information.

Sered, Susan Starr: **The Liberation of Widowhood**. Boston, MA: **Journal of Cross Cultural Gerontology**, 2, April 1987, 139-150.

Sered, Susan: **Conflict, Complement and Control: Family and Religion among Middle Eastern Jewish Women in Jerusalem**. Newbury Park, CA: **Gender and Society**, 5, 1991, 10-29.

Shalvi, Alice: **Equality for Women in Today's Israel: Still an Ideal. Middle East Review**, 20, Summer 1988, 21-25.

Shalvi, Alice: **Varying Points of View**. Washington, D.C.: **Off Our Backs**, 22, Feb 1992.

Shaviv, Yehuda: **Women and War**. Zomet Institute, Gush Etzion, Israel: **Crossroads**, 2, 1988, 237-244.

Solomon, Alisa: **Building a Movement: Jewish Feminists Speak out on Israel**. Eugene, OR: **Bridges**, 1, Spring, 1990, 41-56.

Stahl, Abraham: **Beliefs of Jewish Oriental Mothers Regarding Children who are Mentally Retarded**. Reston, VA: **Education and Training in Mental Retardation**, 26, December 1991, 361-9.
"Beliefs of Israeli residents of Oriental (North African or Middle Eastern) origin regarding mentally retarded children...and interviews with 40 mothers."

Strum, Philippa: **Women and the Politics of Religion in Israel**. Human Rights Quarterly: **11**, Baltimore, MD, 1989, 483-503.

Svirsky, Gila: **Women in Black**. New York: **Present Tense**, 16, May/June 1989, 52-3.

Tal, Zohar & Dabad, Elisha: **The Teacher's Pet Phenomenon: Rate of Ocurrence, Correlates, and Psychological Costs**. Washington, D.C.: **Journal of Educational Psychology**, 82, December 1990, 637-45.

Studies in Israeli classes to ascertain whether female teachers were more likely to favor good students than male teachers.

Ungar, Carol Green: **The Politics of Population**. New York: **The Reporter: Women's American ORT**, Fall 1990, 12-13,29.

> Statistics on Jewish births in Israel vs. Arab births; predictions for the future, "out-numbering of Jews"; various political and policy inducements and alignments to push for larger Jewish families. Quotes from Yehuydit Shilat, "sloganeer for larger families, and the Israeli Association of Large Families." Also quotes some male heads of families on subject.

Women in Israel: Studies of Israeli Society. New Brunswick, NJ: **Transaction**, 6, 1993.

Yuval-Davis, Nira: **Women/Nation/State: The Demographic Race and National Reproduction in Israel**. Somerville, MA: **Radical America**, 21, Nov/Dec 1987, 37-59.

> "Looks at ways in which Jewish women and childbearing have been..constructed in the process..of Israeli Jewish collectivity development...its effects on the social and legal position of women in Israel."

VII
Other Countries

A. Books

Abrahamson, Glenda, ed.: **Blackwell Companion to Jewish Culture: From the Eighteenth Century to the Present**. Oxford: Basil Blackwell, 1989.

A source for information on and about Jewish women during the stated period.

Adelman, Howard: **The Educational and Religious Activities of Jewish Women in Italy: in: Aharon Oppenheimer et al, eds.: Shlomo Simonsohn Jubilee Volume**. Tel Aviv: Tel Aviv University Press, 1993, 9-23.

Appignanesi, Lisa & Forrester, John: **Freud's Women**. New York: Basic Books, 1993.

Women in Freud's life; his family, friends and patients; many who were Jewish, are examined in the context of early psychoanalysis.

Araten, Rachel Sarna: **Michalina: Daughter of Israel**. Jerusalem: Feldheim, 1986.

The biography of a Polish Jewish woman.

Arendt, Hannah/Jaspers, Karl: **Correspondence 1926-1969**. New York: Harcourt Brace Jovanovich, 1992.

Highly recommended correspondence between the historian Hannah Arendt and philosopher Karl Jaspers in which her Jewish identity is well articulated.

Baker, Adrienne: **The Jewish Woman in Contemporary Society: Transitions and Traditions**. New York: New York University Press, 1993.

Rethinking issues of sexuality and redefining sex roles through the perspective of women's experiences.

Blond, Elaine: **Marks of Distinction: The Memoirs of Elaine Blond**, London: Valentine, Mitchell, 1988.

Blond, a Jewish-British social worker in the 1920s, was a leader of the birth control movement in Manchester, England.

Brownstein, Rachel M.: **Tragic Muse: Rachel of the Comedie-Francaise**. New York, Knopf, 1993.

Burman, Rickie: **She Looketh Well to the Ways of Her Household: The Changing Role of Jewish Women in Religious Life, c.1880-1930**. in: **Malmgreen, Gail, ed.: Religion in the Lives of English Women, 1760-1930** Bloomington, IN: Indiana University Press, 1986, 234+.

"Remarkable shifts in the actual significance of Jewish women's domestic religious practices." This study of late 19th c. women in Manchester explores female religious practices as core rather than peripheral to Jewish identity.

Cohen, Judith R.: **Ya Salio de la Mar: Judeo-Spanish Wedding Songs among Moroccan Jews in Canada**. in: **Women and Music in Cross Cultural Perspective: Koskoff, Ellen, ed.** New York: Greenwood Press, 1987, 213-223.

Eyck, Frank: **A Diarist in Fin-de-siecle Berlin and her Family: Helene, Joseph and Erick Eyck**. in: **Leo Baeck Institute Yearbook: Vol.XXXVII** London: Secker & Warburg, 1992, 287-307.

Article about the diary of the author's grandmother. "A vivid picture of the life of an educated German-Jewish family..."

Friedlander, Judith: **The Anti-Semite and the Second Sex: A Cultural Reading of Sartre and Beauvoir**. in: **Women in Culture and Politics: A Century of Change.** Bloomington, IN: Indiana University Press, 1986, 81-96.

Generations of Memories: Voices of Jewish Women. London: Women's Press, 1989.

Gerber, Jane S.: **The Jews of Spain**. New York: Free Press, 1992.

Barely five pages concern women in this important book. See 166-168;183-4 and several interesting illustrations. Judge for yourself.

Hoffman, Charles: **Gray Dawn: The Jews of Eastern Europe in the Post-Communist Era**. New York: Aaron Asher/Harper Collins, 1992.

"Interviews with Jewish women and men reveal how Eastern European Jews have coped with a history of persecution and indoctrination, and are now discovering Judaism's heritage...."

Jordan, William Chester: **Women and Credit in Pre-Industrial and Developing Societies**. Philadelphia, PA: University of Pennsylvania Press, 1993.

Jewish women are included in this book about "women and their relation to credit in the period before industrialization." Often as widows, or as within networks of female society they enter the financial world in Europe becoming part of the economic fabric of their communities.

Kaplan, Marion: **The Making of the Jewish Middle Class: Women, Family and Identity in Imperial Germany**. New York: Oxford University Press, 1991.

Reappraisal of German-Jewish history in "light of women's experiences." Jewish women are viewed as minority women, yet within the Jewish and German bourgeoisie between 1861 and 1918.

Krasno, Rena: **Strangers Always: A Jewish Family in Wartime Shanghai:1937-1945**. Berkeley, CA: Pacific View Press, 1992.

Kuzmack, Linda Gordon: **Woman's Cause: The Jewish Woman's Movement in England and the United States, 1881-1933**. Columbus, OH: Ohio State University Press,1990.

Focuses on women whose feminist activities directly affected the Jewish community and the mainstream in both countries.

Levine-Melammed, Renee: **Some Death and Mourning Customs of Castillian Conversas: In: Aharon Mirsky, ed., Exile and Diaspora: Studies in the History of the Jewish People presented to Professor Haim Beinard**. Jerusalem: Ben-Zvi Institute, 1991, 157-67.

Lixl-Purcell, Andreas, ed.: **Women of Exile: German-Jewish Autobiographies since 1933**. New York: Greenwood Press, 1988.

"Emigre history" from the female point of view. Womens' personal experiences and political beliefs recorded in order to leave written evidence for future generations.

Neiman, Susan: **Slow Fire: Jewish Notes from Berlin**. New York: Schocken Books, 1992.

Neiman's impressions of living in Berlin in the 1980's as a Jewish woman, an outsider and observer of the present time, notes residues of the Holocaust.

Nudel, Ida: **A Hand in the Darkness: The Autobiography of a Refusnik**. New York: Warner Books, 1990.

Rachlin, Rachel & Israel Rachlin with de Weille, Birgitte M., tr.: **Sixteen Years in Siberia: Memoirs of Rachel and Israel Rachlin**. Tuscaloosa, AL: University of Alabama Press, 1988.

A Jewish family's exile from Lithuania told in a first-person account about life in a remote area. Highlights emotions of displacement and solidarity.

Saghal, Gita: **Jewish Fundamentalism and Women's Empowerment** (British Orthodox Jewish women), see Author index or Religion section.

Sebag-Montefiore, Ruth: **A Family Patchwork: Five Generations of an Anglo-Jewish Family**. London: Weidenfeld and Nicolson, 1987.

The history of an upper middle-class family during the 20's and 30s, told by the daughter of a well known Anglo-Jewish family.

Shelomay, Kay Kaufman: **Music, Ritual, and Falasha History**. East Lansing, MI: African Studies Center, Michigan State University, 1986.

Althought this fascinating book does not focus on women: several pages do have interesting items on women in monastic orders, women at weddings, and in other rituals (see 72-3,85-6,88-9 and 98).

Simon, Rachel: **Change Within Tradition Among Jewish Women in Libya**. Seattle, WA: University of Washington Press, 1992.

"Changes influencing Jewish women in Libya in the mid 19th century ...these include changes in status in family life, work, education and participation in public life."

Suhl, Yuri: **Ernestine L. Rose: Women's Rights Pioneer**. New York: Biblio Press, 1990 (rept.).

Updated edition of the 1959 biography of this important Jewish woman social reformer/suffragist in the international arena, born in Poland, died in England.

Suzman, Helen: **In No Uncertain Terms: Memoirs**. London: Sinclair-Stevenson, 1993.

Autobiography of this remarkable woman, her background and upbringing as well as participation in South Africa's government. (review: Jewish Quarterly, vol 40, Spring 1994 pp.34-5)

B. Articles

Abramowitz, Yosef I.: **Where are the Women?** Jerusalem: **Israel Scene**, 10, January 1989, 24.

Jewish women's status in Britain, the empowerment of women of other faiths and in other countries, with focus on students.

Adelman, Howard: **Rabbis and Reality: Public activities of Jewish women in Italy during the Renaissance and Catholic Restoration**. Haifa: **Jewish History**, 5, Spring 1991, 27-40.

Compares the public and personal/business lives of Jewish women during the Renaissance.

Adelman, Penina V.: **Out of Africa: A Jewish Woman's Modern Day Exodus**. New York **Lilith**, 18, Spring 1993, 6-11,26.

> Moving account of an Ethiopian Jewish woman's exodus from Ethiopia, through the Sudan and Germany, and finally, to Beersheva in Israel.

Agosin, Marjorie: **I am a Woman, a Jew, a Chilean**. New York: **Lilith**, 15, Summer 1990, 12-15.

Agron, Laurence: **A Landmark Gathering**. New York: **Midstream**, XXXV, May 1989, 26-32.

Alexander, Tamar & Hasan-Rokem, Galit: **Games of Identity in Proverb Usage: Proverbs of a Sephardic-Jewish Woman**. Bern, NY: **Proverbium**, 5, 1988, 1-14.

Another First: Jewish Women Gather in Kiev. New York: **Lilith**, 18, Fall 1993, 5.

Bahloul, Joelle: **Female Emancipation and Marriage Strategies: North African Jewish Women in France**. Oberlin, OH: **Jewish Folklore and Ethnology Review**, 12, 1990, 23+.

Berkovic, Sally: **London: Jewish Women's Aid**. New York: **Lilith**, 18, Fall 1993, 4-5.

Berkovits, Berel: **Divorce and Gittin in the 1990s** (English divorce laws compared with Jewish laws) see Author index or Religion sections..

Breger, Jennifer: **Role of Jewish Women in Hebrew Printing. AB Bookman's Weekly**, 91, March 29, 1993, 1320-1329.

> Original and well researched article on Jewish women who published important Judaic works, either as the wives or widows of printers, or often, in their own right.

Cohen, Judith R.: **Judeo-Spanish Songs in Montreal and Toronto**. Oberlin, OH: **Jewish Folklore and Ethnology Review**. 12, 1990, 26+.

Cutting-Gray, Joanne: **Hannah Arendt, Feminism and the Politics of Alterity: What Will We Love If We Win?**. Bloomington, In: **Hypatia**, 8, Winter 1993, 35-54.

> "Arendt's perspective on female otherness and Jewishness in the light of her own personal interest in Rahel Varnhagen, a German Jewish woman."

European Judaism, special issue devoted to Jewish, Christian and Muslim women, see Subject in index.

Gilman, Sander L.: **Salome, Syphilis, Sarah Bernhardt and the "Modern Jewess."** Cherry Hill, NJ: **The German Quarterly**, 66, Spring 1993, 195-211.

Ginsberg, Alice: **A Feminist Confronts her Identity in Germany**. New York: **Lilith**, 21, Sept. 1988, 29-30.

Hareven, Gail: **From Russia with Luggage: Absorbing the Exodus**. Oakland, CA: **Tikkun**, 6, March/April 1991, 39-42;90-2.

From point of view of a Russian-Jewish woman, the apparent pressure that Russian Jews feel to emigrate to Israel.

Haas, Peter J.: **Women in Judaism: Re-examining an Historical Paradigm**. West Lafayette, IN: **Shofar**, 10, Winter 1992, 35-52.

Power relations in patriarchal societies which seems to be ignored in traditional literature.

Hendel, Yehudit: **Near Quiet Places: Twelve Days in Poland**. New York: **Lilith**, 15, Spring 1990, 16-21.

Hertz, Deborah: **Why Jewish women Rebelled In Old Regime Berlin**. Oakland, CA: **Tikkun**, 3, July/August 1988, 33-35.

Dorothea Mendelssohn, Rahel Levin Varnhagen, Henriette Herz, Amalie Beer, Sara and Marianne Meyer, Sara Levy and Rebecca Friedlaender, all wealthy Jewish women rebelled against the traditional German-Jewish life in different ways.

Isaac, Jeffrey C.: **At the Margins: Jewish Identity and Politics in the Thought of Hannah Arendt**. Oakland, CA: **Tikkun**, 5, Jan/Feb 1990, 23-26,86-92.

Jewish Women: Special issue. Johannesburg: **Jewish Affairs**, 48, Winter 1993.

Lackow, Manya Prozanskaya: **In the Russian Gymnasia**. New York: **Lilith**, 15, Winter 1990, 15-20.

Lieberman, Rhonda: **Glamorous Jewesses**. New York: **Artforum**, 31, Jan 1993, 5-6.

Women depicted in art.

Marr, Lucille: **If You Want Peace, Prepare for Peace: Hanna Newcombe, Peace Researcher and Peace Activist**. Ontario History: **Willowdale, Ontario**, 84, 1992, 263-281.

Nahai, Gina Barkhordar: **A Wedding in Persia: Ceremonies of Innocence and Experience**. New York: **Lilith**, 16, Summer 1991, 14-17.

Norwich, Rose: **Jewish Women in Early Johannesburg**. Johannesburg: **Jewish Affairs**, 48, Winter 1993, 89-99, 152.

Ockman, Carol: **Two Large Eyebrows a l'Orientale: Ethnic Sterotyping in Ingre's Baronne de Rothschild**. London/Boston: **Art History**, 14, Dec 1991, 521-539.

Rapoport, Natalya: **The Doctors' Plot of 1953: A Daughter Remembers**. New York: **Lilith**, 17, Winter 1992, 20-24.

> Rapoport, a scientist "describes her ordeal as a 14 year old who is the daughter of the only survivor of the notorious (Stalinist) 'doctor's plot'."

Sabar, Shalom: **Bride, Heroine and Courtesan: Images of the Jewish Woman in Hebrew Manuscripts of the Renaissance in Italy**. Jerusalem: **World Congress of Jewish Studies**, 10, 1990, 63-70.

Sacks, Maurie: **Problems in the Study of Jewish Women's Folk Culture**. Waltham, MA: **Contemporary Jewry**, 10, 1989, 95-104.

Samuels, Gayle: **A Tale of Two Women**. New York: **Women's American ORT Reporter**, Summer 1992, 6+.

> Comparison of two Russian women emigres, one of 1913, the other in the wave of 1880-1920; the latter grandmother of the writer, both immigrants seemingly driven here via antisemitisim.

Schlesinger, Benjamin: **Jewish Mother-Headed One-Parent Families: Impressions From a Canadian Study**. New York: **Journal of Psychology and Judaism**, 14, 1990, 169-188.

Shorter, Edward: **Women and Jews in a Private Nervous Clinic in Late Nineteenth-Century Vienna**. London: **Medical History**, 1989, 149-183.

> Interactions between culture and biology: Study of types of nervous problems in Jewish women and their treatment at a Viennese clinic.

Taitz, Emily: **Kol Ishah - The Voice of Woman: Was it Heard in Medieval Europe**? New York: **Conservative Judaism**, 38, Spring 1986, 46-57.

> It is known that women sang in public during the Middle Ages. Jewish women were barred from singing and dancing in public as opposed to the same at home, at weddings or as mourners.

Weiss-Rosmarin, Trude: **Sigmund Freud's "Infamous Exasperated Question"**. Santa Monica, CA: **Jewish Spectator**, 53, Sept.1988, 6-7.

Wenger, Beth S.: **Radical Politics in a Reactionary Age: The Unmaking of Rosika Schwimmer, 1914-1930**. Bloomington, IN: **Journal of Women's History**, 2, 1990, 66-99.

Wernick, Laura & Wice, Leila: **Twelfth International Conference of Gay and Lesbian Jews**: Eugene, OR: **Bridges**, 2, Fall 1991, 129-30.

Zellin, Agnes: **I'm Polish Too**. Eugene, OR: **Bridges**, 2, Spring 1991, 40-7.

> Polish Jewish women who are also lesbians.

Zolty, Shoshana Pantel: **Beyond the Veil**. New York: **Jewish Action**, Winter 1993-4, 14-18.

> Historical overview of outstanding Jewish women: scholars, teachers, copyists and publishers/printers in Kurdistan. Special mention of Asenat.

VIII
Literature 1986-93

A. Books—Fiction

Appelfeld, Aharon: **Katerina**. New York: Random House, 1992.

Asher, Carol: **The Flood**. Freedom, CA: Crossing, 1987.

Barkhordar, Gina: **Cry of the Peacock**. New York: Crown, 1991.

Bayer-Berenbaum, Linda: **The Blessing and the Curse**. Philadelphia, PA: JPS, 1988.

Birnhak, Alice: **Next Year, God Willing**. New York: Shengold Publishers, 1992.

Birstein, Ann: **The Last of the True Believers**. New York: Norton, 1988.

Bogen, Nancy: **Bobe Mayse**: **A Tale of Washington Square**. New York: Twickenham Press, 1993.

Brown, Rosellen: **Before and After.** New York: Farrar Straus & Giroux, 1992.

Buck, Pearl S.: **Peony**. New York: Bloch/Biblio, 1990 (Rept.).

Chernin, Kim: **The Flame Bearers**. New York: Perennial Library, 1987.

Dworkin, Andrea: **Mercy**: **A Novel**. New York: Four Walls Eight Windows, 1991.

Dworkin, Andrea: **Ice and Fire**: **A Novel**. New York: Weidenfeld & Nicolson, 1987.

Dworkin, Susan: **Stolen Goods**. New York: Newmarket, 1988.

Edelson, Majorie: **Malkeh and Her Children**. New York: Ballantine Books, 1992.

Feinberg, Leslie: **Stone Butch Blues**. Ithaca, NY: Firebrand, 1993.

Fink, Ida Weschler with Joanna & Francine Prose, trs.: **The Journey**. New York: Farrar, Straus & Giroux, 1992.

Finkelstein, Barbara: **Summer Long-a-coming**. New York: Harper, 1987.

Gerber, Merrill Joan: **Kingdom of Brooklyn**. Atlanta, GA: Longstreet, 1992.

Gerber, Merrill Joan: **King of the World: A Novel**. Wainscott NY: Pushcart Press, 1989.

Goldreich, Gloria: **Mothers**. New York: Bantam Books, 1992.

Goldstein, Rebecca: **The Dark Sister**. New York: Viking, 1991.

Goldstein, Rebecca: **Late-Summer Passion of a Woman of Mind**. New York: Farrar, Straus & Giroux, 1989.

Gordimer, Nadine: **A Sport of Nature**. London: Jonathan Cape, 1987.

Gruber, Ruth: **Raquela, A Woman of Israel.** New York: Biblio Press/Hadassah, 1993 (rept.).

Gur, Batya: **The Saturday Morning Murder**. New York: Harper Collins, 1992.

Hareven, Shulamith with Halkin, Hillel, translator: **City of Many Days**. San Francisco, CA: Mercury House, 1993.

Hareven, Shulamith with Halkin, Hillel, tr.: **The Miracle Hater**. San Francisco, CA: North Point Press, 1988.

Hareven, Shulamith: **The Prophet: A Novel**. San Francisco: North Point Press, 1990.

Horowitz, Eve: **Plain Jane**. New York: Random House, 1992.

Isaacs, Susan: **After All These Years**. New York: Harper Collins, 1993.

Isaacs, Susan: **Shining Through**. New York: Harper, 1988.

Katz-Loewenstein, Judith: **Running Fiercely Toward a High Thin Sound**. Ithaca, NY: Firebrand, 1992.

Kellerman, Faye: **Day of Atonement**. New York: Morrow, 1991.

Kellerman, Faye: **Grievous Sin**. New York: Morrow, 1993.

Kellerman, Faye: **Milk and Honey**. New York: Ballantine, 1991.

Kellerman, Faye: **The Quality of Mercy**. New York: Morrow, 1989.

Kellerman, Faye: **The Ritual Bath**. New York: Ballantine, 1987.

Kellerman, Faye: **Sacred and Profane**. New York: Arbor, 1987.

Konecky, Edith: **Allegra Maud Goldman**. Philadelphia: Jewish Publication Society, 1987.

Konecky, Edith: **A Place at the Table**. New York: Random House, 1989.

Kornblatt, Joyce Reiser: **Breaking Bread**. New York: Dutton, 1987.

Krich, Rochelle Majer: **Til Death Do Us Part**. New York: Avon, 1992.

Kupfer, Fern: **Surviving the Seasons**. New York: Laurel, 1989.

Lentin, Ronit: **Night Train to Mother**. Pittsburgh, PA: Cleis Press, 1989.

Lerman, Rhoda: **God's Ear**. New York: Henry Holt, 1989.

Lesser, Ellen: **The Other Woman**. New York: Washington Square, 1989.

Levin, Jenifer: **The Sea of Light**. New York: Dutton, 1993.

Levin, Jenifer: **Shimoni's Lover**. San Diego, CA: Harcourt, Brace, Jovanovich, 1987.

Levine, Faye: **Solomon and Sheba**. New York: St. Martin's, 1986.

Levy, Amy with New, Melvin, ed.: **The Complete Novels & Selected Writings of Amy Levy: 1861-1889**. Gainesville, FL: University Press of Florida, 1993.

> A late Victorian, assimilated Anglo-Jewish writer resurrected (wrote 3 novels and short stories, essays and poetry). See review by Linda Hunt: Women's Review of Books, May 1993, p.28.

Lipman, Elinor: **Then She Found Me**. New York: Washington Square, 1991.

Lipman, Elinor: **The Way Men Act**. New York: Bantam, 1993.

Malkiel, Theresa Serber: **The Diary of a Shirtwaist Striker**. Ithaca, NY: ILR Press, 1990.

Minco, Marga with Clegg, Margarett, tr.: **An Empty House**. Chester Springs, PA: Dufour Editions, 1991.

Minco, Marga with Ringold, Jeanette Kalker, tr.: **The Fall**. Chester Springs, PA: Dufour Editions, 1990.

Mosco, Maisie: **Out of the Ashes**. New York: Harper, 1989.

Moszkiewiez, Helene: **Inside the Gestapo: A Jewish Woman's Secret War**. New York: Dell, 1987 (rept.).

Nachman, Elana/Dykewomon: **Riverfinger Women**. Tallahassee, FL: Naiad Press, 1992 (rept.)

Nason, Tema: **Ethel, A Fictionary Autobiography: A Novel of Ethel Rosenberg**. New York: Delacorte Press, 1991.

Newman, Leslea: **In Every Laugh a Tear**. Norwich VT: New Victoria Publishers, 1992.

Norman, Hilary: **Chateau Ella.** New York: Delacorte, 1988.

Fiction about Hungarian-Jews in New York.

Oz, Amos: **To Know a Woman**. London: Vintage, 1992.

Ozick, Cynthia: **The Messiah of Stockholm**. New York: Knopf, 1987.

Ozick, Cynthia: **The Shawl**. New York: Alfred A. Knopf, 1989.

Piercy, Marge: **Gone to Soldiers**. New York: Summit Books, 1987.

Piercy, Marge: **He, She and It**. New York: Alfred A. Knopf, 1991.

Piercy, Marge: **Summer People**. New York: Summit Books, 1989.

Piesman, Marissa: **Unorthodox Practices**. New York: Pocket, 1989.

Plain, Belva: **Blessings**. New York: Delacorte Press, 1989.

Plain, Belva: **Golden Cup**. New York: Delacorte, 1993.

Probst Solomon, Barbara: **Smart Hearts in the City**. New York: Harcourt Brace Jovanovich, 1992.

Prose, Francine: **Judah the Pious**. Boston: G.K.Hall, 1986.

Ragen, Naomi: **Jephte's Daughter**. New York: Warner Books, 1990.

Raskin, Barbara: **Hot Flashes**. New York: St. Martin's, 1988.

Ratner, Rochelle: **The Lion's Share**. 27 N.4th St, Minneapolis, MN: Coffee House Press, 1992.

Reich, Tova: **Master of the Return**. New York: Harcourt, 1988.

Roiphe, Anne: **Lovingkindness**. New York: Summit Books, 1987.

Rosen, Norma: **John and Anzia: An American Romance**. New York: Dutton, 1989.

Schwartz, Lynne Sharon: **Leaving Brooklyn**. Boston: Houghton Mifflin, 1989.

Shankman, Sarah: **Let's Talk of Graves**. New York: Pocket, 1990.

Shulman, Alix Kates: **In Every Woman's Life**. New York: Ballantine, 1988.

Silva, Linda Kay: **Tory's Tuesday**. San Diego, CA: Paradigm Publishing Co, 1992.

Sinclair, Jo: **Anna Teller**. New York: Feminist Press, 1992.

Singer, Brett: **Footstool in Heaven**. New York: Donald Fine, 1986.

Stevens, Serita & Moore, Rayanne: **Bagels and Tea**. New York: St. Martins Press, 1993.

Storey, Alice: **First Kill All the Lawyers**. New York: Pocket, 1988.

Storey, Alice: **Then Hang All the Liars**. New York: Pocket, 1989.

Sunshine, Linda: **The Memoirs of Bambi Goldbloom: Or, Growing Up in New Jersey**. New York: Simon, 1987.

Szeman, Sherri: **The Kommandant's Mistress**. New York: Harper Collins, 1993.

Tax, Meredith: **Rivington Street**. New York: Avon, 1990.

Wagman, Frederica: **Peach**. New York: Soho Press, 1992.

Wasserstein, Wendy: **Bachelor Girls**. New York: Knopf, 1990.

Weil, Grete: **The Bride Price**. Boston: David R. Godine, 1991.

Wolitzer, Meg: **This is Your Life**. London: Sceptre, 1990.

B. Books—Poetry

Adler, Frances Payne: **Raising the Tents**. Corvallis, OR: Calyx Books, 1993.

Alkalay-Gut, Karen. **Mechitza.** Merrick, N.Y.: Cross-Cultural Communications, 1989.

American Jewish Poets Experience Israel. Los Angeles, CA: Shirim, XII, December 1993, 36 pages.

A good sampling of Jewish women poets: Rich, Ostriker, Schulman, Klepfisz, Falk, Starkman, Hellerstein, Sklarew, Pastan; with biographical notes.

Dame, Enid: **Anything You Can't See**. Albuquerque, NM: West End Press, 1992.

Dizhur, Bella & Bliumis, Sarah W., tr.: **Shadow of a Soul**: **Collected Poems**. Mt. Kisco, N.Y.: Moyer Bell Ltd., 1990.

Poems that speak of Jewishness and humanity, of pain and heroism, especially of Janusz Korczak who perished with 200 orphans at Treblinka.

Fainlight, Ruth: **Sibyls**: **A Book of Poems**. Northampton, MA: Gehenna Press, 1991.

Fainlight, Elaine: **This Time of Year**: **A Collection of Poems**. London: Sinclair-Stevenson, 1993.

Feinstein, Elaine: **City Music**. London: Hutchinson, 1990.

Feinstein, Elaine: **P.E.N.**: **New Poetry II**. New York: Quartet, 1988.

Feldman, Ruth: **Birthmarks.** Merrick, N.Y.: Cross-Cultural Communications, 1993.

Gluck, Louise: **Wild Iris**. Hopewell, NJ: Ecco Press, 1993.

Goldberg, Leah Sivan & Miriam Billig, tr.: **On the Blossoming**. New York: Garland, 1992.

Granirer, Pnina: **The Trials of Eve**. Vancouver, BC: Gala Press, 1993.

Herman, Grace: **Set Against Darkness**. New York: Jewish Women's Resource Center, 1992.

Holender, Barbara D.: **Ladies of Genesis**: **Poems**. New York: Jewish Women's Resource Center, 1991.

Kaufman, Shirley: **Rivers of Salt**. Port Townsend, WA: Copper Canyon Press, 1993.

Klepfisz, Irena with introduction by Adrienne Rich: **A Few Words in the Mother Tongue**: **Poems Selected and New (1971-1990)**. Portland, OR: Eighth Mountain Press, 1990.

Kumin, Maxine: **Looking for Luck**: **Poems**. New York: W.W.Norton, 1993.

Mandel, Charlotte: **The Marriages of Jacob**: **A Poem-Novella**. Marblehead, MA: Micah Publications, 1991.

Literature

Metzger, Deena: **A Sabbath Among the Ruins**. P.O. Box 7355, Berkeley, CA: Parallax Press, 1992.

Newman, Leslea: **Sweet Dark Places**. Santa Cruz, CA: Her Books, 1991.

Newman, Leslea: **Love Me Like You Mean It**: **Poems**. San Diego, CA: Clothespin Fever Press, 1993.

Newman, Leslea, ed.: **Bubbe Meisehs by Shayneh Maidelehs**: **An Anthology of Poetry by Jewish Granddaughters about our Grandmothers**. Santa Cruz, CA: Her Books, 1989.

Nordhaus, Jean: **Quarterly Review of Literature**: **Poetry Series X**. Princeton, NJ: QRL, 1991.

> Includes poetry by Jean Nordhaus together with other poets.

Paley, Grace: **Long Walks and Intimate Talks**. New York: Feminist Press, 1991.

Pastan, Linda: **Heroes in Disguise**: **Poems**. New York: W.W. Norton, 1991.

Pastan, Linda: **The Imperfect Paradise**: **Poems**. New York: W.W.Norton, 1988.

Pastan, Linda: **Mother Eve**. Dallas: Northouse and Northouse, 1988.

Piercy, Marge: **The Earth Shines Secretly**: **Book of Days**. Cambridge, MA: Zoland Books, 1990.

Piercy, Marge: **Mars and Her Children**. New York: Alfred A. Knopf, 1992.

Piercy, Marge: **Sisters of the Earth**. New York: Vintage, 1991.

Ratner, Rochelle: **Someday Songs**: **Poems Toward a Personal History**. Athens, GA: University of Georgia Press, 1992.

Ravikovitch, Dahlia & Zelda: **Three Israeli Poets**. **IX** Los Angeles, CA: Shirim, December 1990, n. p.

> The three poets sampled here include Dahlia Ravikovitch, Zelda and Tuvya Ruebner, male.

Raz, Hilda: **The Bone Dish**. Brockport, NY: State Street Press, 1989.

Raz, Hilda: **What is Good**. Winnetka, IL: Thorntree Press, 1988.

Rubin, Gertrude: **Passover Poems.** Evanston, IL: Evanston Publishers, 1991.

Saxton, Marsha & Howe, Florence, eds.: **With Wings: An Anthology of Literature by and about Women with Disabilities**. New York: Feminist Press, 1991.

> Poems and short pieces on and about women with disabilities "or who have a physical difference", including Muriel Rukeyser and Adrienne Rich.

Scheindlen, Raymond P.: **Wine, Women and Death: Medieval Hebrew Poems on the Good Life.** Philadelphia, PA: JPS, 1986.

Simon, Maurya: **Days of Awe.** Pt. Townsend, WA: Copper-Canyon Press, 1989.

Sklarew, Myra: **Altamira**. Washington, DC: Washington Writer's Publishing House, 1987.

Spiegel, Marcia Cohn: **Words and Spirit: Poems and Prayers of Jewish Women**. IX Los Angeles, CA: Shirim, March 1990, 21 pages.

> A selection from Spiegel's "Women Speak to God" poems by Jewish women, with an introduction by her explaining the impetus for this genre.

Starkman, Elaine Marcus & Schweitzer, Leah, Eds.: **Without a Single Answer: Poems on Contemporary Israel.** Berkeley, CA: Judah L. Magnes Museum, 1990.

> Collection of poems which give equal representation to women poets.

Tussman, Malka Heifetz with Falk, Marcia, tr./ed.: **With Teeth in the Earth: Selected Poems**. Detroit, Michigan: Wayne State University Press, 1992.

The Poetry of 3 Generations of Israeli Women. Los Angeles, CA: Shirim, Summer 1993.

> The entire issue of this Jewish poetry journal is devoted to Rachel Bloustein, Zelda Shneurson Mishkowsky and Yona Wallach, by various translators. Books by each, in Yiddish and Hebrew are listed.

Wenkart, Henny: **Sarah's Daughters Sing: A Sampler of Poems by Jewish Women**. Hoboken, N.J.: KTAV, 1990.

> Selection of poems on biblical women, Yiddishkeit, women's life cycles, etc.

Whitman, Ruth: **Hatshepsut, Speak to Me**. Detroit: Wayne State University Press, 1992.

Whitman, Ruth: **Laughing Gas: Poems, New and Selected**. Detroit: Wayne State University Press, 1990.

Zisquit, Linda: **Ritual Bath**. Seattle, WA: Broken Moon Press, 1993.

C. Books—Short Stories

Antler, Joyce, ed.: **America and I**: **Short stories by American Jewish Women Writers**. Boston, MA: Beacon Press, 1990.

Dische, Irene: **The Jewess**: **Stories from Berlin and New York**. London: Bloomsbury, 1992.

Felman, Jyl Lynn: **Hot Chicken Wings**. San Francisco: Aunt Lute Books, 1992.

Fink, Ida Levine, Madeline & Francine Prose, trs.: **A Scrap of Time and other Stories**. New York: Random House, 1987.

Gold, Doris B. & Lisa Stein, compilers: **From the Wise Women of Israel**: **Folklore and Memoirs, Introduction by Livia Bitton-Jackson**. New York: Biblio Press, 1993.

A collection of old and modern tales showing Jewish women's ingenuity, resourcefulness and down-right *chutspeh!*

Goldstein, Rebecca: **Strange Attractors**. NY: Viking, 1993.

Goodman, Allegra: **Total Immersion**. New York: Harper & Row, 1989.

Hareven, Shulamith: **Twilight and Other Stories**. San Francisco: Mercury House, 1992.

Holoch, Naomi & Nestle, Joan: **Women on Women**: **An Anthology of American Lesbian Short Fiction**. New York: Plume, 1993.

Short stories of women with different ethnic backgrounds.

Kantrowitz, Melanie Kaye: **My Jewish Face & Other Stories**. San Francisco, CA: Spinsters/Aunt Lute Book Co., P.O. Box 410687, 1990.

Katzir, Yehudit: **Closing the Sea**. New York: Harcourt Brace Jovanovich, 1992.

Loewenstein, Andrea Freud: **The Worry Girl**. Ithaca, NY: Firebrand, 1992.

Moskowitz, Faye: **And the Bridge is Love**: **Life Stories**. Boston: Beacon Press, 1991.

Newman, Leslea: **Letter to Harvey Milk**. Ithaca, N.Y.: Firebrand Books, 1988.

Newman, Leslea: **Secrets**: **Short Stories**. Norwich, VT: New Victoria Publishers, 1990.

Niederman, Sharon, ed.: **Shaking Eve's Tree: Short Stories of Jewish Women**. Philadelphia, PA: Jewish Publication Society, 1990.

Paley, Grace: **Long Walks and Intimate Talks**. New York: Feminist Press, 1991.

Rothchild, Sylvia: **Family Stories for Every Generation**. Detroit, MI: Wayne State University Press, 1989.

Sherman, Josepha: **A Sampler of Jewish American Folklore. American Folklore Series**. Little Rock, AR: August House, 1992.

Solataroff, Ted & Nessa Rapoport, eds: **Writing Our Way Home: Contemporary Stories by American Jewish Writers**. New York: Schocken Books, 1992.

Sturgis, Susanna J., Ed.: **Tales of Magic Realism: By Women**. Freedom, CA: Crossing Press, 1991.

> Included in a collection of stories from different cultures are several by Jewish women

Weinbaum, Batya: **The Island of Floating Women**. San Diego, CA: Clothespin Fever Press, 1993.

Yezierska, Anzia: **How I Found America: Collected Stories of Anzia Yezierska**. New York: Persea Books, 1991.

Zahava, Irene, ed.: **My Mother's Daughter: Stories by Women**. Freedom, CA: Crossing Press, 1991.

> Includes several stories by Jewish women authors.

D. Books—Fiction Collections

Aglietti, Susan L. ed.: **Filtered Images: Women Remembering their Grandmothers**. Orinda, CA: Vintage'45 Press, 1992,

Kaye/Kantrowitz, Melanie, ed.: **Tribe of Dina: A Jewish Women's Anthology**. Boston: Beacon Press, 1989.

> New edition of this important collection of poems, essays, stories, etc.

Micah Publications: **The Global Anthology of Jewish Women Writers.** Marblehead, MA: Micah Publications, 1993.

> "This anthology explores what the modern world has made of the Jewish woman and what the Jewish woman has made of modernity...from ghetto to world traveler, revolutionary to housewife."

Saxton, Marsha & Howe, Florence, eds.: **With Wings: An Anthology of Literature by and about Women with Disabilities**. see Author index.

Schwertfeger, Ruth: **Else Lasker-Schuler: Inside This Deathly Solitude**. New York: Berg/St. Martin's Press, 1991.

E. Books—Criticism

Adler, Carol: **Jewish Poetry's Quantum Leap: The Illusion of Holiness in: Jewish Book Annual. 49** New York: Jewish Book Council, 1991-92, ,121-131.

>A woman reviewer summarizes Jewish content in six modern American Jewish poets' work and includes only one woman, Louise Gluck.

Arcana, Judith: **Grace Paley's Life Stories: A Literary Biography**. Champaign, IL: University of Illinois Press, 1993.

Burstein, Janet Handler: **In the Twilight of Tradition: Trying the Myths in Jewish-American Short Stories. in: Yivo Annual: Volume 19** Evanston, IL: Northwestern University Press, 1990, 107-117.

>Discussion of Tillie Olsen's short story "Tell me a Riddle" (part of chapter).

Criswell, Jeanne Sallade: **Cynthia Ozick and Grace Paley: Diverse Visions in Jewish and Women's Literature. in: Since Flannery O'Connor: Essays on the Contemporary American Short Story. Logsdon, Loren & Charles W. Mayer, eds.** Macon, IL: Western Illinois University, 1987, 93-100.

Cronin, Gail, Hall, Blaine H. & Lamb Connie: **Jewish American Fiction Writers: An Annotated Bibliography**. New York: Garland, 1991.

>Includes: E.M.Broner, Edna Ferber, Fannie Hurst, Erica Jong, Tillie Olsen, Cynthia Ozick, Grace Paley, Susan Fromberg Schaeffer, Alix Kates Shulman, Tess Slesinger, Susan Sontag and Anzia Yezierska.

Dearborn, Mary V.: **Pocahontas's Daughters: Gender and Ethnicity in American Culture**. New York: Oxford University Press, 1986, See Introduction, Chapters 2,4,5,7 and Afterword.

>Important analysis of Mary Antin, Yezierska and Gertrude Stein; and other Jewish women writers in context of "ways in which gender and ethnicity function in American culture."

Fishman, Sylvia Barack: **American-Jewish Fiction Turns Inward, 1960-1990**: 91 New York, American Jewish Committee: American Jewish Year Book, 1991, 46-7;57-67.

This overview of modern fiction has but two brief paragraphs on feminism and a substantial comment on Cynthia Ozick, 2+ pages on Rebecca Goldstein. (See Fishman's <u>Breath of Life</u> for more complete survey).

Fishman, Sylvia Barack, ed.: **Follow My Footprints**: **Changing Images of Women in American Jewish Fiction**. Waltham, MA: Brandeis Universitry Press, 1992.

Fried, Lewis, Chief ed., Brown, Gene; Chametzky, Jules & Harap Louis, Advisory Eds.: **Handbook of American-Jewish Literature**: **An Analytical Guide to Topics, Themes, and Sources**. New York: Greenwood Press, 1988.

Includes many women writers: especially A Question of Tradition: Women poets in Yiddish by Kathryn Hellerstein, pp.195-237; Bilik on Fiction of the Holocaust, pp.415-440; and p. 104 on the Deborah Project: Jewish women playwrights.

Fuchs, Esther: **Israeli Mythogonies**: **Women in Contemporary Hebrew Fiction**. Albany, NY: State University of New York Press, 1987.

"Perspectives and protest concerning the treatment of the female character in Hebrew fiction."

Hadda, Janet: **Passionate Women, Passive Men**: **Suicide in Yiddish literature**. Albany, NY: State University of New York Press, 1988.

Henriksen, Louise Levitas & Boydston, Jo Ann: **Anzia Yezierska**: **A Writer's Life**. New Brunswick, NJ: Rutgers University Press, 1988.

Kamel, Rose Yalow: **Aggravating the Conscience**: **Jewish-American Literary Mothers in the Promised Land**. New York: Lang, 1988.

Kamel addresses the dearth of critical materials [in 1988] on Jewish-American literary writers. Book includes "Maimie Pinzer", Yezierska, Tillie Olsen, Grace Paley and E.M. Broner.

Kielsky, Vera Emuna: **Inevitable Exiles**: **Cynthia Ozick's View of the Precariousness of Jewish Existence in a Gentile Society**. New York: Lang, 1989.

Lerner, Anne Lapidus; Sokoloff, Naomi & Norich, Anita, eds.: **Gender and Text in Modern Hebrew and Yiddish Literature**. New York: Jewish Theological Seminary, 1992.

Lichtenstein, Diane in Warren, Joyce W.: **The (Other) American Traditions: Nineteenth-Century Women Writers**. New Brunswick, NJ: Rutgers University Press, 1993.

"By adopting a principle of inclusivity" Lichtenstein discusses 19th century American Jewish women writers as "whole and legitimate subjects" rather than as lesser authors or subjects for critical analysis. See also: **Lichtenstein: Writing Their Nations.**

Lichtenstein, Diane: **Writing Their Nations: The Tradition of Nineteenth-Century American Jewish Women Writers**. Bloomington, IN: Indiana University Press, 1992.

Women writers such as Emma Lazarus found both their American and Jewish voices as writers, thus "celebrating" both identities.

Lowin, Joseph: **Cynthia Ozick**. Boston: Twayne, 1988.

Nevin, Thomas R: **Simone Weil: A Portrait of a Self-Exiled Jew**. Chapel Hill, NC: University of North Carolina, 1991.

Ozick, Cynthia: **Metaphor and Memory**: New York: Vintage, 1989.

Pacernick, Gary (Layle Silbert Photos): **Sing a New Song: American Jewish Poetry Since the Holocaust**. Cincinnati, OH, American Jewish Archives, 1991.

A very good overview which includes, among other male Jewish poets, critiques on Irena Klepfisz, Adrienne Rich, Marge Piercy, Denise Levertov, Muriel Rukeyser, Linda Pastan and Maxine Kumin.

Pinsker, Sanford: **Jewish American Fiction: 1917 - 1987**. New York: Twayne Publishers, 1992.

This survey of American-Jewish fiction highlights only Ozick and Tova Reich. "New Directions" is a chapter about Ozick, but mentions other women writers.

Pinsker, Sanford: **The Uncompromising Fictions of Cynthia Ozick**. Columbia, MO: University of Missouri Press, 1987.

Rosen, Norma: **Accidents of Influence: Writing as a Woman and a Jew in America. SUNY Series in modern Jewish literature and culture.** Saratoga Springs, NY: State University of New York Press, 1992.

Schulman, Sarah: **Empathy: Lesbian and Jewish Identity Issues**. New York: Dutton, 1992.

Seligman, Dee: **Jewish Mothers' Stories: Rosellen Brown's The Autobiography of My Mother. in: Mother Puzzles: Daughters and Mothers in Contemporary American Literature. Pearlman, Mickey, ed.** Westport, CT: Greenwood, 1989, 115-122.

Sinclair, Jo: **The Seasons: Death and Transfiguration: A Memoir.** New York: Feminist Press, 1993.

> Sinclair's story includes her early years, her relationship with Helen Buchman and her personal and writing challenges.

Stora-Sandor, Judith: **From Eve to the Jewish American Princess: The Comic Representation of Women in Jewish Literature. in: Semites and Stereotypes: Characteristics of Jewish Humor. Ziv, Avner & Zajdman, Anat, eds.** Westport, CT: Greenwood, 1993, 131-141.

Strickland, Stephanie: **The Red Virgin: A Poem of Simone Weil.** Madison, WI: University of Wisconsin Press, 1993.

> "Strickland provides a portrait of Weil that goes beyond the limits of biography."

Tax, Meredith: **I Had Been Hungry All those Years.** see Author Index.

Turiansky, Charles, ed.: **Model of the Yiddish Lullaby:** Jerusalem: Studies in Yiddish Literature and Folklore, 1986, 208-35.

Uffen, Ellen Serlen: **Strands of the Cable: The Place of the Past in Jewish American Women's Writing.** New York: Peter Lang, 1992.

> Evidence shown of the women writers selected who retain Jewish traditions while adjusting and assimilating to American life.

Yaeger, Patricia: **Honey-Mad Women: Emancipatory Strategies in Women's Writing.** New York: Columbia University Press, 1988.

> Images created by women writers "can help us focus on those pleasurable, powerful aspects of women's orality we have hitherto neglected." This book places the issues that Jewish women writers voice into a broader context.

F. Articles—Literary Criticism

Aarons, Victoria: **Talking Lives: Storytelling and Renewal in Grace Paley's Short Fiction.** Kent, OH: **Studies in American Jewish Literature**, 9, Spring 1990, 20-35.

Aarons, Victoria: **The Tune of the Language: An Interview with Grace Paley**. Kent, OH: **Studies in American Jewish Literature**, 12, 1993 (No.2), 50-61.

In this interview of Paley, Aarons gives us a sense of her formative years—of Yiddish and Russian and her grandparents who were immigrants; her family and her education, of being a Jew and a feminist.

Adler, Ruth: **Mothers and Daughters: The Jewish Mother as Seen by American Jewish Women Writers**. Flushing, NY: **Modern Jewish Studies Annual**, VI, 1987, 87-92.

Allen, Prudence: **Plato, Aristotle, and the Concept of Woman in early Jewish Philosophy**: Ottawa, Ontario: **Florilegium: Carleton University Annual Papers on Late Antiquity and the Middle Ages**, 9, 1987, 89-111.

Ariel, M.: **Female and Male Stereotypes in Israel Literature and Media: Evidence from Introductory Patterns**. New York: **Language and Communication**, 8, 1988, 43-68.

Aschkenasy, Nehama: **Women in the Double in Modern Hebrew Literature**. Baltimore, MD: **Prooftexts**, 8, 1988, 113-128.

Baba, Minako: **Faith Darwin as Writer-Heroine: A Study of Grace Paley's Short Stories**. Kent, OH: **Studies in American Jewish Literature**, 7, Spring 1988, 40-54.

"Paley tries to understand people, particularly the underdog." The character Faith provides Paley an opportunity to do a "variation on the Jewish-American dream and its failure."

Bassman, Michael F.: **The Woman in the Shtetl as Seen in Yiddish Literature**: Pocatello, ID: **Selecta**, 11, 1990, 25-28.

Berger, Alan L.: **Jewish Identity and Jewish Destiny, The Holocaust in Refugee Writing: Lore Segal & Karen Gershon**. Kent, OH: **Studies in American Jewish Literature**, 11, Spring 1992, 83-95.

Bilik, Dorothy: **Jewish Women and Yiddish Literature: Gluckel of Hameln**. Bristol, UK: **Studies on Voltaire and the Eighteenth Century**, 265, 1989, 1217-1220.

Bodoff, Lippman: **Kabbalistic Feminism in Agnon's Betrothed**. .New York: **Judaism**, 42, Fall 1993, 423-437.

Agnon's use of the Shekhinah in The Betrothed adds a "feminine spiritual" dimension to his novel and gives readers a good example of the power and richness of the Shekhinah.

Brown, Erella: **The Ozick-Bloom Controversy: Anxiety of Influence, Usurpation as Idolatry, and the Identity of Jewish American Literature**. Kent, OH: **Studies in American Jewish Literature**, 11, Spring 1992, 62-82.

Burch, C. Beth: **Johanna Kaplan's "O My America!": The Jewish Female Claim to America**. Kent, OH: **Studies in American Jewish Literature**, 9, Spring 1990, 36-47.

Burch, C. Beth: **Mary Antin's "The Promised Land" and the Unspoken Failure of Assimilation**. Kent, OH: **Studies in American Jewish Literature**, 12, 1993, 36-41.

Antin's autobiography—a story of contrasts from shtetl to Barnard, of Americanization and loss of Jewishness.

Burstein, Janet: **Jewish-American Women's Literature: The Long Quarrel with God**. Kent, OH: **Studies in Jewish-American Literature**, 8, Spring 1989, 9-25.

Fiction and poetry of Jewish-American women: what it tells us about traditions, values and about their lives. References to work by Ozick, Paley and Tillie Olsen.

Cantalupo, Barbara: **Reclaiming the Inadvertent: Olsen's Visceral Voice in Yonnondio: From the Thirties**. Kent, OH: **Studies in American Jewish Literature**, 11, Fall 1992, 128-139.

Olsen's novel "confronts the false security of closed systems by uncovering the frailty of their promises...by allowing the inner voice to emerge..voices of women resisting."

Cohen, Sarah Blacher: **Living and Writing the Jewish-American Play: "The Ladies Locker Room"**. Kent OH: **Studies in American Jewish Literature**, 11, Fall 1992, 204-214.

Cohen's collaboration with Isaac Bashevis Singer on the play "Shlemiel the First" led to her own play about women of different ages, ethnicities and religions coming together and baring their souls. Includes excerpts.

Contemporary Women Writers. Kent, OH: **Studies in American-Jewish Literature**, 11, Fall 1992, Special issue: see individual articles for pages.

Includes articles about Tillie Olsen's "Yonnondio", Grace Paley, four Holocaust writers, Ozick, Rosen and Rebecca Goldstein, Anne Roiphe's "Lovingkindess," Allegra Goodman, Faye Kellerman, and excerpt from Sarah Blacher Cohen's "The Ladies Locker Room", and a prayer by Alicia Ostriker.

Cronin, Gloria L.: **Melodramas of Beset Womanhood: Resistance, Subversion, and Survival in the Fiction of Grace Paley**. Kent, OH: **Studies in American Jewish Liteature**, 11, Fall 1992, 140-149.

"Melodramas of beset womanhood"....marginalized, often ethnic minority women, but, not, as author says, an altogether pessimistic story. Paley shows through her stories the strength of women in mother-daughter bonds, in friendship and in survival.

Dalin, David G.: **Jewish Historiography of Hannah Arendt**. New York: **Conservative Judaism**, 40, 1988, 47-58.

Falk, Marcia: **Marcia Falk: Sexy Lyrics from the Bible**. New York: **Lilith**, 16, Summer 1991, 18-19.

Falk, Marcia: **Mother Nature and Human Nature: The Poetry of Malka Heifetz Tussman**. New York: **Lilith**, #17, Fall 1987, 20-21.

Falk eulogizes the Yiddish poet Malka Heiftez Tussman soon after her death.

Feldman, Yael S.: **Feminism under Siege: The Vicarious Selves of Israeli Women Writers**. Baltimore, MD: **Prooftexts**, 10, September 1990, 493-514.

Consideration of characteristics common to contemporary Israeli novels and novelists—"introspection and self analysis." Author asks if Israeli women writers create cross-gender subjects in their life-stories?

Ferraro, Thomas J.: **Working Ourselves Up in America: Anzia Yezierska's Bread Givers**. Durham, NC: **South Atlantic Quarterly**, 89, 1990, 547-581.

Fishman, Sylvia Barack: **Imaging Ourselves: Cynthia Ozick's "The Messiah of Stockholm"**. Kent, OH: **Studies in American Jewish Literature**, 9, Spring 1990, 84-92.

Fried, Lewis: **Living the Riddle: The Sacred and Profane in Anne Roiphe's "Lovingkindness."** Kent, OH: **Studies in American Jewish Literature**, 11, Fall 1992, 174-181.

Lovingkindess is, for Roiphe "our acting with and for others to help them develop their humanizing capacities." It is a story of mother and daughter, but in broader sense of self and of others and of Creation.

Fuchs, Esther: **Amalia Kahana-Carmon and Contemporary Hebrew Women's Fiction**: Chicago, IL: **Signs**, 13, Winter 1988, 299-310.

Article based on Fuch's research on women in Hebrew fiction; here on Kahana-Carmon.

Glazer, Miriam: **The Will to Be Known**: **An Introduction to Contemporary Jewish-American Women Writers**. Kent, OH: **Studies in American Jewish Literature**, 11, Fall 1992, 125-127.

Glazer, Miryam: **Male and Female, King and Queen**: **The Theological Imagination of Anne Roiphe's "Lovingkindness"**. Kent, OH: **Studies in American Jewish Literature**, 10, Spring 1991, 81-91.

Golan, Patricia: **Contemporary Mythogynies in Israel Fiction**. New York: **Lilith**, #20, Summer 1988, 24-25.

Greenstein, Michael: **The Muse and the Messiah**: **Cynthia Ozick's Aesthetics**. Kent, OH: **Studies in American-Jewish Literature**, 8, Spring 1989, 50-65.

"The aggadic or imaginative nature" of Ozick's stories is discussed.

Halfmann, Ulrich & Gerlach, Philipp: **Grace Paley**: **A Bibliography**. Tulsa, OK: **Tulsa Studies in Women's Literature**, 8, Fall 1989, 339+.

Hallisey, Joan F.: **Denise Levertov's "Illustrious Ancestors" Revisited**: Kent, OH: **Studies in American Jewish Literature**, 9, Fall 1990, 163-175.

Hellerstein, Kathryn: **Songs of Herself**: **A Lineage of Women Yiddish Poets**. Kent, OH: **Studies in American Jewish Literature**, 9, Fall 1990, 138-150.

The poetry of Malka Tussman carries on the tradition of Yiddish women poets.

Henderson, Katherine & Usher Piercy, Marge: **Interview with Marge Piercy**. Arlington, VA: **Belles Lettres**, 4, 1989, np.

Interesting factual interview in which Piercy speaks of her Jewish family, and a *siddur* project she joined with Reconstructionists in Wellfleet, MA., where she lives.

Horowitz, Sarah R.: **Portnoy's Sister - Who's Complaining**: **Contemporary Jewish-American Women's Writing on Judaism**. New York: Jewish Book Council.: **Jewish Book Annual**, 51, 1993-4, 26-41.

Comparison of Malamud's 1950s depiction of Jewish women and the recent novels of Anne Roiphe, Nessa Rapoport, Vanessa Ochs and Allegra Goodman and their portrayals of contemporary women within different Jewish worlds.

Images and Voices of Jewish Women. London: **Jewish Quarterly**, 39, Autumn 1992, Special issue.

Kauvar, Elaine M.: **Courier for the Past**: **Cynthia Ozick and Photography**. Kent, OH: **Studies in American Jewish Literature**, 6, Fall 1987, 129-146.

Klingenstein, Susann: **Destructive Intimacy: The Shoah between Mother and Daughter in Fictions by Cynthia Ozick, Norma Rosen, and Rebecca Goldstein**. Kent, OH: **Studies in American Jewish Literature**, 11, Fall 1992, 162-173.

> The ability of getting at truths through fiction, that speak of loss, suffering, and evil, that are impossible otherwise.

Kossick, Shirley: **Writing with Heart: Some South African Jewish Women Novelists**. Johannesburg: **Jewish Affairs**, 48, Winter 1993, 120-126.

Kremer, S. Lillian: **Holocaust-Wrought Women: Portraits by Four American Writers**. Kent, OH: **Studies in American Jewish Literature**, 11, Fall 1992, 150-161.

> Particular effects of Holocaust on women—as shown in the fiction of Susan Fromberg Schaeffer, Cynthia Ozick, Marge Piercy and Ilona Karmel.

Lichtenstein, Diane: **Fannie Hurst and her Nineteenth-Century Predecessors**. Kent, OH: **Studies in American Jewish Literature**, 7, Spring 1988, 26-39.

> Discussion of questions that Hurst as well as her predecessors, Rebecca Gumpert Hyneman (1812-75) and Emma Wolf (1865-1932) examined about assimilation and intermarriage, Jewish/American and female identities.

Lyons, Bonnie: **Grace Paley's Jewish Miniatures**. Kent, OH: **Studies in American-Jewish Literature**, 8, Spring 1989, 26-33.

> Jewishness and humor—evocative of American-Jewish life as seen in Paley's stories.

Lyons, Bonnie: **Cynthia Ozick as a Jewish Writer**. Kent,OH: **Studies in American Jewish Literature**, 6, Fall, 1987, 13-23.

Mintz, Alan & Roskies, David G., eds: **The Representation of Women in Jewish Literature**. Baltimore, MD: **Prooftexts**, 8, Special issue: 1988, np.

Novershtern, Abraham: **"Who Would Have Believed That a Bronze Statue Can Weep": The Poetry of Anna Margolin**. Baltimore, MD: **Prooftexts**, 10, September, 1990, 436-467.

> Rosa Lebensboym (1887-1952), modern Yiddish poet, speculation about her identity, her personality, but mainly her writing career.

Molodowsky, Kadye with Peczenik, F., tr.: **Encountering the Matriarchy: Kadye Molodowsky's Women's Songs**. Flushing, NY: **Yiddish**, 7, 1988, 170-87.

Pinsker, Sanford: **Satire, Social Realism, and Moral Seriousness**: **The Case of Allegra Goodman**. Kent, OH: **Studies in American Jewish Literature**, 11, Fall 1992, 182-194.

Insightful article about the young Jewish-American author Allegra Goodman. "Comic portraiture..penetrating...stories about Hawaiian Jews, turning the strange into the familiar and the familiar into the strange."

Pitock, Todd: **Forgotten Singer, Forgotten Song**: **Hinde Esther Singer Kreitman**. Johannesburg: **Jewish Affairs**, 48, Winter 1993, 127-33.

Raphael, Phyliss: **The World of Wendy Wasserstein**: New York: **Congress Monthly**, 18, May/June 1993, 14-17.

Reinharz, Shulamit. **Feminist Biography, The Pains, the Joys, the Dilemmas, in: Exploring Identity and Gender: The Narrative Study of Lives,** Amia Lieblich & Ruthellen Josselson, eds. Thousand Oaks, CA: Sage publications, 1993.

Regenbaum, Shelly: **Art, Gender, and the Jewish Tradition in Yezierska's Red Ribbon on a White Horse and Potok's "My name is Asher Lev."**. Kent, OH: **Studies in American Jewish Literature**, 7, Spring 1988, 55-66.

The isolation of the Jewish woman artist—rejection, conflict of identity and finally, self-acceptance (article compares her to Potok's Asher Lev).

Rich, Adrienne: **Stepmother Tongues**: **On the Poetry of Irena Klepfisz**. Oakland, CA: **Tikkun**, 5, 1990, 103-104.

Rose, Elisabeth: **Cynthia Ozick's Liturgical Postmodernism**: **The Messiah of Stockholm**. Kent, OH: **Studies in American Jewish Literature**, 9, Spring 1990, 93-107.

Rosen, Tova : **On Tongues Being Bound and Let Loose**: **Women in Medieval Hebrew Literature**. Baltimore, MD: **Prooftexts**, 8, 1988, 67-87.

Roshwald, Miriam : **Feminism and Hebrew Literature**. Santa Monica, CA: **Jewish Spectator**, 52, 1987, 42-45.

Rovit, Earl : **The Two Languages of Cynthia Ozick**. Kent, OH: **Studies in American-Jewish Literature**, 8, Spring 1989, 34-49.

Grief, rage and satire in the writings of Cynthia Ozick.

Saltzman, Rachelle H.: **Folklore, Feminism, and the Folk**: **Whose Lore Is It?**. Durham, NH: **Journal of American Folklore**, 100, Oct/Dec 1987, 548-562.

Sandberg, Elisabeth: **Jo Sinclair: A Gardener of Souls**. Kent, OH: **Studies in American Jewish Literature**, 12, 1993, 72-78.

>Good biographical information on Jo Sinclair (nee Ruth Seid); her ethnic and sexual identity and her writing.

Setton, Ruth Knafo: **Anzia Yezierska: A Hunger Artist**. New York: **Midstream**, XXXV, F/Mr 1989, 50-54.

Shapiro, Ann R.: **The Novels of E.M.Broner: A Study in Secular Feminism and Feminist Judaism**. Kent, OH: **Studies in American Jewish Literature**, 10, Sept.1991, 93-103.

Sinclair, Clive: **Esther Singer Kreitman: The Trammeled Talent of Isaac Bashevis Singer's Neglected Sister**. New York: **Lilith**, 16, Spring 1991, 8-9.

>A short biography of Hinde Esther—I.B. Singer's sister, and a talented writer.

Sokoloff, Naomi B.: **Imagining Israel in American Jewish Fiction: Anne Roiphe's "Lovingkindness" and Philip Roth's "The Counterlife"**. Kent,OH: **Studies in American Jewish Literature**, 10, Spring 1991, 65-80.

Sokoloff, Naomi B.: **Narrative Ventriloquism and Muted Feminine Voice: Agnon's "In the Prime of Her Life"**. Baltimore, MD: **Prooftexts**, 9, May 1989, 115-137.

>Central concern of Agnon's "Bidmi yameha" (In the prime of her life) with the "silencing and sounding of female voice." The story is told as though it was the voice of the woman, a daughter telling of her mother's sad life plus her own struggles.

Sokoloff, Naomi B.: **Reinventing Bruno Schulz: Cynthia Ozick's "The Messiah of Stockholm" and David Grossman's "See Under:Love"**. Cambridge, MA: **Journal of the Association for Jewish Studies**, XIII, Spring/Fall 1988, 171-184.

Stephens, Anthony: **Else Lasker-Schuler and Nelly Sachs: Female Authority and Jewish Identity**. Bundoora, Vic.: **Menorah/Australian Journal of Jewish Studies**, 2, 1988, 37-50.

Taking the Fruit: Modern Women's Tales of the Bible. San Diego: **Woman's Institute for Continuing Jewish Education**, 1989.

>Interpretations or "midrashim" of Biblical women's texts by women.

Ucko, Greenbaum Lenora: **Who are the Wives? Who are the Husbands: A Study of Marriage Roles in Jewish Classical Folktales**. Oberlin, OH: **Jewish Folklore and Ethnology Review**, 12, 1990, 5-10.

Portrayals of wives in traditional folktales range from the pious "Shekhinah" figure to the devil incarnate "Lilith" as an evil being.

Uffen, Ellen Serlen: **The Orthodox Detective: Novels of Faye Kellerman**. Kent OH: **Studies in American Jewish Literature**, 11, Fall 1992, 195-203.

Crime fiction and Orthodox Judaism — not a likely combination; but Uffen describes how in fact the "detective novel is a most orthodox literary form." Revealing insights on women and orthodoxy, on mikvehs and adherence to orthodox sexual norms

Uffen, Ellen Serlen: **The Novels of Fannie Hurst: Notes Toward a Definition of Popular Fiction**. Bowling Green, OH: **Journal of American Culture**, 1, Fall 1987, 574-583.

Umansky, Ellen: **Representations of Jewish Women in the Works and Life of Elizabeth Stern**. Baltimore, MD: **Modern Judaism**, 13, 1993, 165-175.

Explores "both the representations of Jewish women in Elizabeth Stern's writings and her own self-representation as a Jew." Reared by Jewish foster parents, Umansky shows that Stern's works are autobiographical novels rather than autobiographies.

Wagner-Martin, Linda: **Racial and Sexual Coding in Hemingway's "The Sun Also Rises."** Ada, OH: **Hemingway Review**, 10, 1991, 39-41.

Waxman, Barbara Frey: **Jewish American Princesses, Their Mothers and Feminist Psychology: A Rereading of Roth's "Goodbye Columbus."**. Kent, OH: **Studies in American Jewish Literature**, 7, Spring, 1988, 90-105.

Evolution of the "Jewish American Princess," portrayed in stories such as "Goodbye Columbus" and the phenomenon that created this stereotype in fiction and in real life.

Weinthal, Edith C.: **The Image of the City in E.M. Broner's A Weave of Women**. Los Angeles, CA: **Response**, 61, Fall 1993, 46-51.

Zierler, Wendy: **The Rebirth of Anzia Yezierska**. New York: **Judaism**, 42, Fall 1993, 414-422.

Yezierska was a very well known writer in the early 1920's, then almost forgotten. Now, there is a renaissance of interest in ethnic/immigrant writings and her work (especially The Bread Givers) has found an ever widening audience.

IX

Recent Titles: 1994-1995

A. Books

Ajzenberg-Selove, Fay: **A Matter of Choices: Memoirs of a Female Physicist**. New Brunswick, NJ: Rutgers University Press, 1994.

Albert, Mimi: **Skirts: A Novel**. Dallas, TX: Baskerville, 1994.

Allen, Diogenes & Springsted, Eric O.: **Spirit, Nature, and Community: Issues in the thought of Simone Weil**. Albany, NY: State University of New York Press, 1994.

Arnold, Roseanne: **My Lives**. New York: Ballantine, 1994.

Ashby, Ruth and Gore, Deborah Ohrn: **Herstory: Women Who Changed the World**. New York: Viking, 1995.

Ashkenazi, Elliott, Ed,: **The Civil War Diary of Clara Solomon: Growing up in New Orleans 1861-2**. Baton Rouge, LA: Louisiana State University Press, 1994.

Baskin, Judith and Tenenbaum, Shelly, eds: **Gender and Jewish Studies: A Curriculum Guide**. New York: Biblio Press, 1994.

"A comprehensive guide for teachers, with readings, approaching gender issues for both men and women"

Baskin, Judith R., Ed,: **Women of the Word: Jewish Women and Jewish Writing**. Detroit, MI: Wayne State University Press, 1994.

Bellis, Alice Ogden: **Helpmates, Harlots, and Heroes: Women's Stories in the Hebrew Bible**. Louisville, KY: Westminster/John Knox Press, 1994.

Berrin, Susan, ed.: **Celebrating the New Moon: A Rosh Chodesh Sourcebook**. New Jersey: Jason Aronson, 1995.

Broner, E.M. & Nimrod, Naomi: **The Women's Haggadah**. San Francisco, CA: Harper, 1994.

Broner, E. M.: **Mornings and Mourning: A Kaddish Journal**. San Francisco, CA: Harper San Francisco, 1994.

Bronner, Leila Leah: **From Eve to Esther**: **Rabbinic Reconstructions of Biblical Women**. Louisville, KY: John Knox: Westminster Press, 1994.

Buchmann, Christina & Spiegel, Celina, eds.: **Out of the Garden**: **Women Writers on the Bible**. New York: Columbine Fawcett, 1994.

Calof, Rachel with Rikoon, Bella & Rikoon, Sanford, J. ed.: **Rachel Calof's Story**: **Jewish Homesteader on the Northern Plains**. Bloomington, IN: Indiana University Press, 1995. (Excerpt, "My Story" by Calof is in Gold & Stein, Biblio Press, N.Y., 1993. see Author index.)

Cantor, Aviva: **Jewish Women, Jewish Men**: **The Legacy of Patriarchy in Jewish Life**. San Francisco: Harper, 1995.

Chernin, Kim: **Crossing the Border**: **An Erotic Journey**. New York: Fawcett Columbine, 1994.

Cohen, Norman and Seltzer, Robert M.: **Americanization of the Jews**: **Chapter on American Feminism and Jewish Women**. New York: New York Press, 1995.

Cohen, Rose: **Out of the Shadow**: **A Russian Jewish Girlhood on the Lower East Side**. Ithaca, NY: Cornell University Press, 1995.

Cohen, Sarah Blacher: **Cynthia Ozick's Comic Art**: **From Levity to Liturgy**. Bloomington, IN: Indiana University Press, 1994.

D'Alpuget, Blanche: **White Eye**: **A Novel**. New York: Simon & Schuster, 1994.

Daniel, Ruby & Barbara Johnson: **Ruby of Cochin**: **An Indian Jewish Women Remembers**. Philadelphia: Jewish Publication Society, 1995.

Dansky, Miriam: **Rebbetzin Grunfeld**: **The Life of Judith Grunfeld, Courageous Pioneer of the Bais Yaakov Movement and Jewish Rebirth**. Brooklyn, NY: Mesorah, 1994.

Davidman, Lynn & Tenenbaum, Shelly: **Feminist Perspectives on Jewish Studies**. New Haven, CT: Yale University Press, 1995.

Delbo, Charlotte: **Auschwitz and After**. New Haven, CT: Yale University Press, 1995.

Diamond, Gila: **Full Circle**. New York: Feldheim, 1994.

Ehrenreich, Barbara: **Kipper's Game**. New York: Harper Perennial, 1994.

Eichengreen, Lucille and Chamberlain, Harriet Hyman: **From Ashes to Life**: **My Memories of the Holocaust**. San Francisco: Mercury House, 1994.

El-Or, Tamar with Watzman, Haim: **Educated and Ignorant: Ultraorthodox Jewish Women and Their World**. Boulder, CO: Lynne Rienner Publishers, 1994.

Falk, Marcia: **Song of Songs: A New Translation**. New York: Random House, 1995.

Felstiner, Mary Lowenthal: **To Paint Her Life: Charlotte Salomon in the Nazi Era**. New York: Harper Collins, 1994.

Ferguson, Kathy E.: **Kibbutz Journal: Reflections on Gender, Race and Militarism in Israel**. Pasadena, CA: Trilogy Books, 1995.

Fogelman, Eva: **Conscience & Courage: Rescuers of Jews During the Holocaust**. New York: Anchor, 1994.

Forman, Frieda, ed.: **Found Treasures: Stories by Yiddish Women Writers**. Toronto: Second Story Press, 1994.

Frank, Anne & Frank, Otto H., Pressler, Merjam, eds.: **The Diary of a Young Girl: The Definitive Edition**. New York: Doubleday, 1995.

Frankiel, Tamar: **The Voice of Sarah: Feminine Spirituality and Traditional Judaism**. New York: Biblio Press:paperback, 1995. (Cloth edition: Harper, 1990)

Ganz, Yaffa: **Cinnamon and Myrrh**. Spring Valley, NY: Feldheim, 1994.

Geras, Adele: **Golden Windows: Collection of Stories**. Portsmouth, NH: Heinemann, 1994.

Gershon, Karen: **A Lesser Child: An Autobiography**. London: Peter Owen, 1994.

Gluck, Louise: **First Four Books of Poems**. Hopewell, NJ: Ecco Press, 1995.

Gluck, Sherna Berger: **An American Feminist in Palestine: The Intifada Years**. Philadelphia, PA: Temple University Press, 1994.

Goldberg, Barbara: **Marvelous Pursuits**. Valdosta, GA: Snake Nation Press, 1995.

Goldberg, Natalie: **Banana Rose**. New York: Bantam Books, 1995.

Goldreich, Gloria: **That Year of Our War**. Boston: Little, Brown, 1994.

Goodkin, Judy & Citron, Judith: **Women in the Jewish community: Reviews and recommendations**. London: Office of the Chief Rabbi, 1994.

Gottlieb, Lynn: **She Who Dwells Within: A Feminist Vision of a Renewed Judaism**. San Francisco: Harper, 1994.

Greenberg, Blu: **Black Bread: Poems, after the Holocaust**. Hoboken, NJ: KTAV, 1994.

Haber, Beth K.: **Drawing on the Bible: Biblical Women in Art**. New York: Biblio Press, 1995.

Heller, Tziporah: **More Precious than Pearls: Selected Insights into the Qualities of the Ideal Woman**. New York: Feldheim, 1994.

Herbsman, Yael: **Women in Israel: A Bibliography: 1980-1991. 52** Westport, CN: Bulletin of Bibliography, March, June 1995.

Heskes, Irene: **Passport to Jewish Music: Its History, Traditions, and Culture**. Westport, CT: Greenwood Press, 1994.

(Includes Chapter 34 on Miriam's Sisters: Jewish Women and Liturgical Music, pp. 325-334).

Hirshfield, Jane, ed.: **Women In Praise Of The Sacred: 43 Centuries Of Spiritual Poetry By Women**. New York: HarperCollins Publishers, 1994.

Hollyday, Joyce: **Clothed With the Sun: Biblical Women, Social Justice and Us**. Louisville, KY: Westminster: John Knox Press, 1994.

Hyman, Paula: **Gender and Assimilation in Modern Jewish History: Roles and Representations of Women**. Seattle, WA: University of Washington Press, 1995.

Ilan, Tal: **Jewish Women in Graeco-Roman Palestine: An Inquiry into Image and Status**. Philadelphia, PA: Coronet, 1994.

Jewish Women's Literary Annual. NCJW-NYC, Vol. 1, No. 1, 1994.

Kabaker, Betty: **The Reasoning & The Seasoning of Jewish Cooking: A Project of the University Women of the University of Judaism**. Malibu, CA: Pangloss Press, 1994.

Kam, Rose Sallberg: **Their Stories, Our Stories: Women of the Bible**. New York: Continuum Books, 1995.

Kates, Judith A., & Reimer, Gail Twersky, eds.: **Reading Ruth: Contemporary Women Reclaim a Sacred Story**. New York: Ballantine Books, 1994.

Knape, Sabine: **The Role of Women's Associations in the Jewish Community: The Example of the Israelitisch-humanitarer Frauenverein in Hamburg at the Turn of the Century, in:Leo Baeck Institute Yearbook: Vol XXXIX** London: Secker & Warburg, 1994, 153-178.

Kopelnitsky, Raimonda with Spiegelberger, William, tr.: **No Words to Say Goodbye: A Young Jewish Woman's Journey from the Soviet Union into America: The Extraordinary Diaries of Raimonda Kopelnitsky**. New York: Hyperion/Little, Brown, 1994.

Kunin, Madeline: **Living a Political Life**. New York: Knopf, 1994.

Lewittes, Mendel: **Jewish Marriage: Rabbinic Law, Legend, and Custom**. Northvale, NJ: J. Aronson, 1994.

Lipman, Elinor: **Isabel's Bed**. New York: Pocket Books, 1995.

Lixl-Purcell, Andreas: **Memoirs as History: Women's Memoirs and the Study of Holocaust History**. in: Leo Baeck Institute Yearbook: Vol XXXIX London: Secker & Warburg, 1994, 227-238.

Lyons, Harriet S., ed. & Roth, Joan, Photos: **Jewish Women: A World of Traditional Changes**. San Diego, Ca: S. Tilatitsky/Yolen Press, 1995.

Margolies-Mezvinsky, Marjorie & Feinman, Barbara: **A Woman's Place: The Freshmen Women Who Changed the Face of Congress**. New York: Crown, 1994.

Marks, Lara V.: **Model Mothers: Jewish Mothers and Maternity Provision in East London: 1870-1939**. Oxford, U.K.: Clarendon Press, 1994.

Mascetti, Manuela Dunn: **Song of Eve: An Illustrated Journey into the Myths, Symbols and Rituals of the Goddess**. London: Aurum, 1994.

Mayer, Tamar, ed.: **Women and The Israeli Occupation: The Politics of Change**. New York: Routledge, 1994.

Meah Berakhot: Benedictions, Selections. Facsimile London: Facsimile Editions, 1994.

Full-color facsimile of a miniature liturgical compendium from 18th-century Europe and intended for women's use.

Meyers, Maan: **The Kingsbridge Plot: An Historical Mystery**. New York: Bantam, 1994.

Minco, Marga with Levitt, Ruth, translator: **The Other Side**. Chester Springs, PA: Dufour, 1994.

Moore, Tracy: **Lesbiot: Israeli Lesbians Talk about Sexuality, Feminism and Judaism**. London: Cassell, 1995.

Morris, Katherine: **Balkan Exile: The Autobiography of Irene Gruenbaum**. in: **Leo Baeck Institute Yearbook: Vol XXXIX** London: Secker & Warburg, 1994, 239-253.

Moskowitz, Faye: **Her Face in the Mirror: Jewish Women on Mothers and Daughters**. Boston: Beacon, 1994.

Nelson, Kay & Hoyle Huse, Nancy: **The Critical Response to Tillie Olsen**. Westport, CT: Greenwood Press, 1994.

Newman, Leslea: **Every Woman's Dream**. Norwich, VT: New Victoria Publishers, 1994.

Orenstein, Rabbi Debra, ed.: **Lifecycles: Jewish Women on Life Passages & Personal Milestones**. Woodstock, VT: Jewish Lights, 1994.

Orenstein, Walter: **Letters to Our Daughters: Fundamental Concepts in Jewish Law and Philosophy**. Northvale, NJ: Jason Aronson, 1995.

Palatnik, Lois: **Friday Night and Beyond: The Shabbat Experience Step by Step**. Northvale, NJ: Jason Aronson, 1994.

Piercy, Marge: **The Longings of Women: A Novel**. New York: Fawcett Columbine, 1994.

Porter, Jack Nusan, ed.: **Women In Chains: A Sourcebook on the Agunah**. Northvale, NJ: Jason Aronson, 1995.

Prell, Riv-Ellen: **Tales of Terror:Growing Up as a Jewish Woman in America, in: Fishkin, Shelly Fisher & Jeffrey Rubin-Dorsky, eds.: Reconfiguring Jewish-American Identity**. Madison, WI: University of Wisconsin Press, 1994, 28 pages.

Radin, Doris: **There Are Talismans-(Poems)**. Upper Montclair, N.J., Saturday Press, 1995.

Ragen, Naomi: **The Sacrifice of Tamar**. New York: Crown Publishers, 1994.

Reed, Barbara: **Today's Jewish Women, in:Sharma, Arvind, ed.: Today's Woman in World Religions**. Albany, NY: State University of New York Press, 1994.

Rudavsky, T.M., ed.: **Gender and Judaism: The Transformation of Tradition**. New York: New York University Press, 1994.

Rush, Barbara: **The Book of Jewish Women's Tales**. Northvale, N.J.: Jason Aronson, 1994.

Sacks, Maurie, Ed.: **Active Voices: Women in Jewish Culture**. Urbana, IL: University of Illinois Press, 1995.

Samsonowitz, Miriam: **Grandma: Mrs. Devorah Sternbuch, Ostrow-Minsk-Zurich-London, 1901-1993. Recollections Prepared by a Grandchild** : New York, Feldheim, 1994.

Schaechter-Gottesman, Beyle: **Lider (Poems):** Bi-Lingual Yiddish/English, Merrick, N.Y.: Cross-Cultural Communications, 1995.

Schreier, Barbara A.: **Becoming American Women: Clothing and the Jewish Immigrant Experience, 1880-1920.** Chicago: Chicago Historical Society, 1994.

Schulman, Sarah: **When We Were Very Young: A Walking Tour Through Radical Jewish Women's History on the Lower East Side 1879-1919 (from The Tribe of Dina, Sinister Wisdom): in: My American History:Lesbian and Gay Life during the Reagan/Bush Years**. New York: Routledge, 1994, 125-148.

Shapiro, Ann R., Ed.: **Jewish American Women Writers: A Bio-Biographical and Critical Sourcebook**. Westport, CT: Greenwood Press, 1994.

Silberstein, Laurence J. & Cohn, Robert L., Editors: **The Other in Jewish Thought and History: Constructions of Jewish Culture and Identity**. New York: New York University Press, 1994.

Sklarew, Myra: **Lithuania: New and Selected Poems**. Washington, DC: Azul Editions, 1995.

Solle, Dorothee: **Great Women of the Bible in Art and Literature**. Grand Rapids, MI: W.B. Eerdmans, 1994.

Solomon, Judith Y.: **The Rosh Hodesh Table: Foods at the New Moon**. New York: Biblio Press, 1995.

Steinsaltz, Adin: **The Woman of Valor: Eshet Hayil**. Northvale, NJ: Jason Aronson, 1994.

Strandberg, Victor: **Greek Mind, Jewish Soul: The Conflicted Art of Cynthia Ozick**. Madison, WI: University of Wisconsin Press, 1994.

Suleiman, Susan Rubin: **Risking Who One Is: Encounters with Contemporary Art and Literature**. Cambridge, MA: Harvard University Press, 1994.

Taitz, Emily: **The Jews of Medieval France: The Community of Champagne**. Westport, CT: Greenwood Press, 1994.

Contains information about medieval Jewish women.

Tarnor, Norman, ed.: **A Book of Jewish Women's Prayers: Translations from Yiddish**. Northvale, NJ: Jason Aronson, 1995.

Tobach, Ethel & Rosoff, Betty, eds. **Challenging Racism and Sexism: Alternative to Genetic Explanations**. New York: Feminist Press, 1994.

Includes essay by Sharoni on sexism and antisemitism.

Toorn, Karel Van der with Denning-Bolle, Sara J., tr.: **From Her Cradle to her Grave: The Role of Religion in the Life of the Israelite and the Babylonian Woman**. Sheffield, UK: JSOT Press, 1994.

Two Halves of a Whole: Torah Guidelines for Marriage. Nanuet, NY: Targum Press, 1994.

Von Kellenbach, Katharina: **"God Does Not Oppress Any Human Being": The Life and Thought of Rabbi Regina Jonas**. in: Leo Baeck Institute Yearbook: Vol XXXIX London: Secker & Warburg, 1994, 213-225.

Wagner, Anneliese: **Murderous Music**. Goshen, CT: Chicory Blue Press, 1995. (Poetry)

Wasserstein, Wendy: **Sisters Rosensweig**. San Diego, CA: Harcourt Brace, 1994.

Whitman, Ruth: **An Anthology of Modern Yiddish Poetry: Bilingual Edition**. Detroit, MI: Wayne State University Press, 1995.

Wolitzer, Meg: **Friends for Life: A Novel**. New York: Crown Publishers, 1994.

Yezierska, Anzia: **Salome of the Tenements.** Intro. by Gay Wilentz. Champaign, IL: Univ. of Illinois Press, 1995. (rept.)

B. Articles

Agosin, Marjorie: **Memoir: A Cross and a Star**. Eugene, OR: **Bridges**, 4, Winter 94/5, 36-48. (Chilean Jews)

Alpert, Rebecca: **If Not Now, When: A Jewish Delegation in Haiti (Visit by women rabbis and rabbinical students)**. Eugene, OR: **Bridges**, 4, Winter/Fall 1994, 89-96.

Altman, Rachel: **Jews Who Choose Jews**. New York: **Lilith**, 19, Summer 1994, 10-14.

Asher, Dana: **Up the Down Staircase: Women, Work and the Glass Ceiling**. New York: **Women's American ORT Reporter**, , Spring, 1994, 24+.

Ashton, Dianne: **Crossing Boundaries: The Career of Mary M. Cohen**. Baltimore, MD: **American Jewish History Quarterly**, Special Issue: Women, 1995.

Avery, Evelyn: **Jewish Women View Marriage**. New York: **Midstream**, XXXX, Dec 1994, 35-36.

Avital, Colette: **The Political Empowerment of Women in Israel**. New York: **Midstream**, XXXX, April 1994, 18-20.

Bal, Mieke: **Head Hunting: Judith on the Cutting Edge of Knowledge**. Sheffield, UK: **Journal for the Study of the Old Testament**, 63, 1994, 3.

Behar, Ruth: **Mi Puente: My Bridge**. Eugene, OR: **Bridges**, 4, Winter/Spring 1994, 63-70.

Bird, Phyllis A.: **Women in the Ancient Mediterranean World: Ancient Israel**. Pulaski, WI: **Biblical Research**, 39, 1994, 31-45.

Bloch, Ariel & Chana Bloch: **From in the Garden of Delights**. New York: **Judaism**, 44, Winter 1995, 36-63.

Blumfield, Hanita & Frymer-Kensky, Tikva: **Breaking Glass: Power in the Jewish Community**. New York: **Hadassah Magazine**, 76, Aug/Sept 1994, 24-26.

Breger, Jennifer: **Jewish Religious Literature for Women**. New York: **AB Bookman's Weekly**, 93, May 23, 1994, 22-48.

Breger, Jennifer: **Women's Devotional Literature: An Essay in Jewish Bibliography**. New York: **Jewish Book Annual**, 52, 1994-5, 73-98.

Brinker, Ludwig: **The Bat Mitzvah of American-Jewish Lesbian Fiction: Newman, Katz and Felman**. Kent, OH: **Studies in American Jewish Literature**, 13, 1994:Special Issue: "New Voices in an Old Tradition", 72-84.

Chevat, Edith: **Artists Talk: Five Artists in Conversation with Edith Chevat**. Eugene, OR: **Bridges**, 4, Winter 94/5, 13-31.

Cohen, Ruth: **Women in Black Step Down**. Eugene, OR: **Bridges**, 4, Winter/Fall 1994, 101-106.

Cwikel, Julie et al: **Past and Present Contraceptive Behavior of New Soviet Immigrant Women in Israel**. Tel Aviv, Israel: **Public Health Reviews**, 22, 1994, 39-46.

Davis, Barry: **Lucy S. Dawidowicz: 1915-1990: American Jewish Women Writers**. London: **Jewish Quarterly**, 40, Spring 1994, 27-31.

Dimitrovsky, Lilly & Schapira-Beck, Ester: **Locus of Control of Israeli Women During the Transition to Marriage**. Provincetown, MA: **Journal of Psychology**, 128, 1994, 537-545.

Dworkin, Andrea: **The Unremembered: Searching for women's experiences at the U.S.Holocaust Museum**. New York: **Ms**, 5, November, 1994, 52-8.

Dworkin, Norine: **Funny Girls**. New York: **Hadassah Magazine**, 76, November, 1994, 36-38.

Dworkin, Norine: **Jewish/Female Dramatists: Looking at Meshugas and Calling it "Family"**. New York: **Lilith**, 19, Winter 1994, 22-26.

Elliott, Roberta: **Stage of Denial**. Jerusalem: **Jerusalem Report**, , Nov.3,1993, 42.

Felman, Jyl Lynn: **If Only I'd Been Born A Kosher Chicken: A Mother's Fears, A Daughter's Longings**. Oakland, CA: **Tikkun**, July/August 1994, 47-50, 78-9.

Felman, Jyl Lynn: **Judy Chicago's Holocaust Project**. New York: **Lilith**, 19, Summer 1994, 15-17.

Felner, Julie: **Bold Type: What's in a Name**, New York: **Ms**, 4, Mar/April, 1994, 75

(Interview with Melanie Kaye/Kantrowitz).

Finkelstein, S. Naomi: **Celebrating Differences or the Difference Between Pain and Oppression**. Eugene, OR: **Bridges**, 4, Winter/Spring 1994, 59-61.

Five Women's Holocaust Stories: And How to Teach Them. (Introduction by Susan Schnur). New York: **Lilith**, Special Issue:19, Winter 1994/95, 9-21.

Frankel, Ellen: **Discovering the Folk Torah**. Port Washington, NY: **Sh'ma**, 25, September 16, 1994, 4-6.

Furstenberg, Rochelle: **Women of the Book**. New York: **Hadassah Magazine**, 76, May 1994, 22+.

Geis, Deborah R.: **And This Strength Is in Me Still: Embodying Memory in Works by Jewish Women Performance Artists**. London: **Yearbook of English Studies**, 24, 1994, 172-79.

Goldstein, Yaacov N.: **The Struggle for Equal Rights for Women in the Early Jewish Defense Underground: Bar Giora and Ha'Shomer, 1907-1918**. New Brunswick, NJ: **Contemporary Jewry**, 15, 1994, 140-156.

Gottfried, Amy: **Fragmented Art and the Liturgical Community of the Dead in Cynthia Ozick's "The Shawl"**. Kent, OH: **Studies in American Jewish Literature**, 13, 1994:Special Issue: "New Voices in an Old Tradition", 39-51.

Gould, Ellen: **On the Making of Bubbe Meises**. Oakland, CA: **Tikkun**, 25, October 14, 1994, 3-5.

Grancell-Frank, Barbara: **For the Sake of the Child**. New York: **Women's American ORT Reporter**, Summer, 1994, 26-27.

Harris, Judith: **Wherever in the Language of Jewish Women a Garden Grows**. Oakland, CA: **Tikkun**, 10, Jan/Feb 1995, 60-62,94.

Hirschberg, Peter: **A Blind Eye to Sexual Harassment**. Jerusalem: **Jerusalem Report**, V, January 26, 1995, 12-14.

ICAR: **International Consultation Ends 'Year of the Agunah'**. Jerusalem: **Israeli Women's Network Newsletter (Networking for Women)**, 7, Summer 1994, 2-4.

Jacobus, Sarah: **Airlift**. Eugene, OR: **Bridges**, 4, Winter 94/5, 64-71.

Kaunfer, Alvan: **Who Knows Four?: The Imahot in Rabbinic Judaism**. New York: **Judaism**, 44, Winter 1995, 94-103.

Khazzoom, Loolwa: **A Bridge Between Different Worlds**, Eugene, OR: **Bridges**, 4,Winter 94/5, 49-56. (Middle Eastern Jewish Culture)

Klepfisz, Irena: **Di mames, dos loshen/ The mothers, the language: Feminism, Yidishkayt and the Politics of Memory**. Eugene, OR: **Bridges**, 4, Winter/Spring 1994, 12-47.

Kogan, Marcela: **Marge Piercy: Feminist Writer with a Jewish Soul**. Washington, DC:**Women's World**, Spring 1994, 3.

Lentin, Ronit: **The (Female) Outsider Within: American Jewish Women Writers**. London: **Jewish Quarterly**, 40, Spring 1994, 24-26.

Levinson, Melanie: **"To Make Myself For A Person": "Passing" Narratives and the Divided Self in the World of Anzia Yezierska**. Kent, Oh: **Studies in American Jewish Literature (special issue) annual 1994**, 13, 1994:Special Issue: "New Voices in an Old Tradition", 2-9.

Linkon, Sherry Lee: **"A Way Of Being Jewish That is Mine": Gender and Ethnicity in the Jewish Novels of Marge Piercy**. Kent, OH: **Studies in American Jewish Literature**, 13, 1994:Special Issue: "New Voices in an Old Tradition", 93-105.

Marks, Marlene Adler: **In the Land of Missed Opportunities**. New York: **Hadassah Magazine**, 76, Aug/Sept 1994, 15-17.

Marks, Marlene Adler: **Staying Power**. New York: **Hadassah Magazine**, November 1994, 14-15.

McDougle, Roger: **Memories of a Jewish Lesbian Evening**. Eugene, OR: **Bridges**, 4, Winter/Spring 1994, 51-58.

Moore, Deborah Dash: **Reading the Akedah as a Mother of Sons**. Port Washington, NY: **Sh'ma**, 25, September 16, 1994, 3-4.

Moskowitz, Faye: **Portnoy's Sister**. Jerusalem: **Jerusalem Report**, 5, October 6, 1994, 52.

> Short but "right on" reassessment of Portnoy's Complaint as if written by his sister Hannah!

Motola, Gabriel: **Miserable Human Merchandise: Women of the Holocaust**. New York: **Midstream**, XXXXI, May 1995, 34-36.

Musleah, Rahel: **Women Rabbis: Turning Newness Into Strength**. New York: **Na'amat Woman**, May/June 1994, 4-7.

> 328 women have become rabbis since 1972. This article overviews several Reform and Conservative women rabbis' experiences.

Nadel, Arl Spencer: **My Dinner with Fat Jewish Dykes**. Eugene, OR: **Bridges**, 4, Winter 94/5, 77-80.

Neusner, Jacob: **The Feminization of Judaism: Systematic Reversals and Their Meaning in the Formation of the Rabbinic System**. New York: **Conservative Judaism**, 46, Summer 1994, 37-52.

Orenstein, Debra & Jay Stein (Rabbis): **Domestic Violence and Jewish Responsibility.** N.Y.: Women's League Outlook, Fall 1995, 23-24.

Parmet, Harriet L.: **Jewish Voices and Themes: Rose Drachler, Julia Vinograd and Linda Pastan**. Kent, OH: **Studies in American Jewish Literature**. 13, 1994:Special Issue: "New Voices in an Old Tradition", 52-58.

Parrish, Timothy: **Whose Americanization: Self and Other in Mary Antin's "The Promised Land"**. Kent, Oh: **Studies in American Jewish Literature**, 13, 1994:Special Issue: "New Voices in an Old Tradition", 27-38.

Parush, Iris: **Readers in Cameo: Women Readers in Jewish Society of Nineteenth Century Central Europe**. Baltimore, MD: **Prooftexts**, 14, 1994, 1-23.

Plaskow, Judith: **Im and B'li: Women in the Conservative Movement**. Oakland, CA: **Tikkun**, 10, Jan/Feb 1995, 55-56.

Praying What We Mean: An Exploration of Some Aspects of Liturgical Change: Havurat Shalom Siddur Project. Port Washington, NY: **Sh'ma**, 25, September 2, 1994, 4-6.

Ragussis, Michael: **Birth of a Nation in VictorianCulture: The Spanish Inquisition, the Converted Daughter, and the "Secret Race"**. Chicago: **Critical Inquiry**, 20, Spring 1994, 477-508.

Rapoport, Tamar; Penso, Anat & Yoni Garb: **Contribution to the Collective by Religious-Zionist Adolescent Girls**. Oxford, UK: **British Journal of Sociology of Education**, 15, 1994, 375-388.

Roth, Joan & Schnur, Susan: **Joan Roth: She Photographs a World of Jewish Women**. New York: **Lilith**, 19, Summer 1994, 17-22.

Roth, Joan: **Jewish Women of the World: Photo Essay**. New York: **Hadassah Magazine**, 76, Aug/Sept. 1994, 34-37.

Schnur, Susan: **A Conference for Children Hidden during the Holocaust**. New York: **Lilith**, 20, 1994, 20-23.

Schram, Peninnah: **The Voice is the Messenger of the Heart**. Oakland, CA: **Tikkun**, 25, October 14, 1994, 5-6.

Schreier, Barbara: **Becoming American: Jewish Women Immigrants 1880-1920**. London: **History Today**, 44, March 1994, 25-31.

On dress and Eastern European immigrants.

Shenhav, Sharon: **The Agunah: An Ancient Problem in Modern Dress**. New York: **Women's League Outlook**, 64, Summer 1994, 18-19,29.

Stein, Arlene: **Report from Warsaw: Back to the Ghetto**. Eugene, OR: **Bridges**, 4, Winter/Spring 1994, 97-100.

Studies in American Jewish Literature: "New Voices in an Old Tradition". Kent, OH: **Studies in American Jewish Literature**, 13, 1994 Annual, Special Issue.

Suzman, Helen with Colin Legum (Interview): **Defender of Human Rights: Helen Suzman**. London: **Jewish Quarterly**, 40, Spring 1994, 32-33.

Vogel, Dan: **Remembering "Marjorie Morningstar."** Kent, OH: **Studies in American Jewish Literature**, 13, 1994, 21-26.

Waldman, Selma: **A Response to Lisa Link's Computer Art Essay, "Warnings"**. Eugene, OR: **Bridges**, 4, Winter 94/5, 8-12.

Wallen, Ruth: **Memory Politics: Implications of Healing from Sexual Abuse**. Oakland, CA: **Tikkun**, 9, Nov/Dec 1994, 35-40.

Wasserfall, Rahel R.: **Continuity and Struggle: Two Generations of Jewish Moroccan Men in a Moshav in Israel**. Malta: **Journal of Mediterranean Studies**, 4, 1994, 300-312.

Weinthal, Edith C.: **The Image of the City in Yezierska's "Bread Givers"**. Kent, Oh: **Studies in American Jewish Literature**, 13, 1994:Special Issue: "New Voices in an Old Tradition", 10-13.

Yanow, Dvora: **Sarah's Silence: A Newly Discovered Commentary on Genesis 22 by Rashi's Sister**. New York: **Judaism**, 43, Fall 1994, 398-408.

Resources   157

X
Resources

For titles of local Jewish papers and magazines which may provide information and news about Jewish women's activities, see **American Jewish Yearbook,** available at most Jewish libraries, published at 165 East 56th Street, New York, 10022. For articles on particular topics see the **Index to Jewish Periodicals** available at your local Judaic library (see Association of Jewish Libraries below to find such a library).

For addresses of other magazines such as Lilith, Moment, Tikkun, etc., see **Ulrichs Guide to Periodicals** at your library or the **American Jewish Yearbook.**

Aleph: through the Internet
  This is the online version of "Rambi" The Index to Articles in Jewish Studies.
  To access: at Telnet prompt, type: aleph.huji.ac.il. At username prompt, type Aleph, if request name type any name; then, script=#2 (Latin only), finally in empty box that appears, type lb/jnl.rbi. You should then be in "Rambi" and can follow menu prompts. To exit: in same "box" type "stop."

American Jewish Congress Commission on Jewish Equality, 15 East 84th Street, New York, 10028.

Association of Jewish Libraries: Directory of Judaica libraries/collections in the USA and Canada, c/o; also, Reviews and articles of interest in Judaica Librarianship and AJL Newsletter. Membership information: Phyllis P. Robarts, c/o University of Miami Libraries, POB 248214, Coral Gables, FL 33124 (Membership in the National organization includes both above mentioned publications.)

Organizations

Association for Jewish Studies: P.O. Box 383089, Cambridge, MA 02238.

B'nai Brith: Jewish Monthly: Article by Zelda Bloom on B'nai Brith Women, March, 1990, pp. 7-9, 11. Good summary of the "divorce" between B'nai Brith Women and B'nai Brith 1985-89 (which is important for understanding the "separatism" of women in this organization).

Center for Jewish Studies: Graduate Center, City University of NY, 33 W. 42nd St., New York, NY 10036. Source for Jewish demographic studies, including women.

Israel Women's Network, POB 3171, Jerusalem 91031, Israel.

Jewish Women's Resource Center, National Council of Jewish Women , 9 East 69th Street, NYC, 10021. Send for their publications list.

Jewish Working Group on Domestic Violence: Jewish Family and Children's Service. 1610 Spruce Street, Philadelphia, PA 19107.

National Center For Jewish Film: Brandeis University, Lown 102, Waltham, MA 02254, (617) 899-7044 (Since 1976 largest library of film and video of Jewish content in the world.) See also Jewish Film Directory, ed. Matthew Stevens, Westport, CT, 1992. (1200 films of Jewish interest)

STAAR: Students Together Against Acquaintance Rape, (student-run, peer-educational group). c/o Office of Health Education, Student Health Service, Box 745, HUP, Philadelphia, PA 19104-4283. (215) 662-7126.

World Union of Jewish Students, Women's Project, P.O. Box 7914, Rechavia, Jerusalem 91077, Israel.

Women's Institute for Continuing Jewish Education, 4126 Executive Drive, La Jolla, CA 92037, Attn: I. Fine.

YIVO Institute for Jewish Research, 555 West 57th Street, Suite 1100, New York, NY 10019
  (For Yiddish Research)

Bulletins/Magazines/etc.

Blett: Newsletter of the Yiddish Women's Literature Network. Frieda Forman, Centre for Women's Studies in Education. 252 Bloor Street West, Toronto, Canada M5S1V6, FAX: (416) 926-4725 (paid subscription).

Bridges. A Journal for Jewish feminists and friends; P.O. Box 24930, Eugene, OR 97402. (See other Resources to find women's magazines).

Cantor, Aviva. (bibliographies/publication database) at the Jewish Women's Resources Center, NCJW, 9 East 69th Street, NYC, 10022. $1.50, 5 pages. (Note Cantor was the compiler of first Jewish Woman Bibliography, 1900-85).

Directory of Little Magazines & Small Presses, from Dustbooks, esp. poetry, POB 100, Paradise, CA 95969.

Feminist Collections, editor: Phyllis Weisbard Holman. University of Wisconsin, Madison, WI (quarterly subscription) See Fall 1993 issue on Idenity, Ceremony, Community: Jewish Women's Spirituality; also Spring, 1991 issue on Women, Race and Ethnicity.

Hadassah Magazine, 50 West 58th Street, New York, 10019; also:

Hadassah Textures: Hadassah National Jewish Studies Bulletin, Education Department, 50 West 58th Street, New York, 10019.

Hadassah: Voices for Change (A study on Future Directions for American Jewish Women) 1995. 135 page report.

Hebrew Women Writers, A Directory, 1994
Institute for the Translation of Hebrew Literature, POB 10051, 52001 Ramat Gan, Israel (The previous Directory of Hebrew Writers had 30 women listed).

Jewish Arts, Etc. P.O. Box 303, Lexington, MA 02173 (617) 861-9679
Occasional bulletin of news of Jewish arts; strong focus on Jewish women artists/artisans. (Paid subscription)

Lilith: The Jewish Women's Magazine, 250 West 57th Street, NYC 10128
Consult Tsena Rena section for many useful resources (quarterly).

Neshama. P.O. Box 545, Brookline, Ma 02146, Marthajoy Aft, editor Newsletter on Jewish Women's spirituality (quarterly).

On The Issues: The Progressive Women's Quarterly, 97-77 Queens Blvd., Forest Hills, NY 11374, indexed in the Alternative Press Index. (Occasional Jewish content)

Shirim: Semi-Annual Review of Jewish Poetry. 4611 Vesper Avenue, Sherman Oaks, CA 91403

Tel Aviv Review, Durham, NC: Duke University Press
English or translations into English of poetry, including poets from Israel, the Middle East as well as Western countries; includes women poets.

Wellsprings Quarterly, Fall 1993. No. 40: Special edition on women. Student Affairs Office of the Lubavitch Youth Organization, 770 Eastern Parkway, Brooklyn, NY 11213
Several interesting book reviews by and about observant women topics and a feature on "Conversations with Chabad women."

Other Useful Publications

Celebration of Jewish Women: A Hillel Program Guide for the Campus Community. **Hillel,** 1640 Rhode Island Avenue, NW, Washington DC, (202) 857-6560

Dovetail, A Newsletter by and for Jewish/Christian families ($4.50 per issue; each on a specific topic). P.O. Box 19945, Kalamazoo, MI 49010.

Israel Yearbook and Almanac. Contains statistics and other useful information on women (e.g., see vol 46, 1991, p.272. Jewish Law and Modern Woman: Can They Be Reconciled?) Australian Institute of Jewish Affairs, GPO Box 540200, Melbourne, Victoria 3001, Australia. Proceedings of a symposium on this central issue in contemporary Jewish life.

Resources

National Women's Studies Association. Jewish Women's Caucus - University of Maryland, College Park, MD 20742. Send for NWSA list of Women's Journals in the USA. (A few occasionally publish reviews and articles on Jewish women).

Poets House, 72 Spring St., New York, NY 10012 (A complete collection of modern poetry books, workshops and events calendar.)

Posner, Marcia W., *How To Start A Jewish Women's Book Collection.* Jewish Book Council, 15 East 26th Street, New York, NY 10010.

Renzetti, C., Segal, M.T. and Ehrlich, H., Eds. *Teaching About and Responding To Hate Crimes On Campus: A Resource Guide.* 1722 N Street, NW, Washington DC 29936, American Sociological Association, Teaching Resource Center. Contains Carnay, J., Paster, L., and Spiegel, M.C., Preparation for Dialogue: "Listening to Our Diversity," adapted from the *Jewish Women's Awareness Guide,* Biblio Press, NY 1992, pp.46-53.

Rosenblatt, Judith Turk., Ed.: *Who's Who in the World of Jewry: A Biographical Dictionary of Outstanding Jews.* Baltimore, MD, 1987. This standard biographic reference tool is a good place to find contemporary Jewish women whether in Israel or the Diaspora. (Since entries were by invitation it is therefore selective.)

Ruud, Inger Marie: *Women and Judaism: A Selected Annotated Bibliography.* Garland Reference Library of Social Science: v. 316, New York: Garland, 1988.
"Provides access to all sorts of works dealing with as many aspects as possible of women's life from ancient to modern times." Period covered (of publications) is 20th century mostly 70's early 80's, through 1986. Bibliography is selective but covers English, German, French, and Scandinavian.

Spiegel, Marcia Cohn. *A Bibliography of Sources on Sexual and Domestic Violence in the Jewish Community.* Updated 12/94. For copy write 4856 Ferncreek Drive, Rolling Hills Estates, CA 90274. (Send a self-addressed, stamped envelope and $2.50).

XI

Errata

Corrections and Omissions

I. Corrections

Diament, Carol, ed., **Jewish Marital Status: A Hadassah Study.** Northvale, NJ: Jason Aronson, 1989.
(*There is an incorrect cross reference to this item in Religion, Books*)

These will complete incorrect cross references:

Religion Books, p. 34
Biale, David. **Eros and the Jews: From Biblical Israel to Contemporary Americas.** New York: Basic Books, 1992.

Bronner, L. article on Biblical Prophetesses was placed in Religion Book section in error.

Religion Books, p. 43
Meyers, Carol. **Discovering Eve: Ancient Israelite Women in Context.** New York: Oxford University Press, 1988.

United States, Articles, p. 92
Hagy, James W.. **Her Scandalous Behavior: A Jewish Divorce in Charleston, South Carolina 1788.** Cincinnati, OH: American Jewish XLI. Fall/Winter 1989, 184-198.

Tax, Meredith, p. 134
Add to citation: in Dubois, Ellen Carol and Vicki L. Ruiz, eds.: **Unequal Sisters: A Multicultural Reader in US History.** New York: Routledge, 1990, 167-175.

II. Omissions

Baskin, Judith R. **Some Parallels in the Education of Medieval Jewish and Christian Women.** Haifa: Jewish History: 5, Spring 1991, 41-51.

Brown, Michael, **The American Element in the Rise of Golda Meir: 1906-1929.** Haifa: Jewish History, 6, 1992, 35-60.

> Meir's rise to a key position in the Jewish community in Israel is due, at least in part, to her being an American; issues of adjustment, later rejection of the U.S., her resilience and pioneer spirit. She also had a power base in U.S. for fund raising, etc.
> (*There is an incorrect cross reference to this item in U.S. section, articles*)

Glazer, Ilsa M., "A Cloak of Many Colors: Jewish Feminism and Feminist Jews in America," in **Women: A Feminist Perspective.** Jo Freeman, ed., New York: Mayfield Publishing Co., 1995.

Gruber, Mayer I., **Women in the Cult According to the Priestly Code, in: Judaic Perspectives on Ancient Israel,** Jacob Neusner, Baruch and Ernest S. Frerichs, eds., Philadelphia: Fortress Press, 1987, 35-48.

Hyman, Paula E. **Gender and Jewish History.** Oakland, CA: Tikkun, 3, Jan/Feb 1988, 35-38.

Mazow, Julia. "Proud Feminist Fighter," (Manya Shochat) **Midstream** Magazine, December, 1992, 41-42.

Schlesinger, Rachel. Volunteers for a Dream. Willowdale, ON. Canadian **Historical Society Journal,** 1988, 20-33 (Hist. of Hadassah)

Schulman, Susan K. "A Physician's Perspective." Brooklyn, NY: Jewish Homemaker, 25, Dec. 1993, 20-22. (Domestic Violence)

Shulman, Sheila. **What Is Our Love: Homosexuality, Jewishness and Judaism.** London: Jewish Quarterly, 40, Autumn 1993, 24-27.

Spiegel, Fredelle Z. "The Impact of Feminism on Jewish Women's Lives." Jewish Spectator, Winter, 1991-2, 52-54 (Reviews books by Kuzmack, Frankiel and David Kraemer)

Zakutinsky, Rivka. **Beyond Pearls and Merchant Ships: Finding the Woman of Valor.** Brooklyn, NY: Aura Press, 1995 (Meditations on biblical women)

Author Index

Authors in all sections of the Bibliography
are listed
in this Index
* Indicates an editor
** Indicates a translator
*** Indicates a compiler

Aarons, Victoria 134,135
Abramov, Tehilla 33
Abramowitz, Molly 31
Abramowitz, Yosef I.116
Abramson, Glenda* 113
Abzug, Bella 84
Ackerman, Susan 33
Adahan, Miriam 85
Adelman, Howard 113,116
Adelman, Penina V.33,51,117
Adler, Carol 131
Adler, Frances Payne 125
Adler, Rachel 51
Adler, Ruth 135
Aglietti, Susan L.*130
Agosin, Marjorie 117,150
Agron, Laurence 85,117
Aiken, Lisa 33
Ajzenberg-Selove, Fay 143
Albert, Mimi 143
Albrecht, Nancy R. 85
Alexander, Caroline 24
Alexander, Tamar 117
Alexy, Trudi 24
Alkalay-Gut, Karen 125
Allen, Diogenes 143
Allen, Prudence 135
Allison, Marla Ruth 52
Alperin, Mimi 85
Alpert, Rebecca 150
Altman, Rachel 150
Amishai-Maisels, Ziva 24
Amt, Emilie 17
Anderson, Sherry Ruth 33
Ankori, Gannit 85
Antler, Joyce*129
Appelfeld, Aharon 121
Appignanesi, Lisa 113
Aptheker, Bettina 85
Araten, Rachel Sarna 113
Arcana, Judith 131
Archer, Leonie J. 17
Arditti, Rita 85
Arendt, Hannah 113
Ariel, M. 135
Arnold, Jane 21
Arnold, Roseanne 143
Arond, Miriam 85
Ascher, Carol 85
Aschkenasy, Nehama 20,135
Ashby, Ruth 143
Asher, Carol 121
Asher, Dana 150
Ashkenazi, Elliott* 143
Ashton, Dianne 49,52,74,150

Austern, Esther 33
Avery, Evelyn 151
Avgar, Amy 106,107
Avital, Colette 151
Axelrad, Albert S.52
Axelrod, Ira 85
Axelrod, Toby 31
Axsom, Richard H.74
Baba, Minako 135
Bach, Alice 33
Baer, Jean 13
Bahloul, Joelle 117
Baizerman, Suzanne 103
Baker, Adrienne 113
Baker, James 33
Bal, Mieke 34,52,151
Balka, Christie 52,74,85
Barkhordar, Gina 121
Barsky, June 85
Barr, Roseanne, see
   Arnold Roseanne
Bart, Pauline 99
Basinger, Suzanne 20
Baskin, Judith, R. 17,143,errata (160)
Bassman, Michael F. 135
Bauman, Janina 24
Bayer-Berenbaum, Linda 121
Bayme, Steven 74
Beck, Evelyn Torton 74,85,86
Behar, Ruth 151
Bell, Roselyn 52,86
Bellis, Alice Ogden 143
Ben-Tov, Sharona 13
Bendet, Billa Tessler 86
Benjamin, Jessica 20,86
Benson, Evelyn R. 20,86,107
Berger, Alan L. 135
Bergman, Miranda 107
Berkovic, Sally 117
Berkovits, Berel 52,117
Berkovits, Eliezer 34
Berkowitz, Adena 52
Berkowitz, Gila 52,86,107
Berkowitz, Linda 107
Berkowitz, William* 34
Berliner, Sherry 93
Berman, Rabbi Donna 53
Berman, Joshua 53
Berner, Leila* 34
Bernstein, Deborah S.* 103
Bernstein, Richard 31
Berrin,Susan* 143
Berrol, Selma 15
Bershtel, Sara 34
Biale, David errata
Biale, Rachel 53
Bilik, Dorothy 53,135
Bird, Phyllis A.53,151
Biren, Joan E. 87
Birger, Trudi 24
Birnhak, Alice 99,121
Birstein, Ann

Bitton, Livia E.,see
   Bitton-Jackson, Livia E.
Bitton-Jackson, Livia E. 15,53
Bletter, Diane 74
Bliumis, Sarah W.**126
Bloch, Ariel and Chana 151
Block, Gay 24
Blond, Elaine 113
Blood, Jenny 68
Bloom, Harold 34
Blum, Julie 74
Blumfield, Hanita Frymer 151
Boas, Jacob 31
Bock, Gisela 25
Bodoff, Lippman 135
Bogen, Nancy 121
Bograd, Michele 87
Bonin, Adelyn I.25
Booker, Janice L.75
Bos, Johanna W.H.53
Boyarin, Daniel 34
Boydston, Jo Ann 132
Bradshaw, Paul F.*35
Braiterman, Zachary 53
Braunstein, Susan L.75
Breger, Jennifer 53,115,117
Breibart, Solomon 13
Breitowitz, Irving A.35
Brenner, Athalya 35
Brettschneider, Marla 54
Brewer, Joan S.75
Bridenthal, Renate 85
Brin, Deborah 54
Brinker, Ludwig 151
Broner, E. M.35,143
Bronner, Leila Leah 35,54,144,
   ERRATA (160)
Brooten, Bernadette J. 54
Brown, Betty Ann 87
Brown, Cherie, R. 75
Brown, Cheryl Anne 17,87
Brown, Erella 136
Brown, Gene* 132
Brown, Michael 160
Brown, Rosellen 121
Brownstein, Rachel M. 113
Broyde, Michael J.54
Bruder, Judith 35
Brumberg, Stephen F.87
Buber-Neumann, Margarete 25
Buchmann, Christina 144
Buck, Pearl S. 121
Buelens, Gert 87
Bulka, Reuven P. 35
Bulkin, Elly 75
Burch, C. Beth 87,136
Burgansky, Michael 107
Burman, Rickie 114
Burns, Rita Jean 35
Burstein, Janet Handler 131,136
Bycel, Lee T. 54
Calof, Rachel Belia 144

Camp, Claudia V. 17,55
Cantalupo, Barbara 136
Cantarow, Ellen 87
Cantor, Aviva 31,87,148,158
Cantor, Carla 88
Cantor, Debra 88
Capra, Joan 88
Cardin, Rabbi Nina Beth*,**36
Carnay, Janet 75
Carter, Carie 55
Casey, Kathleen 75
Chalmer, Judith 55
Chamberlain, Harriet Hyman 144
Chambers, Tod S. 95
Chametzky, Jules* 132
Chayat, Sherry 88
Chernin, Kim 75,88,121,144
Chertok, Haim 55
Chevat, Edith 151
Chicago, Judy 25,88
Chiswick, Barry R. 88
Christ, Carol* 45
Ciolkowski, Laura E. 88
Citron, Judith 145
Clar, Reva 89
Clegg, Margarett** 123
Clines, David J.A. 36,55
Cohen, Diane 55
Cohen, Janet 89
Cohen, Judith R. 114
Cohen, Norman 15,144
Cohen, Rose 144
Cohen, Ruth 151
Cohen, Sarah Blacher 136,144
Cohen, Sharon 55
Cohen, Shaye J.D 15,17.
Cohen, Steven M. 17,18
Cohn, Josephine 89
Cohn, Robert L.* 149
Cole,Ellen*83
Conrad, Gertrude 89
Cooper, Aaron 89
Coss, Clare 76
Cowan, Jennifer 36,55
Cowan, Rachel and Paul 36
Criswell, Jeanne Sallade 131
Cronin, Gail 131
Cronin, Gloria L. 137
Cruise, P.E. 20
Cutting-Gray, Joanne 117
Cwikel, Julie 151
D'Alpuget, Blanche 144
Dabad, Elisha 111
Dalin, David G.137
Dame, Enid 126
Damian, Natalia 15
Daniel, Ruby 144
Daniels, Doris Groshen 76
Dansky, Miriam 144
Darr, Katheryn Pfisterer 36
Davidman, Lynn 36,55,144
Davidoff, Donna J.89
Davies, Christie 89
Davis, Barry 151
Davis, Karen 56,89
Day, Peggy L.*36

Dayan, Yael 110
de Weille, Birgitte M.**115
Dearborn, Mary V.131
deBeer, Elizabeth R.89
Delbo, Charlotte 25,144
Dengelegi, Lidia 76
Denning-Bolle, Sara J.** 150
Deutschkron, Inge 25
Diament, Carol* 160
Diamond, Gila 144
Dicker, Shira 56
Dimitrovsky, Lilly 151
Dinai, Amilia 107
Diner, Hasia R. 76
Dische, Irene 129
Distelheim, Rochelle 107
Dizhur, Bella 126
Dobson, Barrie 18
Dombey, Rav Moshe 38
Dotan, Amira 108
Dresner, Samuel H.56
Drucker, Malka 24
Drucker, Olga Levy 25
Drucker, Sally Ann 89
Dubinki, D. 103
Dubofsky, Melvyn 89
Dubowsky, Hadar 89
Dubrovsky, Gertrude 90
Dworkin, Andrea 121,152
Dworkin, Norine 152
Dworkin, Susan 121
Eck, Diana 37
Eckardt, A. Roy 76
Edelson, Majorie 121
Ehrenreich, Barbara 144
Ehrlich, H.*159
Eibeschitz,Jehoshua,**,***25
Eichengreen,Lucille 144
Eilberg-Schwartz, Howard* 37
Eilenberg-Eibeschitz, Anna,**,***25
Eisen, Arnold 56
Eisen, Geroge 20
Eliahu, Edna 110
El-Or, Tamar 56,145
Elkin, Michael 90
Elliman, Wendy 90,108
Elliott, Roberta 152
Elwell, Sue Levi 59
Elwell, Sue Levi***76
Epstein, Dena J. Polacheck*81
Erpel, Simone 25
Exum, J.Cheryl 37
Eyck, Frank 114
Fainlight, Ruth 126
Falbel, Rita 103
Falk, Marcia 37,56,57,137,145
Falk, Marcia, **/*128
Feeley-Harnik, Gillian 57
Feinberg, Leslie 121
Feingold, Henry L.77
Feinhor, Noam 57
Feinman, Barbara 147
Feinstein, Elaine 126
Feldman, Yael S.126,137
Felman, Jyl Lynn 31,90,152
Felner, Julie 152

Felstiner, Mary Lowenthal 145
Ferguson, Kathy E.103,145
Ferraro, Thomas J.137
Fewell, Danna Nolan 37,57
Fine, Irene 37 37
Fink, Ida 121
Finkelstein, Barbara 121
Finkelstein, Rabbi Baruch 38
Finkelstein, S. Naomi 121,152
Fiorenza, Elizabeth Schussler 38
Fischel, Jack 77
Fishbane, Simcha 57
Fishman, Gella Schmid** 43
Fishman, Sylvia Barack, 38, 77, 90, 108, 132,137
Fishman, Sylvia Barack* 132
Fishman, Talya 57
Flesher, Paul Virgil McCracken 18,38
Fogelman, Eva 145
Forman, Frieda* 145
Forrester, John 113
Foster, Barbara and Michael 90
Foster, Edith 26
Frager, Ruth A. 20
Frank, Anne 26,145
Frank, Otto H.145
Frank, Shirley 90
Frankel, Ellen 152
Frankel, Estelle 90
Frankiel, Tamar 38,145
Freedman, Marcia 103
Fried,Lewis 137
Fried, Lewis* 132
Friedan, Betty 90
Friedlander, Judith 114
Friedman, Peska 26
Friedman, Reena Sigman 15,77,91,108
Friedman, Saul S. 26
Friedman, Theodore 20,57,58
Frishtik, Mordechai 58
Fromm, Bella 26
Frondorf, Shirley 77
Frymer-Kensky, Tikva 38,58
Fuchs, Esther 58,132,137
Fuchs, Rav Yitzchak Yaacov 38
Fuchs-Kreimer, Nancy 31,58
Furman, Nelly 58
Furstenberg, Rochelle 152
Games, Sonia 26
Gangelhoff, Bonnie 91
Ganz, Yaffa 104,145
Garb, Yoni 155
Geffen, Rela Monson 77
Geffen, Rela Monson* 38
Geis, Deborah R. 152
Geller, Laura 59
Gelles, George 16
Geras, Adele 145
Gerber, Jane S.114
Gerber, Merrill Joan 13,121,122
Gerlach, Philipp 138
Gershon, Karen 145
Gies, Miep 26
Gilad, Lisa 104
Gilman, Sander L.31,188
Gilson, Estelle 91

Ginsberg, Alice 118
Ginsburg, Faye 91
Girvan, Lois Brier 78
Glancy, Jennifer 59
Glazer, Miriam 138
Glenn, Susan A. 78
Gluck, Louise 126,145
Gluck, Sherna Berger 145
Goitein, Shlomo Dov 18,59
Golan, Galia 108
Golan, Patricia 138
Gold, Alison Leslie 26
Gold, Doris B.***129
Gold, Michael 59,78
Gold, Yeshara 39
Goldberg, Barbara 145
Goldberg, Leah Sivan 126
Goldberg, Natalie 145
Goldblum, Naomi**30
Goldenberg, Myrna 26
Goldenberg, Naomi Ruth 91
Goldman, Ari L. 59
Goldman, Herbert G. 78
Goldman, Karla 59
Goldman, Nechama 59,108
Goldreich, Gloria 122
Goldscheider, Calvin 91
Goldstein, Alice 91
Goldstein, Rabbi Elyse M. 59
Goldstein, Rebecca 122
Goldstein, Yaacov N. 152
Goldston, Ruth Berger 59
Good, Edwin M. 60
Goodkin, Judy 145
Gordimer, Nadine 122
Gordis, Robert 60
Gordon, Haim *39
Gordon, Harvey L. 60
Gore, Deborah Ohrn 143
Gornick, Vivian 78,91
Goss, Julie 60
Gottfried, Amy 152
Gottlieb, Freema 39
Gottlieb, Lynn 39
Gould, Ellen 152
Graetz, Naomi 60
Grancell-Frank, Barbara 153
Granirer, Pnina 126
Graubard, Allen 34
Green, Jeffrey M. 24
Greenbaum, Joanne 108
Greenberg, Barbara W.
Greenberg, Blu 39,60,61,146
Greenberg, Irving 39
Greenberg, Simon*39
Greene, Susan 107
Greenstein, Edward L. 39
Greenstein, Michael 138
Greisman, Nechama 39
Gribetz, Judah 18
Grinker, Lori 74
Grob, Leonard 39
Grossman, Avraham 20
Grossman, Barbara W. 78
Grossman, Lawrence 61,92
Grossman, Naomi 61,108

Grossman, Susan 40
Gruber, Mayer I. 49, 160
Gruber, Ruth 122
Guberman, Jayne Kravetz 91
Gunn, David M. 40
Gur, Batya 122
Gurock, Jeffrey 40
Gutman, Janice 92
Haas, Peter J. 40,118
Haber, Beth K. 146
Haberman, Bonne Devora 61
Hachen, Debra 61
Hadda, Janet 132
Hagy, James W. 160
Hahn, Deborah Fuller 92
Halfmann, Ulrich 138
Halkin, Hillel**122
Hall, Blaine H. 131
Hallisey, Joan F. 138
Hammer, Viva 61
Hanft, Sheldon 92
Harap Louis* 132
Hardy, Jan*78
Hareven, Gail 108,118
Hareven, Shulamith 122
Harris, Judith 153
Hasan-Rokem, Galit 117
Hassan, Riffat 39
Hauptman, Fred 92
Hauptman, Judith 61,62
Haut, Rivka* 40
Hay, Peter 27
Hefter, Wendy C. 78
Heinemann, Marlene E. 27
Heinze, Andrew 79
Helfgott, Esther Altshul 62
Heller, Fanya Gottesfeld 27
Heller, Janet Ruth 62
Heller, Tziporah 146
Hellerstein, Kathryn 138
Hellig, Jocelyn 62
Hendel, Yehudit 118
Henriksen, Louise Levitas 132
Henry, Sondra 79
Herbsman, Yael 146
Herman, Grace 126
Hertz, Deborah 21,118
Hertzberg, Arthur 40
Heschel, Susannah 92
Heskes, Irene 146
Hirschberg, Peter 153
Hirshan, Marjorie Schonhaut 92
Hirshfield, Jane* 146
Hoffman, Charles 114
Hoffman, Lawrence A.*35
Hoffman, Michael 92
Holender, Barbara D. 126
Hollander, Vicki 62
Hollyday, Joyce 146
Holman, Phyllis Weisbard* 40
Holoch, Naomi 129
Horn, Dara 21
Horowitz, Eve 122
Horowitz, Herman L. 15
Horowitz, Sarah R. 138
Hostein, Lisa 46

Hottelet, Richard 109
Howe, Florence*128
Hurwitz, Janet Cohen 89
Huse, Nancy 148
Huwiler, Elizabeth 41
Hyman, Frieda Clark 62
Hyman, Miryam 62
Hyman, Paula E. 18,41,146,errata
Iannone, Carol 93
Ilan, Tal 146
Isaac, Jeffrey C. 118
Isaacs, Susan 122
Isaacson, Judith Magyar 27
Isser, E.R. 31
Izraela, Dafna N. 109
Jacob, Walter 41
Jacobs, Lynn Dimarsky 93
Jacobs, Rebecca 62
Jacobus, Sarah 153
Jain, Devaki*37
Jaspers, Karl 113
Jeansonne, Sharon Pace 41
Johnson, Barbara 144
Johnson, David 41
Jobling, David 41
Jochnowitz, Carol 63,93,109
Jones, Hettie 79
Jordan, William Chester 114
Josefowitz, Rachel 93
Joselit, Jenna Weissman 79
Jurman-Appelman, Alicia 27
Kabaker, Betty 146
Kahn, Annette 27
Kahn, Yoel H. 93
Kalechofsky, Robert errata
Kalechofsky Roberta errata
Kalib, Goldie Szachter 27
Kalib, Sylvan 27
Kam, Rose Sallberg 146
Kamel, Rose Yalow 132
Kaminetsky, Ellen 79,93
Kaplan, Bernice 21
Kaplan, Betsy 63
Kaplan, Lou**104
Kaplan, Marion 31,85,115
Karayanni, Mousa 110
Karsh, Audrey R. 93
Kass, Leon R. 63
Kates, Judith A.*146
Katz-Loewenstein, Judith 122
Katzir, Yehudit 129
Kaufman, Debra Renee 41,63
Kaufman, Michael 42
Kaufman, Shirley 126
Kaunfer, Alvan 153
Kauvar, Elaine M. 138
Kaye, Evelyn 42
Kaye/Kantrowitz, Melanie 79,93,104,130
Kayfetz, Ben 63
Keane, Ellen Marie 100
Keeney, Bradford 80
Keller, Rosemary Skinner* 47
Kellerman, Faye 122
Kempner, Vitke 31
Kenel, Mary Elizabeth 63
Kent, D. 94

Kent, Evelyn Julia 29
Khazzoom, Loolwa 153
Kidder, Louise H.76
Kielsky, Vera Emuna 132
King, Andrea 109
King, Stella 13,27
Klagsbrun, Francine 63
Klepfisz, Irena 80,103,126,153
Kliger, Hannah 94
Klingenstein, Susanne 139
Klirs, Tracy Guren***43
Knape, Sabine 146
Knight, Chris 63
Kofsky, Alina Semo 63
Kogan, Marcela 153
Koltuv, Barbara Black 42
Konecky, Edith 123
Koonz, Claudia 21,27
Kopelnitsky, Raimonda 147
Koppelman, Susan* 13
Kornblatt, Joyce Reiser 13,123
Koskoff, Ellen 42
Kosmin, Barry A.94
Kossick, Shirley 139
Kozodoy, Neal 32
Kraemer, David C.64
Kraemer, Ross Shepard 21,42
Kramer, William M.94
Kranzler, Gershon 64,94
Krasner-Davidson, Haviva 64
Krasno, Rena 115
Krause, Corinne Azen 13
Krause, Deborah 42
Krauss, Chaim 42
Kravath, Tania 04
Kray, Susan 21,94
Kremer, S. Lillian 139
Kremsdorf, Deborah Lipton 48
Krich, Rochelle Majer 123
Krois, Hayim ben Y.42
Kron, Inge Deutsch 27
Krutein, Eva 28
Kubar, Zofia S. 28
Kumin, Maxine 126
Kun, Rita 28
Kunin, Madeline 147
Kupfer, Fern 123
Kuzmack, Linda Gordon 80,115
Lackow, Manya Prozanskaya 118
LaCocque, Andre 43
Lamb, Connie 131
Lamb, Lynette 94
Lamont, Rosette**25
Lamoree, Karen M.94
Land, Randi Jo 64,109
Langford, J.K. 94
Lantos, John D.95
Lassner, Jacob 18,43
Latting, Jean Elizabeth 95
Lebow, Barbara 28
Lefkovitz, Lori 64
Legum, Colin 155
Lehrer, Ruth 95
Leibowitz, Nathaniel 65,109
Leibowitz, Shira 65,109
Lemish, Dafna 104,105

Lentin, Ronit 123,153
Leon, Masha 109
Lepon, Shoshana 43
Lerenthal, Tamar 111
Lerman, Rhoda 123
Lerner, Anne Lapidus 65,132
Lerner, Gerda 19
Lerner, Harriet Goldhor 95
Lesser, Ellen 123
Lev Ari, Ronit 104
Levin, Jenifer 123
Levine, Elizabeth Resnick*43
Levine, Faye 123
Levine, Madeline** 121
Levine-Melammed, Renee 65,115
Levinson, Melanie 153
Levitan, Tina 80
Levitt, Ruth**147
Levy, Amy 123
Levy, Diane 65
Levy, Naomi 109
Lewis, Frieda 95
Lewis, Helen 28
Lewittes, Mendel 147
Lichtenstein, Diane 133,139
Lieberman, Rhonda 118
Linafelt, Tod 43
Linden, R.Ruth 28
Lindwer, Willy 28
Linkon, Sherry Lee 153
Lipman, Beata 104
Lipman, Elinor 123,147
Lipstadt, Helena 95
Lisle, Laurie 80
Litman, Jane 65
Lixl-Purcell, Andreas 147
Lixl-Purcell, Andreas*115
Lobel, Thelma C.109
Loewenstein, Andrea Freud 129
Long, Asphodel P.43
Lowin, Joseph 133
Lowy, Beverly 32
Lubitch, Rivkah 65
Lustig, Vera 32
Lyons, Bonnie 139
Lyons, Harriet S.*147
Mack, John E.28
MacLean, Nancy 95
Magnus, Shulamit 21
Malkiel, Theresa Serber 123
Malmgreen, Gail*43
Mamlak, Gershon 65
Mandel, Charlotte 126
Manes, Edna 32
Manheim, Ralph**25
Mar'i, Mariam 108
Maranz, Felice 109
Marcus, Ivan G.22
Marcus, Jacob Rader 80
Marder, Janet 65
Margolies-Mezvinsky, Marjorie 147
Markowitz, Ruth Jacknow 80
Marks, Lara V.95,147
Marks, Marlene Adler 153
Marr, Lucille 118
Martin, Douglas 95

Mascetti, Manuela Dunn 147
Mason, Ruth 65,110
Mayer, Tamar* 147
Maynard, Fredelle Bruser 95
Mazabow, Gerald 65
McDougle, Roger 154
Medjuck, Sheva 95
Meersschaert, Alison**
Melammed, Renee Levine 22
Merbaum, Michael 55
Meschel, Susan V.22
Metzger, Deena 65,104,127
Meyers, Carol errata
Meyers, Maan 147
Milgrom, Jo 66
Miller, Judith 28
Miller, Rabbi Judea B.15
Miller, Yisrael 43
Min-Hahar, Shlomo 22
Minco, Marga 28,123,147
Mintz, Alan*139
Mintz, Jacqueline A. 16
Mitchell, Pam 95
Monson, Rela Geffen, see Geffen
Montel, Jessie 110
Moore, Carey A.66
Moore, Deborah Dash 154
Moore, Rayanne 125
Moore, Tracy 147
Morris, Bonnie 96
Morris, Katherine 148
Morrison, Abby 96
Mosco, Maisie 123
Moses, Jennifer 96
Mosher, William D.96
Moskowitz, Faye 148,154
Moszkiewiez, Helene 123
Motola, Gabriel 154
Murphy, Cullen 66
Murphy, Marjorie 96
Musleah, Rahel 66,96.154
Myerhoff, Barbara G.80
Nachman, Elana/Dykewomon 124
Nadel, Arl Spencer 154
Nadell, Pamela S.44,70,80,96
Nahai, Gina Barkhordar 119
Nason, Tema 124
Navaretta, Cynthia 96
Neiman, Susan 115
Nelson, Kay Hoyle 148
Nelson, Sara 96
Nestle, Joan 129
Neuman, Shoshana 110
Neusner, Jacob 154
Nevel, Donna 103
Nevin, Thomas R. 133
New, Elisa 96
New, Melvin*123
Newman, Leslea 124,127,148
Newman, Leslea*127
Newsom, Carol A.*44
Niditch, Susan 44
Niederman, Sharon*129
Nimrod, Naomi 143
Nirenberg, David 66
Noam, Rahel 44

Nordhaus, Jean 13,127
Norich, Anita*132
Norman, Hilary 124
Norwich, Rose 119
Novack, Judith 28
Novershtern, Abraham 139
Nudel, Ida 115
Ochs, Vanessa 44,66,97
Ockman, Carol 119
Offner, Stacy K.95
Olsen,, Tillie* 13
Orenstein, Rabbi Debra*66,148,154
Orenstein, Walter 148
Orfali, Stephanie 19
Ornish, Natalie 81
Orr, Emda 110
Ostriker, Alicia 14,44,66
Oz, Amos 124
Ozick, Cynthia 133
Palatnik, Lois 148
Paley, Grace 127,130
Pantel, Pauline Schmitt*19
Pardes, Ilana 19,45
Parent, Gail 14
Parks, Tim**29
Parmet, Harriet L.154
Parrish, Timothy 154
Parush, Iris 154
Pasten, Linda 127
Paster, Laura Wine 75
Patai, Jennifer 45
Patai, Raphael 45
Peczenik, F.**139
Pefferman, Naomi 97
Penso, Anat 155
Pfeffer, Leo 97
Pheterson, Gail 97
Phipps, William E.45
Piercy, Marge 14,124,127,148
Piesman, Marissa 124
Pinsker, Sanford 77,133,140
Piotrkowski, Chaya 81
Pirani, Alix 45
Pitock, Todd 140
Plain, Belva 124
Plaskow, Judith 45,66,67,81,154
Plaskow, Judith*45
Pogrebin, Letty Cottin 97
Polacheck, Dena J.*81
Polacheck, Hilda Satt*81
Popkin, Zelda 14
Porter, Jack Nusan*148
Posner, Marcia W. 159
Prager, Karen 97
Pratt, Minnie Bruce 75
Prell, Riv-Ellen 46,81,97,148
Pressler, Merjam *145
Prince-Gibson, Etta 110
Probst Solomon, Barbara 124
Prose, Francine 124
Prose, Francine**121
Rachlin, Rachel & Israel 115
Radcliffe, Sarah Chana 46
Radin, Doris 148
Ragen, Naomi 124,148
Ragussis, Michael 155

Raphael, Chaim 19
Raphael, Phyliss 140
Rapoport, Natalya 119
Rapoport, Nessa 97,110
Rapoport, Nessa*130
Rapoport, Tamar 155
Rapoport-Albert, Ada*46
Rashkow, Ilona N.46
Raskin, Barbara 124
Ratner, Rochelle 124,127
Rattok, Lily 90,108
Raven Arlene 87
Ravikovitch, Zelda Dahlia 127
Ravitz, Abe C. 81
Raz, Hilda 127
Redman, Dina 107
Reed, Barbara 148
Regenbaum, Shelly 140
Reich, Tova 124
Reimer, Gail Twersky*146
Reimers, Paula 67
Reines-Josephy, Marcia 98
Reis, Pamela Tamarkin 67
Reisenberger, Azila Talit 67
Renzetti, C.*159
Resnick, David A.67
Rich, Adrienne 121,140
Richardson, Brenda 14
Rikoon, J. Sanford*144
Ringe, Sharon*44
Ringelheim, Joan 16,29,32
Ringold, Jeanette Kalker**123
Rinn, Miriam 87,98
Riskin, Shlomo 46
Rittner, Carol*29
Roberts, Marlene 98
Rogers, Rita S.28
Rogow, Faith 81,98
Roiphe, Anne 98,124
Romanoff, Lena 46
Rook, James 68
Rose, Andy*74
Rose, Elisabeth 140
Rosen, Norma 82,125,133
Rosen, Tova 140
Rosenberg, Blanca 29
Rosenberg, David**34
Rosengarten, Sudy 47
Rosenheim, Judith 68
Rosenthal, Rabbi
   Dovid Simcha 47
Rosenwasser, Penny 104
Roshwald, Miriam 140
Roskies, David G.*139
Rosoff, Betty*150
Ross, Tamar 68
Ross, Wendy 68
Rotenberg, Mattie 98
Roth, Joan 147,155
Roth, John K.*29
Rothchild, Sylvia 130
Rothstein, Gideon 68
Rovit, Earl 140
Rozenzweig, Michael L.68
Rubin, Julie H.
Rubin, Gertrude 128

Rubin, Stephen J.*82
Rubinstein, Judith Allen 98
Rudavsky, T.M.*148
Ruddick, Sara 14,105
Ruether, Radford Rosemary 47
Rush, Barbara 148
Ruud, Inger Marie 159
Sabar, Shalom 47,119
Sachar, Howard M. 82
Sacks, Maurie 98
Sacks, Maurie*148
Safir, Marilyn P.
Sahgal, Gita 47,116
Salkin, Jeffrey K.68
Saltzman, Cynthia 68
Saltzman, Rachelle H.140
Samith, Barbara
Samsonowitz, Miriam 149
Samuels, Gayle 119
Sandberg, Elisabeth 141
Sanford, J.*144
Sanua, Marianne 98
Saper, Bernard 99
Sara, Elizabeth 47,69
Sarna, Jonathan D.99
Saxton, Marsha*128
Scarf, Mimi 82
Schaechter-Gottesman, Beyle 149
Schapira Beck, Ester
Schechter, Cathy 84
Scheindlen, Raymond P.128
Schlesinger, Benjamin 119
Schlesinger, Rachel
Schloss, Eva 29
Schneider, Susan Weidman 22,47,99,110
Schneyer, Mark 99
Schnur, Susan 69,99,100,155
Schoenfeld, Stuart 47
Schonberg, David*40
Schorsch, Ismar 69
Schram, Peninnah 155
Schreier, Barbara A.155
Schulman, Sarah 133,149
Schulman, Susan K. errata
Schwalb, Susan J.82
Schwartz, Lauren 32,99
Schwartz, Lynne Sharon 125
Schwartz, Martha 69
Schwarz, Renee Fodor 29
Schweitzer, Leah*128
Schwertfeger, Ruth 29,131
Scolnic, Benjamin E.69
Scult, Mel 99
Sebag-Montefiore, Ruth 116
Sedlacek, William C.82
Segal, M.T.*159
Seginer, Rachel 110
Seidman, Naomi 69
Selevan, Ida Cohen**43
Seligman, Dee 134
Seligman, Ruth 110
Sella, Shelley 110
Seller, Maxine S.99,100
Seltzer, Robert M.144
Semyonov, Moshe 111
Sendyk, Helen 29

Sered, Susan Starr 47,69
Setton, Ruth Knafo 141
Shain, Ruchoma 105
Shalvi, Alice 111
Shankman, Sarah 125
Shapiro, Ann R.*149
Shapiro, Ann R.141
Shapiro, Edward S.82
Shapiro, Sarah*82
Shargel, Baila R.99
Shaviv, Yehuda 111
Shelemay, Kay Kaufman 116
Shenhav, Sharon 155
Shepard, Sanford 16
Shepherd, Naomi 16
Sheres, Ita 48
Sherman, Josepha 130
Shizgal Cohen, Elaine 70
Shluker, Zelda 100
Shneiderman, S.L.14
Shorter, Edward 119
Showalter, Elaine 82
Shulevitz, Marion 70
Shulman, Alix Kates 125
Shulman, Sheila 160
Shuster, Claudia Kramer*83
Sidransky, Ruth 83
Siegel, Hannah Tiferet 48,100
Siegel, Rachel Josefowitz 93
Siegel, Sheila Jubelirer 70
Silber, Ellen 100
Silberstein, Laurence J.149
Silva, Linda Kay 125
Silverstein, Olga 80,100
Simon, Kate 83
Simon Maurya 128
Simon, Rachel 116
Simon, Rita J.70
Simons, Howard 83
Sinclair, Clive 14,141
Sinclair, Jo 125,134
Singer, Brett 125
Sinkoff, Nancy B.100
Sivan, Miriam Billig** 126
Sklarew, Myra 128,149
Slobin, Mark 48
Smith, Ann 70
Smith, Barbara 75
Sofer, Barbara 70
Sokoloff, Naomi B.141
Solle, Dorothee 149
Solomon, Alisa 111
Solomon, Barbara Miller 14
Solomon, Judith 149
Solotaroff, Ted*130
Sorin, Gerald 14
Spencer, Gary 100
Spiegel, Celina*144
Spiegel, Fredelle Zaiman 70
Spiegel, Marcia Cohn 48,71,75,100,159
Spiegel, Marcia Cohn*128
Spiegelman, Donna 85
Spitzer, Rabbi Julie 48
Springstend, Eric O.143
Stahl, Abraham 71,111
Stanger, Sheila 100

Starkman, Elaine Marcus*128
Stein, Arlene 155
Stein, Rabbi Jay 154
Stein, Lisa***129
Stein, Regina 18
Steinberg, Jean**27
Steinberg, Naomi 71
Steinsaltz, Adin 149
Stephens, Anthony 141
Stern, Chaim*48
Stern, Norton B.94
Sternberg, Meir 15
Stevens, Serita 125
Stieglitz, Maria 101
Stone, Amy 101
Stora-Sandor, Judith 134
Storey, Alice 125
Stow, Kenneth 22
Strandberg, Victor 149
Strickland, Stephanie 134
Strube, Michael J.55
Strum, Philippa 105,111
Sturgis, Susanna J.*130
Suchow, Betty 101
Suchow, Phil 101
Suhl, Yuri 83,116
Suleiman, Susan Rubin 149
Sunshine, Linda 125
Suzman, Helen 116,155
Svirsky, Gila 111
Swirski, Barbara 105
Swirsky, Joan 101
Szeman, Sherri 29,125
Szwajger, Adina Blardy 29
Taitz, Emily 79.119,149
Tal, Zohar 111
Tallan, Cheryl 19,22
Tarnor, Norman*149
Tavris, Carol 101
Tax, Meredith 125,134
Taylor, Jacqueline 83
Tedeschi, Guiliani 29
Tenenbaum, Shelly 101,144
Tenenbaum, Shelly*143
Teubal, Savina J.48
Teutsch, David A.*49
Tidhar, Chava E. 104,105
Tobach, Ethel*150
Tobias, Marlene 107
Tobin, Gary A.71
Toll, William 84,101
Toorn, Karel Van der 150
Torjesen, Karen J.49
Trible, Phyllis 71
Turiansky, Charles*134
Tussman, Malka Heifetz 128
Ucko, Greenbaum Lenora 142
Uffen, Ellen Serlen 134,142
Umansky, Ellen M.23,49,
  71,101,142
Ungar, Carol Green 112
Van der Rol, Ruud 30
Van der Toorn, Karel 71
Van Dijk-Hemmes, Fokkelien 35
Vanderkam, James C.49
Verdoner, Yoka*30

Verdoner Kan, Francesca*30
Verdoner-Sluizer, Hilde 30
Verhoeven, Rian 30
Vincie, Catherine 100
Visotzky, Burton L.71
Vogel, Dan 155
Von Kellenbach,
  Katharina 150
Wachsberger, Ken 27
Wagman, Frederica 125
Wagner, Anneliese 150
Wagner-Martin, Linda 142
Waldman, Nahum 71
Waldman, Selma 155
Waldstreicher, David 23
Walfish, Barry Dov 49
Wallach, John and
  Janet 105
Wallach, Rachel 128
Wallach, Zelda,
  and Yona 128
Wallen, Ruth 156
Walters, Stanley D.71
Wandor, Michelene 15
Wardi, Dina 30
Wasserfall, Rahel R.156
Wasserstein, Wendy 125,150
Waterford, Helen H.30
Watzman, Haim**145
Waxman, Barbara Frey 142
Weatherford, Doris 19
Weems, Renita J.49,71
Wegner, Judith Romney 49,72
Weil, Grete 125
Weinbaum, Batya 106,130
Weinberg, Abigal 75
Weinberg, Sidney Stahl 84,101,102
Weinthal, Edith C.142,156
Weisberg, Ruth 84
Weisman, Celia 102
Weiss, Avraham 50
Weiss-Katz, Miriam 72
Weiss-Rosmarin, Trude 120
Weissler, Chava 23,50,72
Weissman, L.M.**103
Wells, D.A.72
Wenger, Beth S.102,120
Wenkart, Henny 128
Wernick, Laura 120
Weschler, Joanna 121
Westheimer, Dr. Ruth 30
Whitman, Ruth 15,128,150
Wice, Leila 120
Wikler, Meir 50
Willey, Patricia K.50
Williams, Linda B.
Wilner, Lori 32
Winegarten, Ruthe 84
Winkler, Gershon 73
Winternight, Nancy 102
Wisenberg, S.L.32
Wisse, Ruth R.102
Wohlgelernter, Maurice 32
Wolf, Laura Belkin 95
Wolf, Sara Lee 73
Wolitzer, Meg 125,150

Wolkstein, Diane 50
Wolowelsky, Joel B.73
Woodman,Donald,
   photography,25
Wouk, Jordan 73
Wyden, Peter 30
Yaeger, Patricia 134
Yagoda, Ben
Yanow, Dvora 156
Yezierska, Anzia 84,130,150
Young, Elise G.51, 106
Young, Serinity*51
Yuval-Davis, Nira 112
Zahava, Irene*130
Zakutinsky, Rivka 51
Zandy, Janet 102
Zassenhaus, Hiltgunt 30
Zellin, Agnes 120
Zerubavel, Yael 102
Zierler, Wendy 142
Zipperstein,
   Steven J.*46
Zipser, Arthur 84
Zipser, Pearl 84
Zisquit, Linda 128
Zivotofsky, Ari Z.73
Zivotofsky,
   Naomi T.S.73
Zolty, Shoshanna
   Pantel 51,120
Zuckerman, Francine*106

Note Corrections to Author Index

Gilman 118 (not 188)
Hyman, P.E. 160 (not errata)
Schulman, S.K. 160 (not errata)
Tax (add p. 160)

Note Corrections to Subject Index

Grandmothers 119 (not 107)

Subject Index

Notes: In most cases the words Jewish and women can be appended to any of these subject headings because of the overall focus of the bibliography. Only The word is added in certain cases where clarification was deemed necessary: Example: Jewish-American women for overviews of this topic, Jewish women writers to distinguish from Israeli women writers. Where HOLOCAUST, FICTION, POETRY, SHORT STORIES are listed they are only from the sections: Additions (I) or 1994 5 (IX). These subjects each have their own chapter in the body of the bibliography and therefore it would be redundant to list in index as such. SEE THE TABLE OF CONTENTS. Furthermore, where the author and subject of a Holocaust narrative is the same, the listing will be found in the Author index. Many can be found under Personal narratives.
**ERIC documents are U.S. Government documents which can be found in large U.S. libraries. Ask your Reference Librarian for help in locating these reports.

Abortion 52,53, 92
Abused Women see
   Domestic violence, rape
Activism 19, 20, 32, 76, 80, 84, 90, 91, 93, 94,96,98,100,101,102,110,113,115,117
Activism - Israel 106
   - Peace 16, 103, 104, 105, 106, 107, 108, 109,118,151
Aged-Jewish Americans 80
   Women in Israel, see
   Israel-Aged
Agnon 135, 141
Aguilar, Grace 52
Agunah 35,46,52,61,67,97,107,110,153,155
Ajzenberg-Selove, Fay 143
Akedah 154,156
Almagor, Gila 109
"American Jewess" 82,133
American Jewish women 13,61,74,77,79,80,82,113.148,150
American Jewish women authors 14, 83, 131,132,133,136,134,136,139,146,149,153,155
Ancient Israelite women 17, 19, 20, 21, 22, 33 ,41,58,146,149,151,160
Andreas-Salome, Lou 113
Anti-semitism 74, 75, 85, 87, 93, 96, 114, 142,149
Antin, Mary 82,89,131,134,136,154
Arab-Israeli relations 106
Arendt, Hannah 26, 113,117,118,137
Arnold, Roseanne 143
Artists, see also Holocaust-Art 14 ,25, 74, 80, 84, 85,87,92,96,98, 102, 107, 138, 145, 155
Asenat 120
Ashkenazi women 17,50,72

Baalot Teshuvah 36,41,44,55,63,69
Babi Yar 153
Barr, Roseanne, see
   Arnold, Roseanne
Beck, Evelyn Torton 80
Bendorf Conferences 56
Bernhardt, Sarah 118
Beruriah 51
Bible-violence in 57
Biblical Studies 15,17,335, 37, 40, 41, 43, 44, 47-50,52,53,55,58,59,62,65,66-71, 72, 73, 137,143,144,151,152
Biblical women 17,20,35-37,42,44-46, 58, 65, 67,68,69,71,143,144,146,149,160
Biographical information 18, 19, 49, 77, 79, 113, 143
Birger, Trudi 31
Bisno, Tess 134
Black-Jewish relations 75,76,97
Blond, Elaine 113
Blue Light, play based
   on Ozick's"The Shawl" 152
B'not mitzvah 41,47,52,65,68
   (pl. of bat mitzvah)
Bonin, Adelyn 31
Brice, Fanny 78
Broner, E.M.132,141,142
Buber-Neumann, Margaret 25
Burial Societies
   (chevra kaddisha) 63,
Calof, Rachel 144
Career women 101,109
Ceti 66
Chana Rochel of Ludomir 73,144
Chernin, Kim 88,144
Chicago, Judy 31,152
Childbearing 21,25,37,56,62,81,84,86,88,94,100,147,151
Childbearing-Israel 106,109,112
Cixous, Helene 149
Clara de Hirsch Home for
   Working girls 100
Clothing 42,58,103,149,155
Cohen, Rose 144
Cohen, Hettie 79
Cohen, Sarah Blacher 136
Cohen, Mary M. 150
Comediennes 90,102,152
Communists 95
Concubinage 45
Cone, Claribel and Etta 14
Conference of Jewish
   Feminists 107
Conservative movement see
   Denominations-Conservative
*Conversas 16,22,24,25,65,94,155
   *Conversas is the female form for
   conversos, also known as Crypto-Jews
   or Marranos.
Conversion 35,36,46
Cooper, Adrienne 101
Daniel, Ruby 144

Daughters of Zelophehad 38
Dawidowicz, Lucy 26,31,32,82,151
Dayan, Yael 109,110
Deafness 83
Deborah 65
Delay, Anna Rael 101
Delbo, Charlotte 25
Demographics 96
Denominations-Conservative 15, 39, 44, 52,55,62,70,99,145,153,154
   -Orthodox 36, 38, 39. 41, 47, 53, 55, 56,60,61,63,64,79,95,98,145,152
   -Reconstructionist 49,114
   -Reform 36,41,42,48,57,59,64
Depression 76,95,99
Deutsch, Helene 113
Dinah 48,63,65,68,104
Diversity-Jewish women 89,152
Divorce (Jewish) 15, 32, 35, 36, 46, 52, 55,61,62,63,72,160
Divorce - Israel 36,52,108
Domestic violence 20,48,58,66,74,82,83,85-90,93,100,104,105,107,109,154
Drachler, Rose (1911-1982) 154
Drama, see also
   Holocaust-drama 132,135,150,152
Drucker, Malka 32
Drug addiction 100
Dulcia 22
Education 14, 39, 40, 47, 51, 52, 62, 64, 66, 75,80,87,92,94,102,110,160
   -Israel 111
Eichengreen, Lucille 143
Elderly Jewish-Americans see Aged
Environmental issues 81
Epstein, Judith 95
ERIC documents 76,81,83
   **See note at beginning of Subject Index.
Esterka (Esther of Opoczno) 14
Esther 16,36,37,39,49,65,68
Evangelism 50,52,68
Eve 42,55,68,75
Eyck, Helene 114
Falashas 116
Falk, Marcia 57,69,137
Families 17, 18, 40, 42, 46, 47, 52, 74, 75, 78,80,81,82,83,88,90, 90, 95, 98, 99, 100, 101, 115119,148,149
Families-Israel 104,153
Feld, Rose 146
Felman, Jyl Lynn 151
Feminine identity, see
   Identity issues
Feminism 20, 21 ,33, 36, 39, 40, 44, 45, 47, 54,55,56,59,65,66,67,75,76,77,81,83,84,85 86, 87, 88, 93, 96, 97, 98, 100, 101, 102, 107,108,111,117,118,132,140,144,145,148,152
   -History 47,77
   -Israel 74,103,105,106,107,108,110,111
   -Yiddish 153
Feminist theology 67,149
Ferber, Edna 82,131
Fertility 42,78,90,96

Fiction 13, 14, 104,143, 144, 145, 147, 148,150,160
-Documentary 122
-Holocaust, see Holocaust-fiction
-Israel, see Israel-fiction
Fogelman, Eva 26
Folklore 18,43,44,119,140,141,142,148,152
Food 69,75,146,149
Frank, Ray 89
Frank, Anne 26,28,30,31,145
Frankiel, Tamar 38
Freud, Anna O. 113
Freud and women 120
Friedan, Betty 79,90
Friedman, Rabbi Dayle 101
Frimkin, Esther 19
Fuch, Esther 139
Ganz, Yaffa 104
Gender issues 21, 23, 36, 40, 58, 66, 72, 82, 94,95,103,109,110,111,118,131,132,133,145 146,148,153
Gershon, Karen 135,145
Get, see Divorce (Jewish)
Gies, Miep 26
Glenn, Susan 89
Gluck, Louise 131
Gluck, Shana Berger 145
Glueckel of Hamlyn 18,19,135
Goddesses 24,33,38,43,45,55,58,96,147
Goldman, Emma 23,82
Goldmark, Josephine 36
Goldreich,Merle 146
Goldschlag, Stella 30
Goldstein Judith 132,139
Goldstein Rebecca 136,139
Goodman, Allegra 139,140
Gornick, Vivian 78,82,91
Grandmothers 13,89,107
Gratz, Rebecca 89
Grossman, Nancy 87
Gruenbaum, Irene 148
Grunfeld, Judith 144
Hadassah 95,107
Hagar 48
Haggadot 35,54,143
Hair coverings 54
Haiti 150
Halacha 34,37,39,40,42,46,50,51,53,57, 60-3,68,73,147,148
Half the Kingdom 101
Hamoy,Carol 151
Hannah 71
Haredi women 145
Hasidic women 42,46,94,103
Havurot 46,50
Health issues 85,95,107,119
Held, Stefanie 101
Heller, Fanya Gottesfeld 27
Hillesum, Etty 31
Hoffman, Eva 82
Holocaust 16, 93, 115, 137, 138, 144, 146,147,150,152,154,155
Holocaust-Art 24,25,31,84,145,152,155
Holocaust-Drama 28,31,32
Holocaust-Fiction 26,123,124,135,139,144,145,147

Holocaust-Personal narratives see Personal narratives
Holocaust Project 25
Holocaust-Rescuers 24,25,26,32,145
Holocaust-Resistance 13,25,27,29
Holocaust-Survivors 25, 28, 29, 30, 31, 32, 80,83
Hostein, Lisa 46
Huldah 38
Hull House 81
Humor 89,102
Hurst, Fannie 139,142
Hyneman, Rebekah Gumpert 139
Identity issues 13, 20, 28, 32, 34, 52, 74, 75, 79,87,88,91,97, 100,115,117,118,135,141,148,149
Immigrants 14,15,17,19,20,32,76-79. 83-5,87,89,91,92,94,9, 100-2, 119, 144, 146,149,155
Inclusiveness 22,37,53,71,80,94,154
Intermarriage 32,45,47,52,71,83,91,93
Internationalism 117,119,120,153
Interpersonal relationships 90,95,97
Intifada 105,145
Israel-aged women 47,105
  -courts 59,108
  -Ethiopians in 109
  -fiction 122
  -immigrants 117,118,151
  -Middle Eastern women 47, 69, 104, 105, 107,111
  -Moroccan women 156
  -poverty 106
  -religion 108,111,155
Israeli poets 127,128
Israeli women 64, 66, 107, 108, 109, 111, 112,138,145,146,147,151,152,153
  -Army 104,108,109,111
  -authors 137
  -politics 103,109,110
Jacobi,Kathy 87
Jacobs, Hannah and Solomon 93
Jael 36
Jephtah's daughter 36,69
"Jewish American Princess" 75, 76, 77, 80, 82, 83,84,85,86,88,91,93-96,98-100 134,142
Jewish American women see American Jewish women
Jewish-American women leaders see Leadership roles
Jewish-American women writers, see American-Jewish women writers
Jewish Daily Forward 99,100
Jewish feminism see Feminism
Jewish identity see identity issues
Jewish Lesbians see Lesbians, Jewish
Jewish lesbian writers, see Lesbian, Jewish - literature
Jewish Nurses, see Nurses
Jewish Women Performance artists 152
Jewish Women's Resource Center 92
Jewish women's studies 76,143,144
Jews in: Boston 94
  Britain 43, 47, 113, 114, 115, 116, 117,138,145,147

California 88,93
Canada 119
Chile 117,150
China 121
Cuba 151
Eastern Europe 114,154
Ethiopia 117
Europe 21,119,120,146
Florida 92
France (North African) 117
Germany 21,22,26,27,31,114,115,118,146
India 144
Italy 35,36,113
Kurdistan 120
Libya 116
New Mexico 101
New Orleans 143
New York 144,149
Philadelphia 74
Poland 15,113,118,120,155
Rhode Island 91
Russia 115,118,119,153
Shanghai 115
South Africa 116,118,119,139
Spain 114
Texas 81,84
Jews for Jesus 79,93
Jonas, Rabbi Regina 150
Jones, Hettie 79
Josephus 17
Judith 49,151
Kahana-Carmon, Amalia 138
Kaminetsky, Ellen 79,93
Kaplan, Johanna 135
Karmel, Ilona 139
Karelitz, Batya 33
Katz, Judith 151
Kaye/Kantrowitz, Melanie 93
Kazimierz,Poland, see Jews in: Poland
Kellerman, Faye 142
Kempner, Vitke 31
Ketubbot, see also marriage 47,71
Klagsbrun, Francine 146
Klepfisz, Irena 80,138,140
Kohut,Rebekah 82 (Rubin book)
Kopelnitsky, Raimonda 147
Kramer,Louise 151
Kreimer Sarah 101
Kreitman, Esther Singer 14,140,141
Kulescroft,Anna 18
Kunin, Madeline 147
Lasker-Schuler, Else 133,141
Lazarus, Emma (1849-1887) 19,133
Leadership roles 49,60,85,86,91-94, 101, 102,151
Leah 55
Lebensboym, Rosa 139
Lebow, Barbara 32
Leitner, Isabella 82
Lesbian/Heterosexual alliances 97
Lesbians, Jewish 37, 69 ,74, 79, 80, 83, 88,89,90,93,98,120,147,153,154,160
  -literature 78,107,129,133,148,151
  -motherhood 85,93
  -synagogue participation 51,56

Levertov, Denise 139
Levin, Nora 26
Levitan, Tina 80
Levy, Amy 123
Lewis, Helen 31
Liben, Laura 101
Lichtenstein, Diane 153
Light 39
Lilith 44,45
Link, Lisa 155
Lubavitch women 76
Lullabies 134
Luxemburg, Rosa 19
Maimie, see Pinzer, Maimie
Margolies-Mezvinsky, Marjorie, U.S.Congress 147
Margolin, Anna 139
Marriage, see also kettubot 42, 46, 50, 58, 59,71,72,74,82,147,150,151,160
Matriarchs 46,94
Media representations 21,94,104,105,109,135,138
Medieval women 17-20,22,119,149,160
Mehitzah 60,87,160
Meir, Golda 82
Menken, Adah Isaacs 71,90
Menstruation 63
Michal 20,97
Middle Eastern Jews, see also Israel-Middle Eastern women 119,153
Midrash 15,43,48,149,156
Mikveh 42,56,59
Minyan 46
Miriam 15,35,60,63,69,71
Misogyny 57
Moise, Penina 13
Molodowsky, Kaye 139
Money lenders 101,114
Monotheism 38,56
Montefiore family 116
Mordecai, Jacob 92
Morton, Leah, see Stern, Elizabeth
Moskowitz, Faye 82
Mother-daughter relationships 78, 101, 135, 152
Mothers 13, 18, 58, 81, 82, 95, 98, 101, 105, 110,111,147,148,149,153,154
Music 16, 42, 78, 92, 98, 101, 114, 116, 117,119,146
Myerhoff, Barbara 80,81
Myerson, Barbara 92
Na'amat see Divorce (Jewish)
Naomi 42,53,57,60
Nasi, Dona Gracia 19
National Council of Jewish Women (NCJW) 102
Nevelson, Louise 80
Newcombe,Hanna 118
Newman, Leslea 151
Noam, Rahel 44
Nobel Prize 81
Nudel, Ida 115
Nurses 20,86,107,108
Ochs,Vanessa L. 44,139,146
Olsen, Tillie 16,131,132,136,148,149

Orfali, Stephanie 19
Organizations/organizational work, see Leadership roles or Volunteerism
Orthodox movement, see Denominations-Orthodox
Ostriker, Alicia 136,146
Ozick, Cynthia 131-134,136-7,139-141, 144, 146,149,152
Paganism 96
Paley, Grace 83,131,132,134,135,137,139
Pappenheim, Bertha 19,113
Pardes 44
Passover 35
Pastan, Linda (1932-)154
Patriarchy 19,118,144
Pembroke College 94
Personal narratives 19,21,24-31, 32, 00, 78, 79, 82, 83, 84, 90, 93, 104, 105, 107, 114,116,119,134,137,144,145,147,148,152
Pesotta, Rose 19
Philanthropy 99
Philo 17
Philosophy-treatment of 135
women
Photography 24,147,148,155
Piercy, Marge 134,139,146,153
Pinzer, Maimie 132
Plaskow, Judith 67
Poems about Israel 126,128
Poetry 13-15, 128, 131, 133, 139, 145, 146, 148,149,150,154
Pogrebin,Letty Cottin 97
Polacheck, Hilda Satt 81
Pollard, Anne 85
Popkin, Jo 134
Prayer groups 50
Prayers 34-36, 38, 42, 72, 128, 145, 147, 151,155
Prayers-Yiddish, see techines
Printing and book publishing 117
Property rights 63
Property, women as 38
Prophets, women, see also Women in Bible
Prostitutes 16,36
Prywes,Raquela 122
Purity Laws 33
Queen of Heaven 33,36
Queen of Sheba 18
Queen Salome Alexandra 38
Rabbinical students 62
Rachel 55,56
Rachel (actress) 113
Rachlin, Rachel 115
Racism 21,75,89,94,97
Rape 23,37,63,99
Rapoport, Nessa 139,146
Reconstructionist movement, see Denominations-Reconstructionist
Reference 18,75-77, 80, 89, 101, 131, 139, 143,146,149
Reform movement, see Denominations-Reform
Religion 144,148
Religious education, see education

Renaissance-Jews in 116,119
Rescuers-see Holocaust-Rescuers
Resistance-see Holocaust-Resistance
Resources 157-159
Retirement 95
Rich, Adrienne 138
Richman, Julia 82
Righteous Ones, see Holocaust-Rescuers
Rituals 32,33,35,37,38,78,119,143,148
Roiphe, Anne 137,139,141
Role models 14
Rose, Ernestine 83,116
Rosen, Norma 81,133,139,146
Rosenberg, Ethel 85,124
Rosenberg, Marilyn R.151
Rosh Chodesh 33,143,149
Roth, Joan 155
Roth, Philip 31,154
Rothchild, Judith 74
Rubin, Anna 101
Rubin, Ruth 101
Rudellat, Yvonne 13
Rukeyser, Muriel 128
Ruth 41,42
Sachs, Nelly 26,141
Salomon, Charlotte 145
Samsonowitz, Miriam 149
Sarah 40,42,156
Schaeffer, Susan Fromberg 16,139
Schecter, Mathilde Roth 99
Scheuer, Mathilda 86
Schneurson,Zelda 62
Schwimmer, Rosika 120,143
Scientists 14,22,81,84
Segal, Lore 135
Self-esteem, see Identity issues
Senesh, Hannah 26,27,32,
Sephardi women 114,117
Sexism 93,97,150
Sexual harassment 109,153,156
Sexuality 37,42,75,93,113,149
Shain, Ruchoma 105
Shekkinah 39,135
Shiloh:Birth control center 109
Shochat, Manya 19
Short Stories 13,145
Siblings 47,67,95
Sidransky, Ruth 83
Silverstein, Olga 100
Simon,Kate 82,83
Sinclair, Beatrice 134
Sinclair, Jo 134,141
Single women 74,83,84,119,153,160
Sisterhoods 36,79,89
Slavery 18
Slesinger, Gertrude 134
Social workers 84,99
Solomon, Clara 143
Sommerfeld, Rose 100
Song of Songs 37,145,151
Sorceresses 41
Sotah 33
Southern-Jewish women 76

Spielrein, Sabina 113
Spier, Bertha (Birdie) 94
Spirituality 24,38,81,145
Sports 20
Spousal abuse see
  Domestic violence
Stein, Gertrude 14,131,142
Stein, Sister Edith 31
Stereotypes 86,87,93,94,111,119,134,135
Sterilization (Holocaust),see
  Childbearing
Stern, Elizabeth (1889-1954)
  89,94,131,134,142
Stodel see Spier
Stokes, Rose Pastor 84
Storytelling 132,155
Suicide 132
Susanna 52,59,66,72
Suzman, Helen 116,155
Synagogues 40,62
Szold, Henrietta 82,89,99
Talmud 18,38
Tamar 40
Tango,Jenny 151
Tax, Meredith 134
Taylor,Elyse 151
**Techines 23,36,37,43,49,50,51,53,72,149
  **Techines are Yiddish prayers
Tekoan woman 50
Therapy 30,80,87,92,93
Theresienstadt 29
Thome, Diane 16,78,92
Tikkun Conference 88
Tisha'B'Av 57
Traditional women 33, 38, 39, 42, 76, 79,
  82, 99,105,106,109,145,148,149,150
Trible, Phyllis 53
Tricksters 44,55,60,71
Tsene-rene, see techines
Turchick, Jacky 101
Tussman, Malka Heifetz 137,139
Twersky, Gail 146
Tzili 26
Vashti 49
Vinograd, Julia 154
Volunteerism 77, 81, 89, 91, 94, 95, 96, 98,
  99,101,102,146
Wald, Lillian 76
War 22,106,111
Wasserstein, Wendy 140
Weil,Simone 20,133,134,143
Weinfeld, Yocheved 85
Weisberg, Ruth 84,87
Westheimer, Dr. Ruth 30
Widows 19, 22,111,114,160
Winternight, Nancy 102
Wolf, Emma (1865-1932)133,139
Women at the Wall 55,61,64
Women authors, see also
  American-Jewish women authors 134,139
Women cantors 48,59,68
Women depicted in art 119,146,149
Women in Black 111,151
*Women in literature 15, 132, 134, 135,
  138, 139,140,142,154
  *Women in literature refers to women as
  depicted in literature

Women Peace activists see
  Activism - peace
Women priests 49
Women rabbis 15,39,89,150,154
Women's Liberation see Feminism
Women's Studies 62,92,100
Wouk, Herman (Marjorie Morningstar)155
Yael 53
Yahil,Leni 26
Yalow, Rosalyn 81
Yemenite Women, see
  Israel-Middle Eastern women
Yemenite girls in Israel, see
  Israel-Middle Eastern women
Yezierska, Anzia 16, 84, 89, 131, 132, 134,
  137,139,140,141,142,153,156
Yiddish literature 132,139,145,150
Yiddish prayers see Techines
Zilberfarb, Chedva 103 (Dubinki book)
Zugsmith, Leane 81

For citations 1900-85 see these Biblio publications:

THE JEWISH WOMAN: 1900-1985
Bibliography *(1986)*
by *Aviva Cantor*

also consult the following:

JEWISH WOMEN AND JEWISH LAW
Compiled by **Ora Hamelsdorf** and **Sondra Adlersberg**
1981, with unbound report of 1986

SEX AND THE MODERN JEWISH WOMAN (1986)
Compiled by **Joan Scherer Brewer, MLS, MA**
With Essays by Lynn Davidman and Evelyn Avery